greece in the euro

economic delinquency or system failure?

Eleni Panagiotarea

ecpr PRESS

First published by the ECPR Press in 2013

The ECPR Press is the publishing imprint of the European Consortium for Political Research (ECPR), a scholarly association which supports and encourages the training, research and cross-national cooperation of political scientists in institutions throughout Europe and beyond.

ECPR Press
University of Essex
Wivenhoe Park
Colchester
CO4 3SQ
UK

Typeset by Anvi

Printed and bound by Lightning Source

British Library Cataloguing in Publication Data

A catalogue record for this book is available from the British Library

Paperback ISBN: 978-1-907301-53-7

www.ecpr.eu/ecprpress

ECPR – Monographs
Series Editors:
Dario Castiglione (University of Exeter)
Peter Kennealy (European University Institute)
Alexandra Segerberg (Stockholm University)
Peter Triantafillou (Roskilde University)

Other books available in this series
Agents or Bosses? (ISBN: 9781907301261) Ozge Kemahlioglu

Causes of War: The Struggle for Recognition (ISBN: 9781907301018)
Thomas Lindemann

Citizenship: The History of an Idea (ISBN: 9780954796655) Paul Magnette

*Coercing, Constraining and Signalling: Explaining UN and EU Sanctions After
the Cold War* (ISBN: 9781907301209) Francesco Giumelli

Constraints On Party Policy Change (ISBN: 9781907301490) Thomas M.
Meyer

Contesting Europe: Exploring Euroscepticism in Online Media Coverage (ISBN:
9781907301513) Pieter de Wilde, Asimina Michailidou & Hans-Jörg Trenz

*Deliberation Behind Closed Doors: Transparency and Lobbying in the European
Union* (ISBN: 9780955248849) Daniel Naurin

Democratic Institutions and Authoritarian Rule in Southeast Europe
(ISBN: 9781907301438) Danijela Dolenec

*Economic Knowledge in Regulation: The Use of Expertise by Independent
Agencies* (ISBN: 9781907301452) Lorna S. Schrefler

*European Integration and its Limits: Intergovernmental Conflicts and their
Domestic Origins* (ISBN: 9780955820373) Daniel Finke

Gender and Vote in Britain: Beyond the Gender Gap? (ISBN: 9780954796693)
Rosie Campbell

Globalisation: An Overview (ISBN: 9780955248825) Danilo Zolo

*Joining Political Organisations: Institutions, Mobilisation and Participation in
Western Democracies* (ISBN: 9780955248894) Laura Morales

*Organising the European Parliament: Committees' Role and Legislative
Influence* (ISBN: 9781907301391) Nikoleta Yordanova

Paying for Democracy: Political Finance and State Funding for Parties
(ISBN: 9780954796631) Kevin Casas-Zamora

*Policy Making In Multilevel Systems: Federalism, Decentralisation, and
Performance in the OECD Countries* (ISBN: 9781907301339) Jan Biela, Annika
Hennl and Andre Kaiser

*Political Conflict and Political Preferences: Communicative Interaction Between
Facts, Norms and Interests* (ISBN: 9780955820304) Claudia Landwehr

Political Parties and Interest Groups in Norway (ISBN: 9780955820366)
Elin Haugsgjerd Allern

Regulation in Practice: The de facto Independence of Regulatory Agencies (ISBN: 9781907301285) Martino Maggetti

Representing Women?: Female Legislators in West European Parliaments (ISBN: 9780954796648) Mercedes Mateo Diaz

The Personalisation of Politics: A Study of Parliamentary Democracies (ISBN: 9781907301032) Lauri Karvonen

The Politics of Income Taxation: A Comparative Analysis (ISBN: 9780954796686) Steffen Ganghof

The Return of the State of War: A Theoretical Analysis of Operation Iraqi Freedom (ISBN: 9780955248856) Dario Battistella

Transnational Policy Innovation: The role of the OECD in the Diffusion of Regulatory Impact Analysis (ISBN:9781907301254) Fabrizio De Francesco

Urban Foreign Policy and Domestic Dilemmas: Insights from Swiss and EU City-regions (ISBN: 9781907301070) Nico van der Heiden

Why Aren't They There? The Political Representation of Women, Ethnic Groups and Issue Positions In Legislatures (ISBN: 9780955820397) Didier Ruedin

Widen the Market, Narrow the Competition: Banker Interests and the Making of a European Capital Market (ISBN: 9781907301087) Daniel Mügge

Please visit www.ecpr.eu/ecprpress for information about new publications.

| contents

List of Figures and Tables   vii

Acknowledgements   ix

Chapter One: Introduction   1

Chapter Two: New Institutionalism at a Crossroads   15

Chapter Three: Greek Policy Formation, 1974–1993: Caught Between a
    Politicised Economy and EC Adjustment   29

Chapter Four: EMU Negotiations, National Strategies and the External
    Constraint   55

Chapter Five: Nominal Convergence and Macroeconomic Policy   73

Chapter Six: The 'Good' EMU Years   97

Chapter Seven: Salvation Does Not Come Cheap   125

Chapter Eight: Conclusion: Owning and Sharing Responsibility   155

Appendix A: Biographical Data   175

Appendix B: List of Interviewees   181

Index   183

| list of figures and tables

Figures

Figure 3.1: The growing gap between public spending and revenue   35

Figure 3.2: Electoral cycles and budget deficits   39

Figure 3.3: Creating the debt burden, general government gross
consolidated debt, 1971–93   52

Figure 5.1: Attaining disinflation: Greece's inflation rate (HICP),
1996–2000   79

Figure 5.2: Exchange-rate stability achieved: spread of GRD *vis-à-vis*
the ERM and ERM II   89

Figure 6.1: Discipline in short supply: budget deficits after the launch
of the euro   109

Figure 6.2: Elections and general government budget deficit, 1999–2010
(% of GDP)   112

Figure 6.3: Joblessness and debt-led growth, 1999–2008   120

Figure 7.1: Greece and PIIGS, 10-year sovereign bond spreads over
German, August 2007–May 2010   140

Tables

Table 4.1: Comparing notes, Greek aspirations and EMU outcomes   63

Table 7.1: How the Stability and Growth Pact failed I, deficit as a
percentage of GDP   152

Table 7.2: How the Stability and Growth Pact failed II, debt as a
percentage of GDP   153

| acknowledgements

Writing about the Greek crisis has brought home a series of personal debts, which I am more than happy to carry. Dario Castiglione embraced the project and the author, creating a matter-of-fact yet supportive bond. The team at ECPR consistently raised the stakes with their professionalism and enthusiasm – special thanks to Mark Kench for his cool juggling of queries and requests and to Laura Pugh, whose cover design breaks all conventions on what 'European' books should look like. In Athens, it took Loukas Tsoukalis's uncompromising style and panache to jazz up the book's title.

I take full 'ownership', as the IMF would have appreciated, for any errors that might appear in the book. I would, however, like to thank Dermot Hodson for his convincing use of the Socratic method- in spite of the fact that I was the Greek in the room- during our long discussion on theoretical frameworks. Kevin Featherstone was incredibly generous, sharing his unparalleled and in-depth knowledge of Greek political economy. I am also grateful to the two anonymous referees for their thoughtful and incisive comments- they helped shake any analytical inertia. My interviewees were kind enough to share their time and insight of one of the most fascinating periods of Greek economic policy, their contribution is more than evident in the way the argument in the book has evolved. In the end, my biggest 'creditor' is Albert Weale. As my long-time mentor and trusted friend, he persuaded me that the book had to be written, provided support during the down times and explained that, unlike non-compliance to the Stability and Growth Pact, non-compliance to the task at hand was not an option.

I have been particularly fortunate to have the friends that I have. In their different ways, Alice, Daphne, Elizabeth, and Melina, all believe in me unconditionally and, as a result, they make me want to do better, just to prove them right. My mother Anna is this unstoppable force, her incredible enthusiasm always lighting up the room and her organisational skills always saving the day. I cannot begin to express my gratitude for her love and support. Sotiris, my husband, knew when to retreat strategically and when to take matters into his hands; he also provided the most credible commentary of where the Greek economy was going. His unwavering faith in my projects and his loving presence have, time and again, given me the strength to spread my wings. Our three children, Anna, Achilleas, and Angelos are our very own triple AAA 'bonds', their qualities and talents shining through every single day.

Eleni Panagiotarea
Athens, August 2013

For Sotiris, Anna, Achilleas, and Angelos

chapter one | introduction

Banking on EMU

In April 2010, the Greek government stood on the brink of insolvency. Confronted with an inability to fund its debt, it called upon help from the European Union and the International Monetary Fund, and sought to implement unprecedented public expenditure cuts and structural reforms that would render its economy competitive within a unified currency zone containing some the world's strongest economies. Strikes, riots on the streets and disruption of public services followed, week after week, month after month.

This was supposed to be a different kind of story. Greece had banked on EMU. Entry to the Eurozone, back in 2001, was its ticket to macroeconomic stability and economic modernisation and its gateway to global markets. With the Eurozone enjoying stable growth and low inflation for most of the decade, this small country on the periphery hardly called for special mention or attention. After all, the Greek economy was also reaping benefits, as real GDP growth averaged, between 2000 and 2008, close to 4 per cent per year – against 2 per cent in the euro area.[1] If the Greek sovereign-debt crisis was a disaster waiting to happen, no one could have suspected it because, quite simply, no one was paying sufficient attention. The financial markets regularly refinanced Greek debt, while the country's Eurozone partners turned a blind eye to its budgetary problems and bad statistics.

When the markets became 'vigilant' again, after an almost decade-long intermezzo, they placed Greece, from September 2009 onwards, in a sovereign risk class of its own: the widening of its spreads in both the Credit Default Swaps (CDS) and the government bond markets constituted sufficient proof. Eurozone authorities failed to grasp both the threat of contagion and the logic of escalation, which might follow a market backlash in a setting of multiple equilibria and self-fulfilling sentiments. In the absence of a crisis-resolution framework, the increasingly frantic effort to restore fiscal sustainability led EMU leaders into a quagmire, exposing governance weaknesses that had long lurked underneath the surface.

The Greek case, special though not unique – if Ireland, Portugal, Spain and Cyprus are anything to go by – shows that EMU was always going to be about owning and sharing responsibility in a less-than-optimal monetary union in a more-than-troubled world. The derailment of Greece's IMF/EU economic adjustment programme of May 2010, the non-implementation of the second adjustment

---

1. European Commission, 'The Economic Adjustment Programme for Greece', *Occasional Papers 61*, May 2010, p. 3.

programme of March 2012, the renewed efforts 'to bring the programme back on track'[2] through a substantial set of reforms as well as a convincing budget for 2013, and the political agreement of 26 November 2012 to create a credible path to Greece's debt sustainability[3] – reveal how Eurozone authorities' inability to grasp the extent of system failure, combined with the delinquent behaviour of Greek policy actors, continue to haunt the political economy of the Eurozone. 'Painful' adjustment has not gone a long way and has certainly not appeased the markets: the economy is contracting for a sixth year; unemployment has soared; and fiscal and external deficits remain, in spite of 'horizontal' cuts in wages and pensions.

Great expectations turn to dust

'Too little, too late' became a standard criticism addressed to European leaders', who had been unable to fathom the risks arising from the high degree of interconnectedness of the EU financial system and unwilling to admit, at least publicly, that the EMU policy framework had failed. The rules – no default, no bail-out, no exit – proved to have been too tightly constructed, while all members had underestimated the level of interdependence among the Eurozone economies – and the fragility that came with it. Greece was not the only country in the periphery to misinterpret interest-rate convergence as an invitation to a free ride. The credit booms, the perverse effects of negative real interest rates and capital flows from northern to southern Europe[4] bred widespread content; Greece and Portugal did their best to avoid fiscal discipline altogether, while housing and asset bubbles began to float in Spain and Ireland. It was easy to point the finger to the GIIPS, regularly anagrammatised in the press and even in academic circles as PIIGS, yet less soul-searching took place in the Eurozone's core. A single monetary policy predictably failed to accommodate all, while important divergences at the national level – in wage arrangements, budgetary policies, and social regulations – eroded competitiveness, as evidenced in the mounting current account imbalances between 'north' and 'south'. Eurozone authorities were evidently misguided in their belief that national leaders who had previously delegated monetary policy-making to a new, centralised authority, would set up, whenever and wherever required, adjustment mechanisms, including wage and price flexibility, to respond

---

2.   'Eurogroup Statement on Greece', 12 November 2012, accessed 13 November 2012, http://www. consilium.europa.eu/uedocs/cms_data/docs/pressdata/en/ecofin/133445.pdf.

3.   The agreement included an important set of measures aimed to reduce Greece's debt burden, including a debt buyback operation, return of Securities Market Programme (SMP) profits to Greece, reduction of Greek Loan Facility (GLF) interest rates, significant extension of GLF and European Financial Stability Facility (EFSF) maturities, and the deferral of EFSF interest-rate payments. See 'Eurogroup statement on Greece', 27 November 2012, accessed 9 December 2012, at http://www.consilium.europa.eu/uedocs/cms_data/docs/pressdata/en/ecofin/133857.pdf.

4.   J. Pisani-Ferry, 'The euro crisis and the new impossible trinity', Bruegel Policy Contribution, 2012, no. 1, p. 2.

to macroeconomic shocks, whether asymmetric or common. Structural reforms were delayed or postponed altogether in a number of member states while wages shot up, without a corresponding hike in productivity.

How did it happen that great expectations turned to dust so quickly? As we shall see in the narrative this book relates, the roots of the Greek problem were deep and persistent, involving long-stranding rigidities and inefficiencies in an economic system in which sectional interests guarded their relative position to the detriment of the general interest and in which a political culture of patronage limited what governments could do. Moreover, the inherited institutional rigidities were complemented by failures of policy reasoning. The 'redistributive Keynesianism' of the Papandreou years of the 1980s – in which the hope was that social justice and economic efficiency could both be enhanced by positive government spending – ended in failure, just as a similar French experiment under Mitterrand was paid for by borrowing.[5] Turning to the European project seemed to offer an alternative but it resulted in a conspiracy of optimism, as both Greek negotiators over EMU and the European Union submerged hard-headed economic calculation in a wider political project that would have predictably (and predicted) uneven effects on member states when the time came for a response to asymmetric shocks.

In an ideal world, the Greeks, with an economy constituting a mere 2 per cent of Eurozone GDP, would have had to clean up their own mess. In the Eurozone world, however, a number of countries saw their government bond yields go up, forcing them, in the context of market appeasement, to contract fiscal policies sharply or, worse, adopt full-scale austerity programmes. European leaders, who had time and again, relegated the efficient management of Europe's monetary union well below political necessity, were now compelled to step in and offer, along with the International Monetary Fund, a Greek Loan Facility, worth €110 billion. The systemic character of the crisis became all too evident when questions were raised – predominantly by the markets' punitive reaction – as to whether the firewalls that had been created with International Monetary Fund aid – the European Financial Stability Facility and the European Financial Stability Mechanism – would prove a sufficient 'safety net' for Ireland, Portugal and Spain if the crisis 'spread'. Ireland negotiated its own support programme soon after and Portugal followed suit. It was then the turn of Spain to agree to a financial assistance programme for the recapitalisation of its financial institutions, while Cyprus has embarked on the euro area's fourth economic adjustment programme.

A process of institutional engineering has been unfolding though more as the result of continuous and relentless pressures from the markets than as the outcome of some grand integration design or strategic plan. The emerging rules-based system has included: a Treaty on Stability, Coordination and Governance (TSCG, popularly known as the 'fiscal compact'); the Stability and Growth Pact reinforced by the 'six-pack', a set of rules for macroeconomic and fiscal surveillance, including a new

---

5. P. A. Hall, *Governing the Economy: The politics of state intervention in Britain and France*, New York, Oxford University Press, 1986.

Macroeconomic Imbalance Procedure (MIP) and its corrective arm, the Excessive Imbalance Procedure (EIP) to identify and correct serious gaps in competitiveness and major macroeconomic imbalances; the 'two-pack' introducing provisions for enhanced monitoring of euro area countries' budgetary policies; and the European Semester (with the integrated Europe Plus Pact to promote stronger economic co-ordination for competitiveness and convergence). These are all supposed to create, by centralising EMU's capability to supervise and 'punish', a path to growth and new jobs for the euro areas and the EU's interdependent economies. Quite how more 'control' and 'sanctions' will produce this outcome has yet to be worked out, particularly with the Commission admitting that 'it will take time to move towards a sustainable recovery'.[6]

Even the creation of the European Stability Mechanism (ESM) – theoretically the cornerstone of the European firewall and an integral component of the attempt to ensure financial stability in the euro area – raises the question of whether lessons have been learned. Complex and punitive demands of conditionality attached to ESM assistance confirm that, while Eurozone authorities rightly seek to safeguard creditors' interests, their political courage and strategic thinking continue to be in deficit. With 'conditionality' steadily forming the *modus operandi* of a crisis-management framework-one only needs to look at the logic behind the European Central Bank's (ECB's) Outright Monetary Transactions (OMT) Programme, which has replaced the Securities Market Programme – and with Eurozone authorities failing to incorporate in the 'new' instruments or tools social objectives, to minimise the risk of social tensions and reverse the decreasing trust in the legitimacy of European institutions, it will be hard to avert the vicious cycle generated by national financial systems in disarray, sovereign-debt market turbulence and low economic growth.

The one and only?

The Greek sovereign-debt crisis may have been the trigger for the big bang but the financial markets and the Eurozone authorities provided the fuel. Greece was a 'catalyst' but not the 'odd man out'.[7] In April 2010, when Greek policy makers applied for the activation of the loan facility, Greece was hardly the only country whose fiscal problems betrayed serious incongruence with the European fiscal framework: the largest government deficits as a percentage of GDP were recorded in Ireland (-14.3 per cent), Greece (-13.6 per cent), Spain (-11.2 per cent), and Portugal (-9.4 per cent). Likewise, the countries with the highest debt-to-GDP ratio were Italy (115.8 per cent), Greece (115.1 per cent), and Belgium (96.7 per

---

6. European Commission, 'Communication from the Commission: Annual Growth Survey 2013', Brussels, COM (2012) 750 final, 28 November 2012, p. 1.

7. L. Tsoukalis, 'Greece in the euro area: odd man out, or precursor of things to come?' In W. R. Cline and G. B. Wolff, (eds), *Resolving the European Debt Crisis: Special Report 21*, Washington, Peterson Institute for International Economics, 2012, p. 19.

cent).[8] Nor was Greece the only country whose twin deficits betrayed mounting internal and external disequilibria – Portugal and, to a lesser extent, Spain and Italy saw their budget and current account deficits feed off each other. What made Greece 'special' was the weakness of its political institutions: official economic statistics lacked credibility, corruption and rent-seeking were endemic and tax collection was, at best, unreliable.

In fact it was the *strength* of its weak institutions, that is, their resilience and tenacity *vis-à-vis* significant pressures for adaptation and change, that made Greece's role 'special' in the unfolding of the Eurozone crisis. The first economic adjustment programme agreed with the country's creditors was officially derailed when it was confirmed that Greece had made mixed progress: after an initial burst, 'reforms adopted since spring 2010 were insufficient in restoring growth and in ensuring fiscal sustainability'.[9] While Greece had achieved a substantial reduction in the general government deficit, from 15.75 per cent of GDP in 2009 to 9.25 per cent in 2011, 'on several occasions, there were legitimate doubts about the ownership of the programme by the Greek Government'.[10] Implementation was burdened by 'political instability, social unrest and issues of administrative capacity'.[11] Worse, the recession was much deeper than Greece's creditors had previously projected. With targets missed and structural reforms derailed, the Parliament had to pass, in June 2011, a €28 billion harsh austerity bill: this was set as a precondition for releasing the next instalment of bail-out loans. By the time that the disbursement of €8.7 billion was released in July, Eurozone officials had agreed to support a new bail-out programme for Greece: this aimed to improve the country's debt sustainability and refinancing profile, through lower interest rates and extended maturities; the maturities of the existing Greek facility would also be extended. Conditional on its approval was a successful debt-exchange offer, involving the voluntary contribution of the private sector; it was made clear that private-sector involvement (PSI) would only be applicable in Greece, which required 'an exceptional and unique solution'.[12]

In the autumn, the government formally announced that it would not meet its 2011 and 2012 deficit targets. Soon after, Greece's membership of the euro was openly called into question. Adopting the second programme had now become a matter of urgency; at the October 26 euro area summit, a 'deeper PSI' was considered vital in 'establishing the sustainability of the Greek debt', with Eurozone

---

8.   Eurostat, 'Provision of deficit and debt data for 2009-first notification', 55/2010 – 22 April 2010 (accessed 12 February 2012). Online. Available: http://epp.eurostat.ec.europa.eu/cache/ITY_PUBLIC/2–22042010-BP/EN/2–22042010-BP-EN.PDF.

9.   European Economy, 'The Second Economic Adjustment Programme for Greece', p. 1.

10.   *Ibid.*

11.   *Ibid.*

12.   'Statement by the Heads of State of Government of the Euro Area and EU Institutions', Brussels, 21 July 2011 (accessed 1 September 2012). Online. Available: http://www.consilium.europa.eu/uedocs/cms_Data/docs/pressdata/en/ec/123978.pdf.

authorities repeating that Greece required 'an exceptional and unique solution'.[13] Greece, private investors and all relevant parties were invited 'to develop a voluntary bond exchange with a nominal discount of 50 per cent';[14] apparently, the loss had to be 'voluntary' to avoid the activation of Credit Default Swaps (CDS). In January 2012, it became clear that the second programme would not go through unless Greece's private-sector bondholders finalised the debt write-down deal; in the proposed PSI+, the 'voluntary' 'haircut' had to reach a magnitude of 70–90 per cent. A month later, the government announced the key terms of the transaction, taking its cue from the October summit statement: the PSI+ was expected to include 'private sector holders of approximately EUR206 billion aggregate outstanding face amount of Greek bonds (excluding treasury bills)'.[15] In the end, the Ministry of Finance calculated that around €199 billion of Greek government debt was restructured, representing 96.9 per cent of the €206 billion of government debt held by private-sector creditors. The congratulatory tones all around could not drown out the 'noise' of a potentially dangerous precedent: the way the seniority issue had been handled in the PSI+ could frighten private investors away from Greece and other periphery countries for years to come.

The difficult deal – the world's largest ever sovereign-debt restructuring – allowed Europe 'to avoid what could have been an enormously costly, disorderly default'.[16] Ensuring that the mistakes of the first economic adjustment programme would not be repeated, the euro area governments insisted that 'further strengthening of Greece's institutional capacity and enhanced on-site monitoring are essential for the full implementation and the success of the second Greek program'.[17] On March 14, the formal adoption of the second adjustment programme, jointly financed by the European Financial Stability Facility (EFSF), which had been fully operational since August 2010 and the IMF, constituted 'a unique opportunity for Greece that should not be missed'. The return of the Greek economy to a sustainable path was 'in the interest of everyone'.[18] Interestingly enough, within four months, talk of a Greek exit or 'Grexit' was increasingly audible throughout the Eurozone and beyond. Two election rounds, in May 6 and

13. *Ibid.*
14. 'Euro Summit Statement', Brussels, 26 October 2011 (accessed 1 September 2012). Online. Available: http://www.consilium.europa.eu/uedocs/cms_data/docs/pressdata/en/ec/125644.pdf.
15. Ministry of Finance, 'PSI Launch Press Release', 21 February 2012, accessed 7 August 2012. Online. Available: http://www.minfin.gr/portal/en/resource/contentObject/id/7ad6442f-1777–4d02–80fb-91191c606664.
16. Quote by Charles Dallara, chief negotiator for Greek bondholders, in Milne, R., Hope, K. and Spiegel, P. 'Greek debt swap support close to 95 per cent', *Financial Times*, March 8 2012.
17. 'Statement Euro Area Heads of State or Government', Brussels 2nd March 2012 (accessed 1 September 2012). Online. Available: http://www.consilium.europa.eu/uedocs/cms_data/docs/pressdata/en/ec/128521.pdf.
18. 'Statement by the President of the Eurogroup, Jean-Claude Juncker', 14 March 2012 (accessed 1 September 2012). Online. Available: http://www.consilium.europa.eu/uedocs/cms_data/docs/pressdata/en/ecofin/128941.pdf .

June 17 2012, sent the economy into 'suspended animation'.[19] After the second election, New Democracy Leader Antonis Samaras was able to form a tri-partite, national unity government, which included New Democracy's traditional political rival, PASOK, and DIMAR (Democratic Left, a social-democratic party), with the mandate to secure Greece's future in the Eurozone. However, election pledges to renegotiate some of the harshest austerity terms, together with the serious political and administrative challenges of re-starting implementation, seemingly preserved an environment of fluidity.

The creditors used the only effective weapon that could shake up Greek inertia; they promptly withdrew the scheduled €31.5bn bail-out disbursement for August 2012, as they waited for a troika review of the country's finances to be completed. Critical to a positive evaluation was agreement on a new €13.8bn package of spending cuts and tax increases that was to be voted on in Parliament in October. The Greek authorities showed their 'resolve to bring the programme back on track' by adopting, on 7 and 11 November, 'a substantial set of reforms as well as a convincing budget for 2013'.[20] To enhance 'the governance of the programme' new instruments were developed, including 'correction mechanisms to safeguard the achievement of the fiscal targets and a significant enhancement of the existing account for debt servicing'.[21]

The question of Greece's debt sustainability continued to cast a long shadow, however, marring troika forecasts and causing public rifts between the IMF and its European partners over Greek debt targets. A 'political agreement' was finally reached on the 26 November 2012, theoretically removing 'the uncertainty that has been hanging over Greece for too long, holding back confidence, investment and growth'.[22] With the explicit aim of 'making a substantial contribution to the sustainability' of Greece's debt, it foresaw a number of drastic initiatives promoted by the Eurogroup, including a Greek debt buy-back operation, the return of profits from the Securities Market Programme (SMP) to Greece, reduction of the interest rates of the Greek Loan Facility (GLF), the significant extension of GLF and European Financial Stability Facility (EFSF) maturities, and the deferral of EFSF interest payments. Conditional on full programme implementation, the debt ratio was expected to decrease to 124 per cent of GDP by 2020, through significant upfront debt-reduction measures of 20 per cent of GDP. Greece's debt was to be brought to below 110 per cent of GDP by 2022.[23]

---

19. 'Wait and flee: electoral uncertainty sends the economy into suspended animation', *Economist*, 16 June 2012.

20. 'Eurogroup Statement on Greece', 12 November 2012 (accessed 13 November 2012). Online. Available: http://www.consilium.europa.eu/uedocs/cms_data/docs/pressdata/en/ecofin/133445.pdf.

21. *Ibid.*

22. 'Speech- Vice-President Rehn's remarks at the Eurogroup Press Conference, Commissioner Olli Rehn', SPEECH/12/868, 27.11.2012 (accessed 9 December 2012). Online. Available: http://europa.eu/rapid/press-release_SPEECH-12–868_en.htm.

23. 'Eurogroup statement on Greece', 27 November 2012 (accessed 9 December 2012). Online. Available: http://www.consilium.europa.eu/uedocs/cms_Data/docs/pressdata/en/ecofin/133857.pdf.

It would seem fair to say that Greece and its creditors have come full circle. If Greece's entry to the Eurozone largely rested on a political decision, keeping Greece in (for the time being) has required another political decision. The conspiracy of optimism, discussed earlier, has raised its head again: every troika review has supposed that Greece will, typically in a two-year frame, return to economic growth, sell off public sector assets, proceed with structural reform and gain access to the private debt markets. At the same time, Eurozone authorities have largely downplayed creditors' mistakes and omissions, as evidenced in badly administered doses of austerity and continuously missed projections. The Greek sovereign-debt crisis serves to remind all parties that they got it wrong and that they keep getting it wrong. As Greek policy makers have been granted a two-year extension in order to implement the tough budget targets associated with the €174 billion bailout programme, there is a clear danger that the circle will turn vicious; of all the parties to the bail-out, only the IMF has publicly admitted, in the October 2012 World *Fiscal Monitor*, that 'a deeper-than-expected recession and slippages in the implementation of fiscal measures will once again complicate attainment of the ambitious deficit reduction targets'.[24] Eurozone authorities refuse to make a connection between the front-loaded austerity measures they have so eagerly required and the dramatic reduction in Greek economic output. As for Greece, it is already paying the price of past indolence: broadening and deepening its adjustment effort seems to be the only way of remaining in the 'club', of maintaining a prospect of long-term economic growth and of keeping its society together.

Research hypotheses

The Greek case, special though not unique as suggested above, shows that national political priorities trump the adjustment process, time and again. How can this be, when Greece joined a monetary union for which entry fees were high, exit was not an option and important instruments of macroeconomic policy were removed, with policy makers' consent, from the public sphere?

In spite of the dictates of EMU governance, the first hypothesis holds that:

H1: national and supranational institutional frameworks still compete for influence over the goals and direction of economic policy, the outcome depending on the compliance mechanisms and the incentives available to policy makers for dodging rules or free-riding.

Policy goals, supposedly aligned with the Broad Economic Policy Guidelines (BEPGs) and the Stability and Growth Pact, are implemented domestically, where they can be hijacked or appropriated by actors that have little to gain from the consolidation of the economy, which would bring about greater accountability, transparency, and the efficient allocation of funds.

---

24. International Monetary Fund, 'Taking stock: a progress report on fiscal adjustment', *Fiscal Monitor*, October 2012, p. 4.

Thus the second hypothesis is that:

H2: It is the capture of reform by powerful political and economic actors rather than its design that deals the fatal blow to policy change.

Whenever this happens, the third hypothesis predicts that:

H3: policy makers' subsequent ability to impose a new policy direction becomes more asymmetric and certainly more costly while the propensity of domestic institutions to breed policy stasis becomes stronger.

Despite an excessively antagonistic political system and the intensification of external pressures, the actors who oppose reform are not swept away but manage to reinvent themselves and keep politically visible by linking their fate to policy makers' seeking election or re-election.

Theories, institutions and complex two-level interactions

The core evidence contained in this book is the narrative of Greece's 'adjustment', up to and following its membership of the Eurozone; it is an 'analytical narrative' in that it seeks to develop systematic explanations based on a case study.[25] It suggests that the actors who created and maintained Greece's reform-proof domestic political system have succeeded, over time, in handling external commitments and obligations defensively, treating them as external impositions. This defensive approach to adjustment has – with the exception of the nominal convergence 'push' between 1997 and 1999 and the concomitant (and common among candidate countries) strategy of treating EMU as an 'external constraint'– magnified the costs of adjustment, jeopardised social cohesion, risked the country's marginalisation and precluded the adoption of a new path, including a new growth model.

The story is told in the light of how historically distinctive patterns of national economic-policy formation persist in the face of significant pressure to change, including the effects of the current crisis. The starting point is two disparate orders, one national and one supranational, which compete for the ownership of policies, paradigms and resources. The institutions which inhabit them tend to generate particular modes of decision-making, carrying actors along established paths, precluding and excluding certain outcomes while promoting others. As actors act and re-act, borrowing elements of one order and transplanting them to the other, they become agents of change, creating critical junctures; after each juncture, institutions and actors reformulate strategic interactions, while possibly being reformulated themselves. The theoretical focus on institutions as 'the humanly devised constraints that shape human interaction'[26] predictably provides one reading of this empirical complexity.

25. R. H. Bates, A. Greif, M. Levi, J. -L. Rosenthal and B. Weingast, *Analytic Narratives,* Princeton, Princeton University Press, 1998.

26. D. C. North, *Institutions, Institutional Change, and Economic Performance,* Cambridge, Cambridge University Press, 1990, p. 3.

In the case of EMU, for which a new supranational economic governance was created, a group of nation-states set out to achieve policy and strategic aims that could not be achieved by members acting alone or with less co-operation. The institutionalisation process of EMU was itself a sequence of actors' moves, involving the development of formal and informal institutions to secure the policy preferences and strategic choices of members who adopted the single currency. Irrespective of how governance regimes such as the EU's monetary union are set up, mishaps can and do happen; implementation 'on the ground', even of rules enshrined in treaties, is far from automatic. Actors will seek to evade and override constraints whenever it seems a good idea to do so. In the analysis of Greek policy behaviour, policy actors need to be assigned their proper role, especially if, by their entrepreneurship, they adhere to a well entrenched domestic system of fiscal laxity and systematic procrastination. Pay-offs and rewards can be linked with unconventional outcomes and behaviour, suggesting that, *pace* rational-choice institutionalism, the Eurozone level may well have constituted an 'opportunity structure' that domestic actors chose not to exploit.[27]

Greece's 'reform capacity' has been empirically questioned, along with the nature of EU 'commitment devices' to stimulate economic and social reform at the domestic level.[28] To explain this aversion to reform, analysis must incorporate an understanding of the state in its political-economy context, particularly in the way state-level political attributes, including continuing national differences in budget rules and industrial relations, affect economic performance. In a monetary union which is not an optimal currency area, members with 'a slow dynamic adjustment and responsiveness'[29] risk losing competitiveness and market share to competitors. As national economies function in their diverse ways, their 'major institutional differences show up in different adjustments on the product, credit, and, of course, labour markets'.[30] In a setting in which real convergence is an aspiration and not a given, however, the absence of institutional complementarities and lack of a comparative advantage comes with considerable costs.

In writing the book, official records and documents were carefully reviewed. Attention paid to public statements revealed interesting antitheses: both stable pressures for adjustment – as exerted in Commission opinions and recommendations, Council decisions, and Euro-summit statements – and a good amount of negligence or inability to follow measures through. Equally, national-level responses and aspirations, surfacing in Stability and Growth Programmes,

---

27. B. Kochler-Koch, and B. Ritterberger, 'Review article: the 'governance turn' in EU studies', *Journal of Common Market Studies*, 2006, vol. 44, Annual Review, p. 38.

28. K. Featherstone, and D. Papadimitriou, (eds), *The Limits of Europeanization: Reform capacity and policy conflict in Greece*, London, Palgrave Macmillan, 2008.

29. F. Mongelli, 'European economic and monetary integration and the optimum currency area theory', *Economic Papers*, February 2008, no. 302, p. 51.

30. R. Boyer, 'The unanticipated fallout of European monetary union: the political and institutional deficits of the Euro', in C. Crouch (ed.), *After the Euro: Shaping institutions for governance in the wake of European monetary union*, Oxford, Oxford University Press, 2000, p. 32.

draft budget laws and parliamentary proceedings, repeated key themes – 'reform', 'overhaul', 'consolidation'– over a long period of time, during which, however, economic performance was generally lackluster and most macroeconomic indicators were trending downwards. The real point of the exercise is to illustrate formal positions and then juxtapose them with revealed preferences and private aspirations. The analysis presented here has profited from more than 40 confidential and semi-structured interviews with the key economic players of the period, including one prime minister, nine ministers of national economy and finance, four deputy ministers, and five governors of the Bank of Greece. Interviewees' accounts have been systematically corroborated with those of other interviewees, statements on record and secondary sources. These have been complemented by interviews with key officials, including the two presidents of the Council of Economic Advisors who negotiated, respectively, Greece's entry in the EMU and the Greek Memorandum. The book also relies on first-hand accounts provided by the representatives of business (Hellenic Federation of Enterprises), and labour (the General Confederation of Greek Workers).

Overview of chapters

Has Greece's experience in the euro been a serious case of economic delinquency or did the country fall victim to systemic failures? In this book, I will argue that it has been a case of both. Greece *was* a repeat fiscal offender; some would argue that, on the basis of its miserable record of compliance with the Stability and Growth Pact, it was the worst offender.[31] On top of disregarding the rules, it also repeatedly lied about 'the facts', that is, its official statistics, succeeding in departing from fiscal discipline and embracing idiosyncratic modes of 'gradual adjustment' for more than a decade. Avoiding hard and politically costly reforms, it blatantly failed to enhance its ability, through restructuring its product and labour markets, to respond to economic shocks. Last but not least, it borrowed and spent beyond its means, in a debt-fuelled consumer boom that was reckless and, eventually unsustainable.

At the same time, the Eurozone system failed Greece – among other countries. The monetary policy implemented by the ECB predictably did not fit diverse underlying economic performances; differences across countries in terms of inflation and unit labour costs were 'substantial' and 'persistent', translating into 'accumulated competitiveness losses and large external imbalances'.[32] Eurozone authorities, who had effectively designed a currency with a central bank but no treasury or automatic transfer mechanism, over-optimistically assumed that participating members would be fiscally prudent and, with the bail-out clause in

---

31. A. Sapir, 'Crisis and the governance of the euro area' in L. Tsoukalis and J. E. Emmanouilidis, (eds), *The Delphic Oracle on Europe: Is there a future for the European Union?*, Oxford, Oxford University Press, 2011, p. 103.

32. European Commission, 'EMU@10: successes and challenges after 10 years of Economic and Monetary Union', *European Economy 2*, 2008, p. 6.

place, avoid free-riding. Insufficient control of data by Eurostat reinforced the belief that budget requirements need not be taken seriously. Reality did not hit them even when, once in, most members' self-discipline, let alone self-policing, failed, quite like the preventive and corrective arms of the Stability and Growth Pact. The naïve idea that peer pressure in the Eurogroup, the cornerstone of economic and financial policy co-ordination in EMU, would arrest public sector excesses went hand in hand with another prevalent misconception, namely, that financial markets had in-built mechanisms for correcting theirs. In their quest for profit-maximisation, however, European financial institutions embarked on inappropriate lending practices, while issuing questionable financial instruments right across the board. As periphery bonds started showing up in the balance sheets of core banks, the sovereign-debt crisis became entwined with a banking crisis.

Chapter Two outlines the conceptual framework adopted in the book. Competent institutionalist perspectives tend to present reform processes in terms of a mix of change and continuity; Greece's institutional resistance to change, however, posits a series of interesting challenges to such analyses.

Chapter Three examines the historical dimensions of Greece's political economy, beginning with 1974, when the state began to have a steady, if not intrusive hand, in national economic development. As its role in the economy expanded, so did the budget deficit. In the first socialist period that followed, between 1981 and 1990, a tale that was to become all too familiar emerged: debt-led growth was followed by stabilisation programmes to secure external debt-servicing; these were swiftly dropped once elections were called and the political system was under the sway of electoral cycles.

Chapter Four traces the negotiations that led to EMU and the domestic construction of an 'external-constraint' strategy. The goal of EMU accession was used as a political device to justify long-awaited and long-postponed domestic reform.

In Chapter Five, the analysis turns to the nominal convergence drive and the eventual Greek entry to EMU. With the convergence criteria fulfilled, Greece was on its way to promoting real convergence and fundamentally reforming the politico-economic apparatus that had arrested the country's economic development for decades.

Chapter Six presents the 'good' EMU years and how they were squandered. Following accession, a not-so-new pattern of 'adjustment' emerged: successive governments pursued a loose fiscal policy under 'strict' Eurozone rules, as patronage politics took over the public sector, at the expense of productive investment and structural reform. When the global crisis reached the Eurozone, Greece's loss of credibility, combined with its twin deficits, budget and current account, cut the country off from the financial markets.

Chapter Seven analyses how, ten years after EMU entry, the country faced a crisis that required, once more, a serious rethinking of the political role of the state in the economy. The fact that public finances were in disarray, debt levels had spiralled out of control and the Greek growth 'model' had collapsed indicated policy makers' complete failure to produce a viable political and economic paradigm thirty-five years after the politicisation of the economy had become institutionalised. In this respect, Greece was indeed a special case. It became special in Europe as well, as the very real fear of contagion turned a national crisis into a systemic one. Responsibility for this development, however, was not rightfully apportioned. Greece was a member to a less-than-optimal monetary union, in which a self-fulfilling market panic could drive a country into default[33] and where the 'softer' options of devaluing the currency or loosening monetary policy were *a priori* precluded.

Chapter Eight brings together the two levels of governance, the national and the EU, reassessing their coexistence. While the institutionalisation of economic governance is being built up, in a far from systematic way, the crux of the problem is still unresolved: is the current monetary union feasible without some form of fiscal and banking union? Has the crisis provided sufficient evidence that the 'original sin' – the absence of a political union[34] – must now be rectified? Greece, a delinquent member and a victim of a failed system is testing Eurozone authorities' ability to negotiate a credible and final solution to the crisis, as well as re-work the Eurozone's relationship with the markets. Increasingly, the crisis appears to be testing the process of European integration itself, touching upon important questions of accountability, solidarity and policy effectiveness.

---

33. P. De Grauwe, 'Managing a fragile Eurozone', *CESifo Forum 2*, 2011.

34. P. De Grauwe, 'What have we learned about monetary integration since the Maastricht Treaty?', *Journal of Common Market Studies*, vol. 44, no. 4, November 2006, pp. 711–30 and P. Krugman, 'What do we need to know about the international monetary system?', Princeton University Essays in International Finance 193, Princeton NJ, Princeton University Press 1993.

chapter two | new institutionalism at a crossroads

Introduction

Greece was hardly the only country in the periphery which rode on a wave of complacency, powered by low interest rates and market confidence that macroeconomic and financial stability was here to stay. When the tide turned, following the financial crisis that started in August 2007, Greece was not the only country in the Eurozone that had lost sight of its fiscal obligations under the Stability and Growth Pact (SGP): many countries had pursued a pro-cyclical fiscal and economic policy during the boom years, running up budget deficits and private and public debt. Finally, even if Greece stood out in its handling of creative accounting, it certainly did not stand alone. What really singled Greece out, turning the country's fiscal woes into the 'Greek trigger', were its political institutions and its policies, combined with its persistent twin deficits (state budget and current account), which outdid those of all other EMU countries.

Dealing with institutions and trying to gauge how they affect economic policy and economic performance has never been an easy or straightforward task. In contrast to conventional wisdom, representative democracy, with its emphasis on the process of social decision-making through democratic institutions, does not guarantee economic growth and technological innovation – institutions might fall prey to abuse of power or become repositories for economic inefficiency[1]. Institutions, writes North, are always 'a mixed bag' of those that increase productivity and social welfare and those that reduce productivity.[2] Dissociating the process of institutional creation from actual operation is, therefore, a necessary step for bringing policy-actors back in and determining what they do with their institution-backed status. Opportunities to triumph or fail are equally distributed but political and economic entrepreneurs 'overwhelmingly favor activities that promote redistributive rather than productive activity, that create monopolies rather than competitive conditions, and that restrict opportunities rather than expand them'.[3] If that is the case and the sanguine notion that the political executive acts in the common interest, promoting 'good' governance and creating a 'rent-free' environment, is thrown out of the window, then it becomes important

---

1. M. Rutherford, *Institutions in Economics: The old and the new institutionalism*, Cambridge, Cambridge University Press, 1994, p. 180.

2. D. C. North, *Institutions, Institutional Change and Economic Performance*, Cambridge, Cambridge University Press, 1990, p. 9.

3. *Ibid.*

to gauge who makes economic policy, under what constraints and following which rules. Obviously, the fact that government intervention is not necessarily a good thing does not imply, by default, that giving the market free rein is. The actual performance of markets is not free from coercion, lack of transparency or inefficiency.

There is a second problem, conceptual this time, in assessing institutional performance and its impact on the economy. Initial formulations which linked differences in the formal organisation of the political economy to economic performance were rather sterile or posited unreal or unattainable environments of strategic interaction. Hall and Soskice were right to point out that institutions are inextricably bound up with a nation's history, even if this often prevented simple attempts to explain causation. While institutions are created in a historic moment in time through actions, statutory or otherwise, it is repeated historical experience that allows actors to co-ordinate effectively, through a periodic affirmation of shared understandings.[4] It all becomes much more complicated, of course, when there are two levels of analysis, with asynchronic movements of institutional creation and operation and actors having little incentive to co-operate.[5] Within the period covered in this book, I distinguish between EMU institutions that have been the product of conscious engineering for the explicit purpose of promoting a particular goal, the creation and operation of the euro for example, and national institutions that have been around for a while in participating member states, their design no longer traceable but their impact still very much relevant, such as the domestic budget process. With institutions generating incentives and constraints in two orders that coexist and with actors moving from one order to another, it is assumed that incentives for and blockages to policy change will also tend to coexist. How can we then gauge institutional impact?

This is a particularly pertinent question. The Eurozone crisis that has been unfolding and shows no signs of abating confirms the worst of all worlds. In the absence of an optimal currency area, economic shocks have asymmetric effects, the degree of wage flexibility and labour mobility remains low and no one wants to pick up the tab. It should have come as no surprise that divergent fiscal, social and political structures in the Eurozone regions/countries would eventually sting in an institutional design that forewent cross-border fiscal flows for stabilisation or redistributive purposes.[6] One-sided adjustment has not been working either, without the surplus countries agreeing to perform some adjustment of their own. In reality, lessons have not been learned, in the Eurozone or its constituent parts. In

4. P. A. Hall and D. Soskice, 'An introduction to varieties of capitalism', in P. A. Hall and D. Soskice (eds), *Varieties of Capitalism: The institutional foundations of comparative advantage*, Oxford, Oxford University Press, 2001, pp. 13–14.

5. P. Pierson, 'The path to European integration: A historical institutionalist analysis' in W. Sandholtz and A. Stone Sweet (eds), *European Integration and Supranational Governance*, Oxford, Oxford University Press, 1998.

6. C. Goodhart, 'Currency unions: some lessons from the Euro-zone', *Revista de Economía – Segunda Epoca*, 2007, vol. XIV , no. 1, Banco Central del Uruguay, p. 14.

fact, while the PIIGS have been expected to stick with austerity, 'new' modes of governance have been replicating the emphasis on discipline, this time peppered with prior vetting of fiscal plans, automatic fines, cuts in development funds and loss of voting rights, without promising some degree of risk-sharing or transfers to compensate for further losses of national sovereignty. In contrast to the current cliché, it really does not seem that the crisis has served as a catalyst for policy change.

It has certainly not changed the ways of Greece. Cut off from the markets, the country is supposedly at the mercy of its creditors, each loan disbursement dependent on the implementation of strict fiscal consolidation and structural adjustment measures. In addition to the conditionality clause permeating the entire loan agreement, the Memorandum provides an ideal external constraint/scapegoat for Greek policy makers hesitant to break with their electoral bases; lately, the Commission-backed Task Force has offered much-needed technical assistance in the difficult areas of strengthening tax administration and sound public financial management. Still, Greece's efforts for the last two and a half years have fallen well short of targets and expectations. This is typical for a country that managed to get away with fiscal havoc from the moment it entered the club in January 2001 right up to 2009, breaching, as it has emerged, the SGP every single year. The important question that arises, therefore, is what makes for successful resistance to change, especially change that that been agreed upon and introduced from above, over a long process of supposed adjustment?

Choosing a framework, defining institutions

A suitable arrangement

Theoretically, new institutionalism is best suited to analysing this resistance to change, with its emphasis on the stability of institutions and how they come to shape outcomes over time. From a new institutionalist perspective, Greek 'adjustment', an externally induced process unfolding over time, has been implemented domestically within a dense network of institutions, replete with rules, norms and regulations, which tend to 'lock in' actors' preferences in decisional environments; policy responses to European pressures for reform are, by implication, both context-specific and sensitive to national path-dependencies. 'Adjustment' is also embedded in a supranational order, which is anchored in a set of institutions yet exhibits, at times, an institutional vacuum, whether by lack of political will (as in the case of enforcing compliance with the SGP) or by lack of design (manifest in the absence of a facility for crisis-management and -resolution).

Asserting the analytical importance of institutions is one thing, determining which institutions matter is another. Those who adopt the institutionalist approach agree to disagree on what counts as an institution and how institutions structure outcomes. Here, institutions will be defined, following Hall, as 'sets of regularized practices with a rule-like quality' that 'structure the behaviour of political and economic actors'.[7] This is a historical institutionalist definition that takes seriously both the past trajectory of a given structure, itself the product of human agency, and the way human interactions are played out over a long period of time, affecting that very structure. To avoid over-emphasising stability to the point of solidity, historical institutionalists have been careful to incorporate power asymmetries in their analysis, as institutional operation generates distributional gains and losses and, hence, produces winners and losers. Contests over power may, in fact, have a much greater impact on the way an economic policy is implemented than intentional design. Dispensing with the rational-choice emphasis on 'choice', historical institutionalists are prone to suggesting that actors are restricted by real constellations of power and interest. Hence, rather than deducing the existence of 'equilibrium' and subsequently interpreting it as the actors' preferred outcome, actors are assumed to be in a contest with others to 'establish rules which structure outcomes to those equilibria most favourable to them'[8].

In this way, historical institutionalism becomes pertinent for two reasons. First, if the form and function of institutions reflect the initial balance of power and if subsequent changes reflect the changing equilibrium or changes in the interests and ideas of the most powerful,[9] then the analysis enables an understanding of 'capture'. Groups with little interest in efficiency, transparency or accountability may locate themselves in a position to appropriate or hijack stability and structural adjustment programmes. This is not such a far-fetched assumption, nor does it lack empirical grounding. In its 2005 *World Economic Outlook: Building Institutions* the IMF holds:

> Political institutions determine the distribution of political power, which includes the ability to shape economic institutions and the distribution of resources [...] As groups grow wealthier they can use their economic power to influence political institutions in their favour [...] Changing institutions can be slow, requiring both significant domestic political will and more fundamental measures to reduce the opportunity and incentives for particular groups to capture economic rents.[10]

Second, policy makers' periodic or, in some cases, fixed resistance to change – in spite of formal rules dictating or directing it – suggests that they in fact may be fine-tuned to the operation of informal institutions. Also understood as structures shaping outcomes, they are the 'socially shared rules, usually unwritten, that are

---

7. P. A. Hall, 'Historical institutionalism in rationalist and sociological perspective', in J. Mahoney and K. Thelen (eds), *Explaining Institutional Change: Ambiguity, agency, and power,* Cambridge, Cambridge University Press, 2010, p. 204.

8. J. Knight, *Institutions and Social Conflict,* Cambridge, Cambridge University Press, 1993, p. 20.

9. K. Thelen, 'How institutions evolve: insights from comparative historical analysis', in J. Mahoney and D. Rueschemeyer (eds), *Comparative Historical Analysis in the Social Sciences,* Cambridge, Cambridge University Press, 2003, p. 216.

10. International Monetary Fund, *World Economic Outlook: Building institutions,* Washington, IMF, September 2005, p. 126.

created, communicated, and enforced outside of officially sanctioned channels'.[11] With patronage, clientelism and nepotism transcending the 'behaviour, legal, and normative distinction between a public and private sphere',[12] their close examination brings to the fore 'the relationships, attitudes, and behaviours that are not fully specified in the formal scheme' yet affect actors' strategies through the operationalisation of norms and exposition of roles.[13]

Some criticisms can still be raised. Institutional analysis may accentuate the stability and persistence of institutions, yet even the most static institutions are expected to alter in one way or another. Once room is allowed for institutional plasticity, however, the important analytical question that arises is when should institutions be conceptualised as 'determinants of behaviour' and when as 'objects of strategic action'?[14] With two institutional orders involved, and actors transferring ideas, policy tools and paradigms from one level to the other, this question becomes even more relevant. Here, European institutions and/or policy instruments are held to generate adjustment pressures on the economic policy-making goals of member states, which are subsequently filtered through domestic institutions; these structure the national response and, with the strategic and intentional action of policy actors, generate or hold back policy change. Therefore, the domestic institutions, which serve as the dependent variable at the first stage of the analysis, become the independent variable at the next.[15.]

Do bring the actors in

Historical institutionalism is good at bringing actors in but less competent in ascribing them a central role as strategic and purposive agents of change, blockage or the in-between stages. Rational-choice theorists, on the other hand, present the simplest and most parsimonious representation of actors' interactions. They consider the players involved in a given interaction, the strategies that are being employed, which jointly determine the outcome, and the payoffs that they receive at the end of their interaction. Rational actors try to maximise the achievement of their goals, or their payoffs, subject to institutional constraints and to what other

11. G. Helmke, and S. Levitsky, 'Informal institutions and comparative politics: a research agenda', *Perspectives on Politics*, 2004, vol. 2, no. 4, p. 727. *See also*, G. Helmke and S. Levitsky, (eds), *Informal Institutions and Democracy: Lessons from Latin America*, Baltimore, Johns Hopkins University Press, 2006.

12. G. O'Donnell, 'Another institutionalization: Latin America and elsewhere', *Working Paper 222*, Helen Kellogg Institute for International Studies, University of Notre Dame, 1996, p. 12.

13. D. Searing, 'Roles, rules and rationality in the new institutionalism', *American Political Science Review*, 1991, vol. 85, no. 4, p. 1241.

14. Hall, 'Historical institutionalism in rationalist and sociological perspective', p. 204.

15. I am borrowing this logic from J. Jupille and J. A. Caporaso, 'Institutionalism and the European Union: beyond international relations and comparative politics', *Annual Review of Political Science*, 1999, vol. 2, p. 439.

actors are doing.[16] Concerned with games that 'real' actors play, Scharpf's actor-centred institutionalism posits actors in institutional settings whose characteristics shape both their interactions and the outcome.[17] If institutional context matters – and Tsebelis, for one, holds that 'since institutions determine the choices of actors, the sequence of moves, as well as the information they control, different institutional structures will produce different strategies of the actors, and different outcomes of their interactions',[18] – then there is an overlap with historical institutionalism that can be fruitfully employed.

This is hardly a novelty. Although the 'three institutionalisms' – rational, historical and sociological – build on diverse disciplinary origins, analytic assumptions and explanatory statements,[19] there have been points of convergence or even examples of joint usage and application.[20] In fact, Hall and Taylor have long argued that 'some intellectual borrowing has been going all around'.[21] Consistent with this position, Hall returns, in his later work, to deploy core insights of historical institutionalism in order to extend a rational model of institutional change. Conceptualising how policy change takes root, he takes as his starting point the assembly of a coalition; this must be in favour of change, sharing instrumental beliefs that limit the uncertainty that arises when the effects of institutional reform are considered. Mobilising actors to take the necessary steps to reform still raises collective-action problems of varying intensity, depending on existing organisational practices. In order to collaborate on new institutions, actors

16. G. Tsebelis, 'Institutional analyses of the European Union', *ECSA Review: Approaches to the Study of European Politics*, Spring 1999, p. 4.

17. Scharpf constructs a game-theoretic conceptualisation of strategic interaction that is not methodologically relevant here. His actor-centered institutionalism, however, is a good fit with the idea that social phenomena are to be explained as the outcome of interactions among intentional actors. F. Scharpf, *Games Real Actors Play: Actor-centered institutionalism in policy research*, Boulder, CO, Westview Press, 1997, p. 1.

18. Tsebelis, 'Institutional analyses of the European Union', p. 5.

19. P. A. Hall and R. C. Taylor, 'Political science and the three "new institutionalisms"', *Political Studies*, 1996, vol. 44, December, pp. 936–57; T. A. Koelble, 'The new institutionalism in political science and sociology', *Comparative Politics*, 1995, vol. 27, no. 2, pp. 231–43; J. Kato, 'Institutions and rationality in politics: three varieties of neo institutionalists', *British Journal of Political Science*, 1996, vol. 26, no. 4, pp. 553–82; R. Goodin, 'Institutions and their design' in R. Goodin (ed.), *The Theory of Institutional Design*, Cambridge, Cambridge University Press, 1996; K.A. Shepsle, 'Institutional equilibrium and equilibrium institutions', in H. Weisberg (ed.), *Political Science: The Science of Politics*, New York, Agathon, 1986; K. A. Shepsle, 'Studying institutions: some lessons from the rational choice approach', *Journal of Theoretical Politics*, April 1989, vol. 1, no. 2, pp. 131–47.

20. Grindle, for example, points to studies that combine varying elements of rational-choice and historical institutionalism in emerging economies. M. Grindle, 'In quest of the political: the political economy of development policy making', in G. Meier and J. E. Stiglitz (eds), *Frontiers of Development Economics: The future in perspective*, New York, Oxford University Press, 2001, pp. 345–80.

21. P. A. Hall and R. C. Taylor, 'The potential of historical institutionalism: a response to Hay and Wincott', *Political Studies*, 1998, vol. 46, pp. 958–62, p. 960.

need to resolve the distributional issue of apportioning costs, benefits and risks. Complications further arise by the fact that the effects of institutional change are multidimensional, as are the preference functions that actors bring to proposals. Even when a new set of institutional practices are instituted, they are still mediated by existing practices that were not the object of reform.[22]

With a view to presenting an analysis that is tractable to manageable empirical reality, Hall posits a number of useful propositions that resonate well here, particularly the idea that 'economies are structured by organized relationships that confer more power to initiate or implement change on some actors than on others'.[23] In this book, a dual focus on both institutional effect and actors' purposive behaviour necessitates the employment of both the historical and rational-choice variants of new institutionalism, following the spirit of Hall's writing, if not necessarily the letter. In this way, two important tests of the two variants will also be conducted. If institutional structures do provide the explanatory setting for policy action, or the lack thereof, then a step will have been taken towards filling in the causal links in actors' behaviour, matching the series of intermediate actions, and gaining a better insight into the causal chain through which institutions affect actors' choices. If actors' preferences and strategic interactions do constitute the stuff of policy choices, then a step will have been taken towards understanding how gaps emerge between rational behaviour and suboptimal policy output.

Policy change

Can path dependence be broken?

New institutionalists are primarily concerned with institutional change, opting, at the best of times, to conceptualise policy change as its corollary. In fact, institutional change might or might not have an effect on policy, the verdict depending on the design, functioning and sanctioning mechanisms as well as the political demand for reform. New institutionalism's blessing and curse in conceptualising the process is a notion of path dependence.[24] Once a path has become visible and actors have chosen to proceed down that path, 'they are likely to find it very difficult to reverse course'. For every path taken, several are abandoned and the political alternatives they represent left unexplored. These may well be lost down the road, particularly if they cease to be policy-relevant or elude policy newcomers seeking to make their mark. According to Pierson and Skocpol, 'path dependence analysis' highlights the role of 'historical causation' in which dynamics triggered by an event or a process at one point in time reproduce themselves, even in the absence of the recurrence of the

---

22. Hall, 'Historical institutionalism in rationalist and sociological perspective', pp. 214–5.

23. *Ibid.*, p. 209.

24. P. Pierson and T. Skocpol, 'Historical institutionalism in contemporary political science', in I. Katznelson and H. V. Milner (eds), *Political Science: State of the discipline*, New York, W. W. Norton, 2002, pp. 693–721.

original event or process'.[25] The Eurozone, for example, has been conceptualised as a particular ECB-centric institutional set-up, negotiated primarily, within the EMS policy network. As such, it has defined inflation and economic stability as 'the central problem', underwritten the power of EU central bankers and promoted a bias towards the formulation of sound money policies, locking-in the policies consistent with its definition of price stability.[26] What would have been required to change that path? Nothing short of a 'critical juncture', institutionalists would rush to respond. Nothing short of a major financial crisis like the one that hit European markets in the August of 2007, in fact.

In creating intervals of institutional formation and separating them from the long periods of institutional stability,[27] critical junctures matter because it is only during such times that actors are truly at liberty to choose between new and competing paths. The junctures are, in fact, 'critical' *because* they put institutional arrangements on trajectories that are subsequently difficult to alter.[28] Post-juncture, the logic of increasing returns comes back with a vengeance, locking actors into their choices. The current Eurozone crisis puts into sharp focus the primacy of agency and choice during such short episodes of 'openness'. In this context, the moves to solidify a new economic governance in EMU, as envisaged in the proposed Treaty on Stability, Coordination and Governance, make for interesting inquiry. Member States of the European Union have agreed 'to strengthen the economic pillar of the Economic and Monetary Union by adopting a set of rules intended to foster budgetary discipline through a fiscal compact, to strengthen the coordination of economic policies and to improve the governance of the euro area, thereby supporting the achievement of the European Union's objectives for sustainable growth, employment, competitiveness and social cohesion'.[29] With the wording of the treaty echoing long-standing themes, the only real difference this time appears to be that the stick is longer and that it is expected to hit harder.

In like manner, the design of the permanent mechanism, the European Stability Mechanism, as 'an *ultima ratio* safeguard against imbalances in individual countries'[30] has adopted a 'punishing' logic, whereby non-compliance with strict conditionality[31] is to be met with sanctions, escalating to *de facto* loss of fiscal

---

25. *Ibid.*

26. K. Dyson, *The Politics of the Euro-Zone: Stability or breakdown?*, Oxford, Oxford University Press, 2000, p. 128.

27. See, for example, the analysis in J. Mahoney, 'Path dependent explanations of regime change: Central America in comparative perspective', *Studies in Comparative International Development*, 2001, vol. 36, no.1, pp. 111–41.

28. P. Pierson, *Politics in Time: History, institutions, and social analysis*, Princeton, NJ, Princeton University Press, 2004, p. 135.

29. 'Treaty on Stability, Coordination and Governance (accessed 2 August 2012) Online. Available: http://www.european-council.europa.eu/media/579087/treaty.pdf.

30. European Central Bank, *Monthly Bulletin*, Frankfurt am Main, July 2011, p. 74.

31. *See* 'European Council Decision of 25 March 2011 amending Article 136 of the Treaty on the Functioning of the European Union with regard to a stability mechanism for Member States

autonomy. While access to funding is being made unattractive, in an attempt to limit moral hazard, the overall aim is to affect the expectations of fiscally undisciplined governments about how the other member states are likely to respond to fiscal irresponsibility. It therefore leaves intact the asymmetric architecture that produced the mismatch between the operation of the original institutional framework and increased economic and financial interconnectedness in the first place.

Irrespective of the intensity of the crisis, and even though it may be premature to try to settle the issue once and for all, 'EMU seems to have followed the same logic of institutional change as in its first eight years'.[32] Even when 'fair-weather' times are compared to 'stormy' times, the overall conclusion is one of evolution through 'gradual on-path changes'.[33] This appears to confirm the work of institutionalists who avoid the trap of thinking only in terms of either 'incremental' or 'radical' change: the former are typically associated with the way gradual pressures can make themselves felt in a given system; the latter with the onset of crisis.[34] Understanding that analysis must focus on that grey area between change that is 'minor and continuous' and change that is 'major and abrupt',[35] some institutionalists admit that there may be continuity in periods of upheaval and gradual change in normal periods.[36]

Stability in periods of change and change in periods of stability

In some of its better versions, new institutionalism presents reform processes in terms of a mixture of continuity and change. Recently, Streeck and Thelen[37] and Mahoney and Thelen[38] have sought to capture how institutions change in slow and piecemeal ways that can be equally as consequential for the pursuit of actors' preferred outcomes as are large-scale transformations. Starting with the idea

---

whose currency is the euro' (2011/199/EU), *Official Journal of the European Communities*, L.91, 6.4.2011.

32. M. Salines, G. Glöckler, Z. Truchlewski and P. del Favero, 'Beyond the economics of the Euro: analysing the institutional evolution of EMU 1999–2010', *ECB Occasional Paper Series NO 127*, September 2011, p. 131.

33. *Ibid.*

34. A. P. Cortell and S. Peterson, 'Altered states: explaining domestic institutional change', *British Journal of Political Science*, 1999, vol. 29, no. 1, pp. 177–203.

35. W. Streeck and K. Thelen, 'Introduction: institutional change in advanced political economies', in K. Thelen and W. Steeck (eds), *Beyond Continuity: Institutional change in advanced political economies,* Oxford, Oxford University Press, 2005.

36. *See* Thelen, *How Institutions Evolve*, p. 292, and M. -L. Djelic and S. Quack, 'Conclusion: globalization and a double process of institutional change and institution building', in M. -L. Djelic and S. Quack (eds), *Globalization and Institutions*, Cheltenham, Edward Elgar, 2003, pp. 309–10.

37. W. Streeck and K. Thelen (eds), *Beyond Continuity: Institutional change in advanced political economies,* Oxford, Oxford University Press, 2005.

38. J. Mahoney and K. Thelen, 'A gradual theory of institutional change', in J. Mahoney and K. Thelen (eds), *Explaining Institutional Change: Ambiguity, agency, and power,* Cambridge, Cambridge University Press, 2010.

that the distribution of power provides a basic motor of change, they argue that institutional outcomes need not reflect the interests of the most powerful but may be the unintended result of conflict, or of ambiguous compromises. Institutions' self-reinforcing nature is, therefore, no longer taken for granted. Where they present compromises or rely on coalitional dynamics to support contested settlements, they are vulnerable to shifts, a view that links change and stability inextricably.[39]

In addition to balance of power contestations, change is also linked to a notion of agency-based 'compliance', whereby actors exploit problems of rule interpretation and enforcement in order to implement existing rules in new ways. Based on the four modal types of institutional change – layering, drift, displacement and conversion – Mahoney and Thelen propose a theory of gradual institutional change that emphasises the interaction between features of the political context, particularly whether it affords strong or weak veto possibilities, and properties of the institutions themselves, characterised in terms of a low or high level of discretion in interpretation/enforcement. Different types of agents – insurrectionaries, symbionts, subversives and opportunists –are expected to arise in different institutional environments[40]. What they can or cannot do, alone or in concert with others, remains a moot point and needs to be determined empirically.

The idea here is to arrive at an institutional explanation of policy outcomes, including policy change or lack of, which is not to be confused with explaining institutional change. This is not as straightforward as it sounds. There is a real possibility that institutional change *per se* will not influence policy, let alone affect policy adjustment, inasmuch as policy inertia may derail institutional evolution. The direction of the relationship needs to be thought through and the Greek case, seemingly reform-resistant, posits a sound question mark. The book seeks to explore the patterns of lack of adjustment that tend to persist and the concomitant role of colluding coalitions in creating very real disruptions to externally imposed policies, as well as to external co-ordination and supervision mechanisms. In a way, the problem of applying new institutionalism here is not arriving at an understanding of how institutional and policy change affects economic performance but explaining why there is so much stability, in spite of institutional and policy change 'from above'.

The Approach of this Book

Rather than espousing a theoretical approach and attempting to conveniently match or contrast theoretical constructs with empirical observations, the book adopts, following Hodson, 'a theory-testing approach'[41] that seeks to challenge specific hypotheses about the way institutions, be they national or supranational,

39. *Ibid.*, p. 9.

40. *Ibid.*, p. 39.

41. D. Hodson, *Governing the Euro Area in Good Times and Bad*, Oxford, Oxford University Press, 2011, p. 15.

affect economic performance, linking institutional dynamism to policy change and institutional stasis to the lack thereof. Filtered through this approach, the central organising principle is to examine the institutional frameworks and concomitant configurations of power, both formal and informal, which shape economic policy goals (including price stability, the growth rate of GDP and GDP per capita, and unemployment rate) and that promote or hinder compliance with the agreed goals, instruments and institutions of EMU governance, including the Broad Economic Policy Guidelines and the Stability and Growth Pact. With ever-present incentives to dodge rules or free ride, how do institutions at the national and supranational levels identify noncompliance and what happens when they trigger contrasting signals regarding the possibility of sanctions? Working with the assumption that 'institutions give some groups or interests disproportionate access to the decision-making process',[42] policy actors who are in a position to act or obstruct because of this power are, in turn, analytically indispensable.

There are two main dimensions here: understanding the Greek state and economy and placing national policy systems in the context of EMU operation. New institutionalism is well suited to analysing policy stability, with its emphasis on the stability of institutions and how they come to shape outcomes over time. It has however, rarely been employed in a two-level, ongoing interaction,[43] whereby supranational and national institutions compete for final control over policy output. Examining the institutional and policy misfit between a centralised monetary policy and an overheating peripheral economy is one thing. When it comes to deciphering the north–south asymmetry, however, and how it impacts on adjustment potential, attention must unavoidably turn to the state in its international political economy context, including how economic size and openness, trade balance, organisation of production, and financial market development affect policy makers seeking co-operation or renewed co-operation in multilateral regimes. Whenever necessary, insights from the study of comparative political economy and international political economy (IPE) will be brought in to help elucidate the relevant hypotheses. This is in line with 'best practices', given the difficulties associated with establishing a definitive pattern of influence in national-EU level interaction.[44]

---

42. Hall and Taylor 'Political science and the three new institutionalisms', p. 941.

43. For an analysis of EU-level processes, *see* S. Bulmer, 'The governance of the European Union: a new institutionalist approach', *Journal of Public Policy*, 1994, vol. 13, no. 4, pp. 351–80; Pierson, 'The path to European integration'; K. A. Armstrong and S. Bulmer, *The Governance of the Single Market*, Manchester, Manchester University Press, 1998.

44. *See*, for example, A. Hurrell, and A. Menon, 'Politics like any other? Comparative politics, in-ternational relations and the study of the EU', *West European Politics*, 1996, vol. 19, no. 2, pp. 386–402, J. Richardson, 'Policy making in the EU: interests, ideas and garbage cans of primeval soup', in J. Richardson (ed.), *European Union: Power and policy-making*, London/New York, Routledge, 1996, p. 21.

The 'varieties of capitalism' approach offers a useful example in this respect.[45] Allowing for the fact that it starts with the firm as a relational network, it seeks to map out the institutional frameworks in which it operates, determining the existence of institutional complementarities and whether these confer comparative advantages to a given country. National political economies are divided along a 'liberal market–co-ordinated market' spectrum, the two poles constituting ideal types. Among the large OECD nations, Hall and Soskice suggest that Greece, France, Italy, Spain, Portugal, and Turkey, are left 'in more ambiguous positions'. Their institutional clustering may, in fact, point to the type of capitalism described as 'Mediterranean', whereby a large agrarian sector and extensive state intervention have provided them with specific kinds of capacities for 'non-market co-ordination' in corporate finance and more 'liberal arrangements' in labour relations.[46] Testing whether the institutional complementarities inherent in the Greek economic model were either immune to EMU-related pressures or ill-suited to accommodate them may offer an explanation for the country's divergent 'adjustment'.[47] Comparative advantage probably turns into disadvantage when, for example, the operation of labour and product markets narrows firms' competitiveness and export activities vis-à-vis their main trading partners.

In like manner, the book cannot overlook the political economy of fiscal institutions, particularly the work on the institutional framework of public budget processes. Following EMU, the decisions that touched upon the crux of the matter, namely, which groups would receive public funding and which would pay for it[48] were theoretically being vetted through the Stability and Growth Pact. Its corrective arm, the Excessive Deficit Procedure, provided a framework for punishing lax states but hardly dictated how states were to maintain fiscal discipline.[49] To link the well documented variable adherence to the Pact with national fiscal rules, Hallerberg and Hallerberg, Strauch and von Hagen propose two institutional approaches, the delegation approach, which 'rests on the delegation of power to the minister of finance to overcome the coordination problem inherent in budgetary decision-making' and the contract approach, which 'hinges on pre-established

---

45. In presenting 'varieties of capitalism' as 'one of the more important theoretical innovations in the comparative social sciences', Hancké writes that, as a toolbox, it is based on the combination of 'systematically constructed micro-foundations, innovations in game theory and historical institutionalism'. B. Hancké, 'Introducing the debate' in B. Hancké (ed.), *Debating Varieties of Capitalism: A reader,* Oxford, Oxford University Press, 2009, p. 5.

46. Hall and Soskice, 'An introduction to varieties of capitalism', p. 21.

47. For a thorough critique on 'varieties of capitalism' and its application to Greek processes of structural reform, *see* K. Featherstone, and D. Papadimitriou, *The Limits of Europeanization: Reform capacity and policy conflict in Greece,* London, Palgrave Macmillan, 2008, pp. 48–57.

48. M. Hallerberg *Domestic Budgets in a United Europe: Fiscal governance from the end of Bretton Woods to EMU,* Ithaca, Cornell University Press, 2004, p. 2.

49. M. Hallerberg, 'Budgeting in Europe: did the domestic budget process change after Maastricht?', *Paper presented at the 2003 EUSA Conference,* Nashville TN, 2003, p. 2.

budgetary targets and rules'.[50] National fiscal governance is effectively linked to the structure of the electoral system and the dominant type of government. Hence, delegation is better suited to single-party majority governments, usually formed under majoritarian electoral systems, while coalition governments emerging in highly proportional electoral systems opt for the contract approach.[51] Greece was one of many delegation states posting excessive deficits, hence the institutional centralisation that would allegedly ensue after EMU accession failed to solve the fiscal co-ordination problem. Moreover, the fact that neither the powers endowed to the finance minister nor the stringent budgetary targets operated as disciplining devices posits an interesting question for the relations between the institutions prescribed by the approach.

The book explores Greece's trajectory in the Euro. Right from the moment of EC entry in 1981, up to 2010, when the country sought the activation of the joint EU-IMF financial instrument, distinctive patterns of national economic policy formation have tended to persist, begging the question of why there is so much stability, as evidenced in the absence of adjustment and reform and the consistently disappointing performance of the economy, in spite of EU-driven institutional and policy change. In seeking to answer whether Greece forms a case of economic delinquency or has fallen victim to systemic failure, the book speaks directly to three debates about the way EMU has redefined the balance between national independence and supranational interdependence: First, whether a more centralised approach to economic policy in the Eurozone will work, where the previous governance method failed to provide a co-ordinated fiscal and monetary response?; second, how has the IMF/EU experiment in problem-solving fared, given the perceived and growing chasm between core and periphery?; third, who makes economic policy in the Eurozone and for whom, when the democratic deficit appears to be widening?

---

50. M. Hallerberg, R. Strauch, and J. von Hagen, 'The design of fiscal rules and forms of governance in European Union Countries', *European Central Bank Working Paper No. 419,* Frankfurt-am-Main, ECB, 2004, p. 7.

51. *Ibid.*

chapter three | greek policy formation, 1974–1993: caught between a politicised economy and EC adjustment

Greece's road to Economic and Monetary Union was paved with mixed intentions. A member of the EC since 1981, Greece was never particularly good at adjustment. In fact, the first ten years of membership saw a clear reversal in the process of catching up economically with the rest of the Community. This was no mean feat, particularly as Greece had been a net beneficiary of the EU budget: its net receipts increased from less than half a per cent of GDP in 1981 to five per cent in 1992.[1] Generous payments from the Structural Fund, the Integrated Mediterranean Programmes and the European Agricultural and Guarantee Fund were, theoretically, handed out to alleviate the burden of accession, brought about by trade liberalisation and the ensuing loss of structural competitiveness. To tackle its balance of payments problem, Greece was also the recipient of two EC loans. By 1993, however, when the Treaty on European Union came into force and the first stage of Economic and Monetary Union began, the country was, by all accounts, both a poor and an unlikely candidate for EMU membership; all that it had to offer was a history of low growth, high inflation, fiscal profligacy and recurring external disequilibria.

In this chapter, I explore the constitutive elements of this pattern of Greek mis-adjustment to EU financial discipline: securing over-generous transition periods; exploiting EC financial assistance granted in order to mitigate the dislocating effects of market corrections; and convenient disregarding of obligations attached to EC loans and treaties. It will be divided into three chronological periods: 1974–81, when unfettered statism first brought into focus the fiscal question; 1981–90, which saw the creation and the accumulation of Greece's large public debt; and 1990–93, when a reform drive to roll back the state ultimately failed. The idea is that Greece's subsequent behaviour as a member of the Eurozone can best be understood if placed in its proper 'historical' and 'political economy' context.

Greek economic-policy formation was in fact, uneasily caught between the politicisation of the economy, which acquired a semi-structural character with the restoration of democracy in 1974, and adjustment to a new policy environment – an obligation that emanated from EEC membership in 1981. The domestic institutional framework interfered adversely with the ability of the economy to adapt, as policy makers failed to redesign institutions in order to improve economic performance. For new institutionalists, in fact, the persistence of institutions over

---

1.   OECD, *Economic Outlook 47*, June 1990, pp. 42–3.

time is related to the way in which they preclude certain goals and strategies or make the adoption of new goals costly.[2]

With major economic policy developments examined from this angle, there is, in parallel, a systematic attempt to trace the 'European dimension' of Greek economic policy. This dimension ensues, analytically, from the role (if any) that EC institutions played in policy formulation during this period and from the corresponding policy responses of key national actors. EC (and subsequently EU) institutions and actors were not good at promoting or enforcing adjustment either. Greece repeatedly got away with a slap on the wrist for 'procrastinating', when, in reality, its implementation record of Community policies and obligations was consistently among the worst. The effectively non-conditional character of EC aid, combined with the substantial transfers that Greece was able to obtain, reinforced the impression of a lax regime of supervision and control; in such a regime, slippages were bound to go unnoticed or, worse, unreported. Why should compliance with the EMU regime have been better, if lessons had not been learned, either at national or at European level?

1974–81: the slow-down in the Greek economy

The period prior to the middle 1970s was one of growth and prosperity for the Greek economy. Appraised in terms of economic indicators, gross domestic product more than tripled in volume between 1960 and 1979. The rate of growth peaked to 7.5 per cent in the first decade while it slowed down, due to the 1973 oil shock, to a rate of 4.5 per cent in the second;[3] the deceleration in its growth rate was, after 1975, stronger than for the OECD area as a whole. The rise in energy and raw materials prices, combined with the recessionary trends in the world economy, placed a significant burden on the economy's growth potential. In the new competitive conditions, in which production moved from labour-intensive to technology-oriented activities, the relative position of Greece, which did not possess the requisite infrastructure or skilled labour force, was further weakened. Greece's economic policy response to the oil shock – an external pressure for adjustment – was slow, inadequate or non-existent.

This was not unrelated to the fact that, on the internal front, the fall of the dictatorship in 1974 and the transition to democracy triggered a major change in Greece's economic governance framework: social restitution and justice became

---

2. S. D. Krasner, 'Review Article: approaches to the state, alternative conceptions and historical dynamics', *Comparative Politics*, 1984, vol. 16, no. 2, p. 240. *See also* King and Rothstein, who suggest that institutions persist beyond the fulfilment of their original purposes; *see* D. S. King and B. Rothstein, 'Institutional choices and labor market policy: a British-Swedish comparison', *Comparative Political Studies*, 1993, vol. 26, no. 2, p. 149.

3. All of the economic data in this section have been taken from OECD, *OECD Economic Surveys Greece 1981–2*, Paris, OECD, May 1982, and European Commission, 'Annual Economic Report 1980–81: The Greek economy and entry into the community', *European Economy 7*, November 1980.

the overriding goals and organising principles. Konstantinos Karamanlis,[4] Prime Minister at the time, set a new direction for economic policy, one that marked a clear departure from the 1954–73 framework and its narrative of development and efficiency. In place of 'commitment and co-ordination mechanisms' that were geared towards high investment and growth, low inflation and high returns to capital accumulation,[5] in the post-1974 framework, state intervention was justified on the basis of equity. In this context, the negative policy patterns that surfaced at the time included: extensive nationalisation and the use of public enterprises as employment instruments; selective provision of funds from state-controlled banks that guaranteed the survival of inefficient productive structures and crowded out modernisation initiatives; and the increasing domination of a particularistic logic[6] in the way the state distributed economic benefits.

The slow-down in growth was accompanied by a worsening of the structural imbalances of the Greek economy, with recurring balance of payments problems providing the most tangible proof that the economy continued to lag behind its major competitors.[7] In 1979, the current account deficit as a percentage of GDP doubled from 2.8 per cent in 1978 to 4.85 per cent. Worse, the public sector deficit, shot to 9 per cent of GDP in 1979. Although public investment was kept at a disproportionately low level, general government current expenditure rose from 28.4 per cent on average during the previous period to 35 per cent in 1979; the increase reflected the redistributive activity of central government and the growth of social security funds. At the same time, the responsiveness of the taxation system to changes in GDP remained fairly low; it weakened further when the growth of public expenditure accelerated. In this context, public debt reached 540.1 billion GRD in 1979; it had stood at 178.6 billion in 1974. The expenditure for the servicing of the public debt rose to 64.7 billion GRD in 1979.[8]

---

4.   *See* Appendix A. Biographical Data.

5.   G. Alogoskoufis, 'The two faces of Janus: institutions, policy regimes and macroeconomic performance in Greece', *Economic Policy*, 1995, vol. 10, no. 20, p. 152.

6.   Diamantouros refers to the particularistic logic that guided the distribution of benefits in society. The process of benefit allocation was not based on universal criteria but on state policies affecting large yet diverse groups in society; *see* N. Diamantouros, 'Greek politics and society in the 1990s' in G. Allison and K. Nikolaidis (eds), *The Greek Paradox: Promise vs. Performance*, Cambridge MA, The MIT Press, 1997, p. 26.

7.   To provide one example, between 1960 and 1979, the fall in the share of agriculture (from 23 per cent to 13 per cent) was matched by a corresponding increase in the percentage of industry and services. Industrial development however, was concentrated on traditional, consumer goods sectors, which, in 1975, accounted for 54.2 per cent of total value added in the manufacturing sector. This figure compared unfavourably with developments in Spain and Portugal. Both countries experienced a decline in the share of traditional consumer goods industries (28.5 per cent and 33.6 per cent of total value added), which was accompanied by an increase in the production of intermediate and capital goods; *see* L. Tsoukalis, *The European Community and its Mediterranean Enlargement*, London, George Allen and Unwin, 1981, pp. 23–5.

8.   OECD, *OECD Economic Surveys Greece 1981–82*, pp. 31–58. *See also* S. Dimeli, T. Kollintzas, N. Christodoulakis, *Economic Fluctuations and Development in Greece and in Europe*, Athens, IMOP, 1997, pp. 36–41 [in Greek].

Leaving aside the effects of the oil shock, inflationary pressures intensified, with poor developments in the productive base of the economy, a swelling public deficit and accelerating wage increases brought about by the income redistribution policy. In the four years to 1978, total average earnings rose at an annual rate of about 21 per cent of GDP, over 8 per cent faster than the rate of consumer price increases; the underlying annual growth of productivity decelerated markedly (from 5 per cent before 1975 to around 2 per cent in 1979) to a rate that fell to almost one-third of the rate of real average earnings. As a result, after 1974, a double-digit rate of inflation came to typify Greece's macroeconomic management.

Turning to the EEC

Arriving at the promised land

During this period, Greece's association agreement with the EEC was reactivated and Greece applied for membership in June 1975. The 'European dimension' of Greek economic policy had begun, in fact, with the signing of the Association Agreement in July 1961. The Agreement stipulated, among other provisions, the establishment of a full customs union, following a two-tier transitional period. Tariffs and quotas were to be abolished within twelve years by both sides. Trade restrictions for a list of products were to be eliminated over twenty-two years. The agreement also envisaged the harmonisation of large sectors of the Greek economy with those of the Community as well as the provision of resources, primarily in the form of loans, to facilitate Greece's adjustment to the objectives of the Association. In the preamble, the Contracting Parties recognised 'that the support given by the European Economic Community to the efforts of the Greek people to improve their standard of living will facilitate the accession of Greece to the Community at a later date'.[9] The Agreement was put into effect in November 1962.

Tariff reductions, each equivalent to 10 per cent of existing duties, were effected in November 1962, May 1964, and November 1965. In 1967, the year that the military dictatorship was imposed, the Agreement 'froze', an EEC reaction to the institutional anomaly caused; this affected the harmonisation of agricultural policies between the two sides and the provision of $56m owed under the Financial Protocol.[10] By 1974, when a democratic regime was reinstated and the New Democracy party came to power,[11] the customs union was the only area

---

9.   Cited in St. Stathatos, 'From association to full membership' in L. Tsoukalis (ed.), *Greece and the European Community*, Farnborough, Saxon House, 1979, p. 3.

10. S. Verney, 'Greece and the European Community', in K. Featherstone and D. Katsoudas (eds), *Political Change in Greece: Before and after the Colonels*, London/Sydney, Croom Helm, 1987, pp. 257–8.

11. New Democracy was the party in government during the 1974–81 period. The party's ideological platform was effectively subjugated to the charismatic personality of its leader, K. Karamanlis, an ardent supporter of the country's pro-EC orientation. In the critical 1977 electoral campaign, ND stressed its strong commitment to Greece's accelerated accession to the EEC. Greece's eventual

where concrete results had been achieved. Duties were completely abolished on two-thirds of Greece's industrial imports from the Community, while they were reduced by 44 per cent on the remaining one-third.

Until the early 1970s, Greece's economic growth offered positive omens for the possibility of Greek EEC membership. The New Democracy government submitted an application for full membership on 12 June 1975. The Governor of the Bank of Greece, Xenophon Zolotas, suggested that the 'figures [of Greek economic performance] provide ample proof of the dynamism of the Greek economy and can serve as an answer to the question of whether Greek industry can sustain competition within the unified European market'.[12] The question of the EEC impact on Greece's undeveloped industrial structure and fragile balance of payments caused uncertainty and confusion at best: some 'sensitive' sectors of the Greek economy were identified, coupled with requests for temporary protection 'to avoid disturbances'.[13] Admittedly, no questions were asked at EC level either, as the treaty of accession failed to formally prescribe a programme of stabilisation or structural adjustment.[14] Due to the grave security considerations[15] that emerged at the time and the political elites' effort to consolidate parliamentary democracy, the issue of EEC membership entered the policy agenda mainly as a political issue.[16]

---

accession was considered a defining moment in the party's political direction. Of the opposition parties, PASOK's quick success (as a new political formation, PASOK doubled its share of the vote from 13.6 per cent in 1974 to 25.3 per cent in 1977) rendered the party's position on the EEC significant. In the event, PASOK's position was flexible, reflecting the predominance and the evolving preferences of A. Papandreou, the other charismatic leader of this period. While PASOK had rejected EEC membership in the 1974 elections, in 1977, it had opted for a loose association agreement on the Norwegian model and holding a referendum. Until 1981, when it came to power, its position on the EC remained unclear and subjugated to 'catch-all' considerations. For a full exploration, see R. Clogg, 'The Greek political context', in L. Tsoukalis (ed.), Greece and the European Community, Farnborough, Saxon House, 1979.

12. X. Zolotas, 'Developments and prospects of the Greek Economy: an address, Bank of Greece', Papers and Lectures No. 30, Athens, 1975, p. 22. The Greek view was not shared by the Commission. According to Commission estimates, the main implications of Greek membership were financial and budgetary. If Greece were to accede in 1976, Community expenditure would have risen by approximately 300 million units of account. These estimates did not include the financial requirements that would accrue from the structural imbalances of the Greek economy. 'Opinion on Greek Application for Membership' (Transmitted to the Council by the Commission on 29 January 1976)', Bulletin of the European Communities, 1976, Supplement, no. 2, pp. 8, 18..

13. The likely impact of accession entered only superficially in the formulation of the country's negotiating position. I. Tsalicoglou, Negotiating for Entry: The accession of Greece to the European Community, Aldershot, Dartmouth, 1995, p. 43.

14. D. Ethier, Economic Adjustment in New Democracies: Lessons from Southern Europe, London, Macmillan, 1997, p. 71.

15. Greece had, at the time, withdrawn from the military wing of NATO. This was related to the fact that NATO had not intervened in the Turkish invasion of Northern Cyprus. Community membership was supposed, therefore, to ease Greece's foreign policy ties with the US. See P. Tsakaloyannis, 'The European Community and the Greek-Turkish dispute', Journal of Common Market Studies, 1980, vol. 19, no. 1, pp. 44–5.

16. In the parliamentary session that preceded the ratification of Greece's accession, Prime Minister

The Treaty of Accession between the member states of the European Communities and Greece, and the Final Act, were both signed in Athens on 28 May 1979. During the ratification period, the parliamentary vote in favour of Greek accession was almost unanimous in most member states, with the exception of France and Denmark. In Greece, the Treaty was ratified by the Greek Parliament on 28 June 1979; the three-fifths majority that was required by the constitution was satisfied. Ninety-three deputies of PASOK (Panhellenic Socialist Party) and eleven deputies of KKE (Communist Party of Greece) decided to boycott the voting session. Greece became a full member in January 1981.

How to fit old conditions into new frameworks?

At the time of EC entry, the country's positive growth differential with the rest of the OECD was eliminated. The pattern of macroeconomic mismanagement had resulted in:

> a postponement of necessary structural adjustments, insufficient modernisation of private industry (where troubled firms took even more debt), persistence of both large current account deficits (from around 6.1 per cent of GDP in 1974 to 5.5 per cent in 1980) and high inflation (rising to 24.9 per cent in 1980) and the continuous expansion of government expenditure (from 21.1 per cent of GDP in 1973 to 33.2 per cent in 1980, causing the budget deficit to grow from 1.4 to 2.9 per cent of GDP).[17]

In fact, this period saw, as Figure 3.1 suggests, the growing gap between public spending and revenue turn into a permanent crack in Greece's fiscal management.

Policy makers, who relied on expansionary demand management policies, failed to attract new investment or overhaul labour and product market rigidities. This was a rather unfortunate state of affairs – economic-policy formation was called to operate under new external parameters with an economy that had not shed its 'backward' structural features: these included the agricultural sector's over-dominant position; the industrial and commercial sectors' low degree of concentration and specialisation; heavy external protection and a regulated financial system which hindered the free determination of the exchange and interest rates.[18]

Karamanlis linked accession with the consolidation of both national independence and democratic institutions. He even suggested that: 'The political advantages that I have mentioned are so grave, that we should have pursued our accession even if we were not to receive any financial benefits' (my translation), *Parliamentary Proceedings* (Session PM'), 26 June 1979.

17. M. Rocas and T. Padoa-Schioppa, 'Economic change and the process of democratization in Southern Europe', in H. Gibson (ed.), *Economic Transformation, Democratization, and Integration into the European Union: Southern Europe in comparative perspective,* London, Palgrave, 2001, p. 57.

18. Commission of the European Communities, *Annual Economic Report 1980–81: The Greek economy and entry into the community,* p. 117.

The Growing Gap Between Public Spending and Revenue
1971- 1993

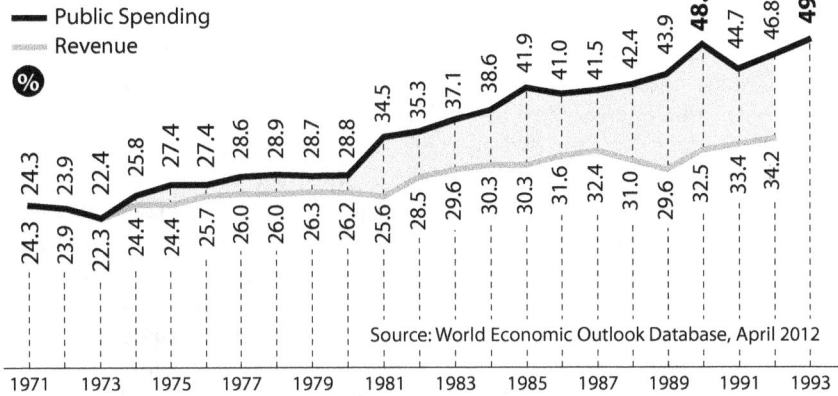

Figure 3.1: The growing gap between public spending and revenue

The post-1974 framework and its operating principle- the legitimisation of the use of the economy for social and political goals-, formed the basis for Greece's major economic policy patterns; it helps explain, in later chapters, their staying power. The notion of a framework refers, analytically, to an historical institutionalist 'overarching context', composed of pre-existing institutions, actors and the ties between them, whose configurations and interactions shape collective choices of adjustment, present and future; it therefore avoids the rational-choice pitfall of focusing on a single institutional or organisational site of political contestation.[19] The sections that follow will provide evidence that this framework subjected the entire economy to an expansionary–contractionary policy cycle that hindered both economic growth and, unavoidably, Greece's adjustment to the EEC.

1981–90: the socialist experiment

Is self-sufficient economic development still possible?

This period is defined by the economic programme of PASOK, the Panhellenic Socialist Movement, which came to power in October 1981. Under the charismatic leadership of Andreas Papandreou,[20] PASOK was the first socialist party to form a government – a transfer of power that was not accompanied, as had been feared, by institutional upheaval. PASOK's economic philosophy had solidified during

---

19. P. Pierson and T. Skocpol, 'Historical institutionalism in contemporary political science' in I. Katznelson and H. V. Milner (eds), *Political Science: State of the discipline*, New York, W. W. Norton, 2002

20. *See* Appendix A. Biographical Data.

its opposition years and, once in power, it swiftly produced a policy agenda that was radical in its aspirations to modernise the economy and transform economic power. The party's analysis of the state of the economy, however, had produced two rather disparate approaches.[21] Structural reform was regarded as the appropriate response to the macroeconomic imbalances of the 1970s and the public deficits generated by the policies of the New Democracy government. Structural reform however, was to be implemented alongside a redistributory social policy and an expansionary fiscal policy, the two main macroeconomic mishaps of the previous period. PASOK economists and party cadres, who had adopted a Greek-style version of Keynesianism,[22] assumed that a boost in demand would strengthen the purchasing power of lower-income groups, which would support, in turn, domestic industry. At the same time, dependency theory and, in particular, the idea that countries in the centre of capitalism imposed on countries of the periphery a type of development that did not correspond to their needs had also shaped the party's platform.[23] Its appeal was evident in Papandreou's commitment to establish an independent route for economic development, through decentralised planning, the socialisation of existing nationalised firms and the introduction of self-management in the workplace.

Competing economic philosophies within the party were imperfectly accommodated in the government's programme; its main thrust consisted of introducing 'compensatory' justice for 'non-privileged Greeks'.[24] This policy was exemplified in a 40 per cent rise in the minimum wage and the establishment of wage indexation. The implementation of both measures had an adverse impact on employment, as unit labour costs rose by 26 per cent in 1982 and a number of small and medium-size firms went out of business. A new policy of nationalisation of the so-called 'ailing firms' was put into effect: these included a number of loss-

21. Tsakalotos provides a detailed review of the ideas that shaped the new government's economic thinking. He suggests that various influential economists, including Gerasimos Arsenis and Yannos Papantoniou (who subsequently became Ministers of National Economy) had pointed out the areas of ambiguity in PASOK's economic strategy. See E. Tsakalotos, *Alternative Strategies to Economic Development*, Aldershot, Avebury, 1991.

22. The view that PASOK experimented with a Keynesian economic policy has been expounded by G. Evdoridis, 'Basic weaknesses of our economy and possibilities to remedy them', *Economicos Tahydromos*, 8 March 1990 [in Greek], and G. Soldatos, 'Why the postwar modernisation of the Greek economy remained unfinished', *Economicos Tahydromos*, 12 October 1989 [in Greek].

23. Opposing the prevailing view that Keynesianism constituted the main economic 'philosophy' behind policy formation, Psalidopoulos asserts that Papandreou's economic thinking was shaped by the dependency theory work of Amin and Frank. See M. Psalidopoulos, 'Keynesianism across nations: the case of Greece', *The European Journal of the History of Economic Thought*, Autumn 1996, vol. 3, no. 3, p. 457.

24. Referring to PASOK's first four years in government, Papandreou asserted that the first economic goal of the 1981–85 government was 'the restoration of social justice, the restitution of the accumulated injustices of the past and the substantial redistribution of income in favour of the weaker strata of the population'. See *Parliamentary Proceedings*, (Session MH'), 6 December 1985. Faced with the economic failure of this policy, he later admitted that 'the redistribution of 1982 was not part of an economic strategy, but part of a policy of social justice'. Cited in Tsakalotos, *Alternative Strategies to Economic Development*, p. 19.

making and bankrupt private firms (including textiles, mining, and shipyards), whose ownership passed on to the Industrial Restructuring Organisation (IRO), a public holding company.

The rapid expansion of public finance failed to strengthen domestic production or create the conditions for GDP growth. While between 1980 and 1982, private consumption rose by 6 per cent in real terms and public consumption by 9, GDP fell by -0.2 per cent in 1981 and -0.1 per cent in 1982. Expansionary policies fuelled inflation, which peaked at 25 per cent, almost double the average rate in OECD and EEC countries.[25] In addition, the restructuring and recapitalisation of non-viable industrial firms failed to trigger, in the absence of any serious structural adjustment measures, a strong supply-side response. Hence, the competitiveness of the economy continued to decline while the fall in private investment was not reversed. The government shifted focus from public- to private-led growth and adopted, in January 1983, a reform programme: its central tenets included the readjustment of the wage indexation system and a devaluation of the currency by 10 per cent. The enactment of Law 1262/82 was to provide a series of incentives for private investment.[26]

Implementation, however, was short-lived. Policy makers proved unable or unwilling to change the system of governance in such a way that public revenue could be raised and private-sector profitability guaranteed, by addressing labour-market rigidities or reducing tax uncertainty.[27] The lack of government commitment was not accidental but symptomatic of a policy pattern that was to become embedded in the framework. The development of a number of economic indicators indicated that an electoral-fiscal cycle[28] was in full operation well before the 1985 elections. 'The timing reflected Prime Minister Papandreou's analysis that the 1984 European elections, which preceded national elections, were critical for PASOK's future in government'.[29]

---

25. OECD, OECD Economic Surveys Greece 1983–1984, Paris, OECD, 1983.

26. Bank of Greece, *Report of the Governor for the Year 1984*, Athens, Bank of Greece, 1985.

27. N. Christodoulakis, 'Fiscal developments in Greece, 1980–93: a critical review', *European Economy 3*, 1994, pp. 97–134.

28. Following Nordhaus, a government seeking electoral gain takes advantage of the short-term trade-off between inflation and unemployment. Prior to the election, the government will create the conditions for an increase in the growth rate of the economy (and a fall in unemployment) at the cost of 'some inflation'. Once elected, it will reduce gross national product during its first years in office in order to reduce inflation. *See* W. D. Nordhaus, 'The political business cycle', *Review of Economic Studies*, 1975, vol. 42, no. 2, pp. 169–90. In his later work, Nordhaus uncovered five different models of electoral cycles, including the 'opportunistic' and the 'ideological' cycles. W. D. Nordhaus, 'Alternative approaches to the political business cycle', *Brooking Papers on Economic Activity*, 1989, no. 2, p. 48. A number of theories have developed since, seeking to explain the occurrence of cycles. Rogoff and Siebert, for example, suggest that electoral cycles emerge due to temporary information asymmetries because voters are imperfectly informed about the competence of politicians. *See* K. Rogoff and A. Sibert, 'Elections and macroeconomic policy cycles', *Review of Economic Studies*, 1988, vol.55, no.1, pp. 1–16.

29. Interview 1.

A short story about Greek electoral cycles

PASOK was hardly the first party in power to generate an electoral cycle. In its bid for re-election in 1981, the ND government had engineered a massive expansion of public spending, under the leadership of Georgios Rallis,[30] – the general government budget deficit shot from 2.6 per cent of GDP in 1980 to 9.0 per cent in 1981. As New Democracy lost the elections, the strategy did not pay off. It did, however, set a precedent for the political manipulation of a number of economic variables; in the post-1974 framework, the line between political management and political manipulation could be easily blurred. The PASOK government followed the trend: prior to elections, it pursued an expansionary fiscal policy (by manipulating government spending, the primary deficit, and taxes) and a loose monetary policy (by manipulating growth in the money supply). Between 1983 and 1985, the budget deficit rose from 8.6 per cent to 14.5 per cent; general government consolidated gross debt followed a similar course, rising from 36.6 per cent in 1983 to 51.6 per cent in 1985; this generated an increase of the net Public Sector Borrowing Requirement (PSBR) to 17.9 per cent in 1985, which triggered, in turn, an acceleration of the growth rate of M3, from 20.3 per cent in 1982 to 29.4 per cent in 1984. In Figure 3.2, the rise in the government budget deficit acquires, in election years, the form of well defined peaks.

In the 1985 elections, the generation of an electoral-fiscal cycle did prove an optimal strategy for staying in office. This was not the case either in the previous election in 1981 or in the elections that followed in 1989, 1990 and 1993. Still, government policy makers chose to persist with this strategy, even if the overriding short term political goal – creating an environment of high growth and low unemployment at the time of the election – came at a steep price. As cycles became more pronounced over time but also more asymmetric, they precipitated the further deterioration of existing macroeconomic imbalances; at the end of each cycle, it became increasingly hard for the economy to return to its initial deficit level.[31] In this context, the electoral-fiscal cycle acted as a sort of negative incentive, with actors and institutions disassociating the economic-policy formation framework from the long-term performance of the economy. The notorious laxity in tax enforcement and the deliberate lags in tax collection, which were typical of election years, affected the credibility of budget implementation; at the same time, use of public enterprises for the satisfaction of clientelistic goals affected their credibility as economic agents.[32]

---

30. When Konstantinos Karamanlis became President of the Republic, Georgios Rallis, Education Minister and Foreign Minister respectively in the Karamanlis governments of 1974 and 1977, was elected leader of the ND party, succeeding Karamanlis as Prime Minister.

31. S. Thomadakis, 'The Greek economy and European integration: prospects for development and threats of underdevelopment', in D. Constas and T. Stavrou (eds), *Greece Prepares for the Twenty-First Century*, Washington, The Woodrow Wilson Center Press, 1995, pp. 108–10.

32. S. Thomadakis and D. Seremetis, 'The destabilizing dynamics of the Greek electoral-fiscal cycle', *Greek Review of Political Science*, 1993, no. 2, p. 81 [in Greek].

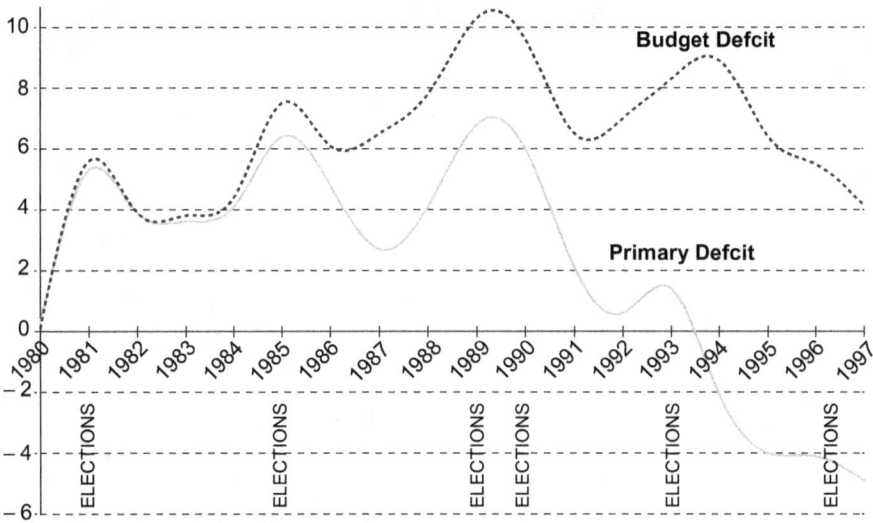

Figure 3.2: Electoral cycles and budget deficits

Greece acquires an EEC orientation: transition as the postponement of adjustment

Greece's accession coincided with a marked deterioration in the Community's external environment. The poor performance of the European economy as a whole commanded restrictive macroeconomic policies, progress towards the convergence of countries and regions of the Community, policy co-ordination in the framework of the European Monetary System (EMS) and a firm application of the market mechanism. The emerging EEC policy frame[33] on 'sound economic management' offered a medium-term strategy[34] for achieving a number of economic policy objectives, including the curtailment of inflation and improvement in price stability and the pursuit of structural change for the promotion of growth and employment.

Disregarding the new frame, which, in the Greek interpretation, lacked institutional back-up,[35] was symptomatic of a more general policy response to the EEC institutional and policy framework. Starting with the obligations of the Treaty

---

33. Rein and Schon define a frame as 'a perspective from which an amorphous, ill-defined problematic situation can be made sense of and acted upon'. In M. Rein and D. Schon, 'Frame-reflective policy discourse', in P. Wagner, C. H. Weiss, B. Wittrock and H. Wollman (eds), *Social Sciences and Modern States: National experiences and theoretical crossroads*, Cambridge, Cambridge University Press, 1991, p. 263.

34. Commission of the European Communities, 'Fifth Medium-Term Economic Policy Programme', *European Economy*, July 1981, no 9, p. 22.

35. Lenschow and Zitro argue that the impact of policy frames on policy outcomes depends on the degree or 'thickness' of their institutionalisation. A. Lenschow and A. R. Zito, 'Blurring or shifting of policy frames? Institutionalisation of the economic-environmental policy linkage in the European Community', *Governance*, 1988, vol. 11, no. 4, p. 420.

of Accession, the government submitted, in 19 March 1982, a Memorandum on Greece's relationship with the European Communities; the economic impact of accession on a weaker member state had to be acknowledged: 'To the extent that the Community enlargement was not accompanied by adjustment and differentiation of its rules, with the aim of protecting the peculiarities of the Greek economy, Greece's entry accentuates some of the country's problems or exacerbates their solution'.[36] Based on this assessment, the government asked for an extension of the transitional period in a number of policy areas, including the temporary protection of newly established industries, the provision of state aid to small and medium-sized exporting companies, the abrogation from production quotas. It also called for increased EC financial transfers to compensate for the negative effects of the liberalisation of markets. Even though the Commission did not grant extended derogations from the application of competition rules, it granted, in February 1983, both the transition period and substantial financial aid.

Admittedly, the economic implications of EEC accession were grave for the Greek economy. In the case of agricultural products, the trade balance with the Community immediately turned negative. Agricultural productivity, which at the time contributed 14 per cent of GDP, was much lower than the Community average, while the guaranteed prices mechanism covered only 40 per cent of Greece's production, in comparison to 70 per cent for the rest of the Community. At the same time, the position of the manufacturing industry in the economy was modest, with simple and unsophisticated industrial products. The alignment on the common external tariff and the gradual elimination of customs duties accelerated the penetration of the domestic market by foreign industrial products, displacing domestic products at a large rate.[37] Greek firms had to compete, for exports, with the highly industrialised Community countries and with those developing countries that had kept low labour costs and adopted competitive technologies.[38]

The over-financing of certain sectors and the crowding-out of private investment, both associated with Greece's highly complicated system of credit controls and regulations had, effectively, failed to strengthen the productive base of the economy.[39] In addition, the stimulus packages, as envisaged in PASOK's

36. 'Memorandum of the Greek Government Regarding the Relationship of Greece with the European Communities (19 March 1982)' [in Greek] in Perrakis and Gregoriou, (eds), *Greece in the Processes of European Integration (1981–1994)*, [in Greek], Athens, Sakkoulas Editions, 1987, p. 22.

37. The most thorough account of import penetration is provided in A. Giannitsis, *Accession in the EC and the Effects on Industry and External Trade* [in Greek], Athens, Foundation of Mediterranean Studies, 1988.

38. Bank of Greece, *Report of the Governor for the Year 1983*, Athens, Bank of Greece, 1984, pp. 12–13.

39. Papademos writes that, at the time, the system was effectively 'repressed'. Its salient features included a) a very small capital market and non-existent, non-bank money market, b) an oligopolistic and largely state-controlled banking industry, c) the administrative setting of interest rates, d) the complex regulations which determined the allocation of financial resources, e) the strict control of all foreign exchange transactions. L. Papademos, 'Monetary policy and financial markets in the 1990s' in T. Skouras (ed.), *Issues in Contemporary Economics, Vol. 5, The Greek Economy: Economic policy for the 1990s*, London, Macmillan in association with the

'Keynesianism', proved unsuccessful in re-engineering economic activity. GDP rose by 4 per cent in the two years to 1985, as 'lack of competitiveness, market rigidities and the associated misallocation of resources weakened the response of the Greek economy to domestic and external stimulus'.[40] With fiscal profligacy unchecked, monetary policy financed, during this period, between two-thirds and three-quarters of the Public Sector Borrowing Requirement. Credit policy arrangements, which provided for the compulsory purchase of Treasury Bills and other government debt, secured the low cost financing of the public deficit.

'Stop-go' is the name of the game: the stabilisation programme of 1986–87 and the first EC loan

PASOK won the parliamentary elections of June 1985. The successful electoral outcome reinforced Prime Minister Papandreou's belief that the ambivalent stance *vis-à-vis* the EC and the fiscal laxity generated in line with the electoral cycle had paid off. In presenting the new government programme to Parliament, he stated: 'We are continuing and intensifying the struggle within the framework of EEC in order to ensure our national economic interest and the gradual convergence of member-states' economies, while at the same time we are firmly promoting options which lead to the country's self-sufficient development'.[41]

Safeguarding the 'national interest' was not necessarily paying off. According to the OECD:

> [...] Up to mid-1985, the development needs of the economy would seem to have been subordinated to the aspirations of the population for continuing rapid increases in living standards at the expense of capital accumulation and external equilibrium.[42]

The marked deterioration of most economic indicators confirmed this assessment. Public expenditure rose to 43 per cent of GDP from 31 per cent in 1980 while private investment fell to 11 per cent. The rate of inflation, which had fallen to 18 per cent in 1984, rose again to 23 per cent in 1986. The expansionary fiscal policy had led to an uncontrollable rise in public debt. In 1985, the foreign-debt component had risen to 24 per cent of GDP compared to 7 per cent in 1980 of the public debt, while by the end of 1985, the current account deficit had reached 9.5 per cent of GDP. Other policy measures, including the reappearance of wage indexation, led to a further rise in unit labour costs and loss of competitiveness. The fixing of the drachma at an excessively high level exacerbated this.[43]

International Economic Association, 1992, pp. 71–2.

40. OECD, *OECD Economic Surveys Greece 1986*, Paris, OECD, 1986, p. 65.

41. Cited in K. Featherstone, *Socialist Parties and European Integration: A comparative history*, Manchester, Manchester University Press, 1988, p. 183.

42. *Ibid*, p. 37.

43. G. Alogoskoufis and S. Lazaretou, *The Drachma: monetary regimes and fiscal distortions in modern Greece* Athens, IMOP, 1997 [in Greek]; G. Alogoskoufis, *The Crisis of Economic Policy,*

In October 1985, the government adopted a two-year stabilisation programme in response to a balance of payments crisis.[44] To correct the external imbalance, the government proposed rapid disinflation, a reduction in the current account deficit and the stabilisation of the country's external debt. An initial devaluation of the drachma by 15 per cent and the introduction of an obligatory, non-interest-bearing deposit on certain imports were considered the right response to Greece's low competitiveness.[45] Central to the new economic direction was the modification of the wage–price indexation system. Wage adjustment would now observe the official forecast of inflation, after deducting the effect of imported inflation; the system was made compulsory for both public- and private-sector employees and entailed significant reductions in real pay. On the fiscal front, the total deficit of the public sector was to be reduced by about 4 per cent of GDP in 1986 and 1987, through a reduction in the rate of increase of regular budget expenditures and an increase in tax revenues and administered prices. Monetary policy would, accordingly, be tightened through a series of measures: reduction in the growth of domestic credit expansion; gradual establishment of positive real interest rates; and rationalisation of the banking system.

Concerned that the persistence of these imbalances could 'jeopardize the proper functioning of the common market', the Community granted a loan of 1,750 million ecus. Article 3 of the Council decision made the loan available on the basis of the Greek commitment 'to implement the economic recovery programme which it has presented'. While the first instalment was paid automatically, the second instalment would be released on the basis of 'the execution of the economic recovery programme'.[46] The EC loan marked, in one interpretation, a shift in Greece's stance and a greater acceptance of the institutional framework and logic of the EEC.[47] Parting with the 'national exceptionalism'[48] of 1981–85,

---

Athens, Kritiki Publications, 1994 [in Greek]; Y. Stournaras, 'Greece on the road to economic and monetary union: problems and prospects', in H. D. Gibson and E. Tsakalotos (eds), *Economic Integration and Financial Liberalisation: Prospects for Southern Europe,* London, Macmillan with St Antony's College, Oxford, 1992.

44. Ministry of National Economy, *Stabilisation Measures for the Greek Economy,* Athens, Ministry of National Economy, Press and Public Relations Office, 1985.

45. Commission of the European Communities, 'Annual Economic Report 1986-7', *European Economy,* November 1986, no. 30.

46. 'Council Decision of 9 December 1985 concerning a Community loan in favour of the Hellenic Republic' (85/543/EEC), *Official Journal of the European Communities,* L341, 19.12.1985, p. 17–18.

47. P. C. Ioakimidis, 'Contradictions between policy and performance', in K. Featherstone and K. Ifantis (eds), *Greece in a Changing Europe: Between European integration and Balkan disintegration?,* Manchester, Manchester University Press, 1996, p. 39.

48. This also came to acquire an ideological dimension. *See,* for example, M. Spourdalakis, *The Rise of the Greek Socialist Party,* London, Routledge, 1998. Pagoulatos proposes an ideational framework of national exceptionalism as a politically beneficial ideological strategy, through which government policy makers perceive their country's position in the European and global sphere. *See* G. Pagoulatos, 'Believing in national exceptionalism: ideas and economic divergence

the government publicly committed to implement a series of measures that would allow for 'the acceleration of the Greek economy's adjustment to the Community rules and regulations'.[49]

Institutional developments at the EC level also affected Greek policy makers' European orientation. The Council of Ministers proceeded, in 1985, with the adoption of the Integrated Mediterranean Programmes (IMPs). During the closing stages of accession negotiations with Spain and Portugal, Greece pressured for a programme that would facilitate the adjustment of the southern parts of the EC to the prospective enlargement. The IMPs were established for seven years (1986–92) and made provision for 4.1 billion ecus in grants and 2.5 billion ecus in loans; their adoption was supposed to have removed one of Greece's grievances regarding the economic effects of Spain's and Portugal's accession.

It was the Single European Act, however, signed at the Luxembourg Council in December 1985, which supposedly signalled the turnabout of Greek policy. The government realised – and various producer groups conceded – that further integration into the European economy was essential to domestic growth in the long run.[50] More importantly, the liberalisation of domestic markets triggered significant dislocation costs in the short run that could only be compensated by EEC development assistance.[51] In the interstate negotiations, the Greek side asserted that the economy would not be able to take advantage of the 'dynamic phenomena' of the single market without the 'strengthening and expansion' of community mechanisms for the transfer of resources and social policies.[52] Article 130a of the Single European Act committed the EC to reforming the Structural Funds, of which Greece was a major recipient.

Back home, Prime Minister Papandreou publicly declared that, in exchange for accepting the single market, Greece was able to advance 'the principle of economic convergence, the convergence of the standards of living'.[53] In the event, the Single European Act was ratified in Parliament on 28 February 1986; although policy makers used the Act to signal their supposed commitment to the new policy direction – associated with the EEC-backed programme – this was hardly accompanied by a new policy approach to adjustment. Policy makers focused, yet again, on the increased EEC transfers that would accompany the programme rather

in Southern Europe', *West European Politics*, 2004, vol. 27, no. 1, pp. 43–68.

49. C. Simitis, Minister of National Economy, granted these assurances in a letter to J. Delors, President of the Commission. Published in *Newspaper Kerdos*, 26 October 1985 [in Greek].

50. I. Hassid and Y. Katsos, *European Integration and Greek Industry: Structure-performances-perspectives*, Athens, Institute for Economic and Industrial Research (IOBE), 1992 [in Greek].

51. G. Garrett, 'International cooperation and institutional choice: the European Community's internal market', *International Organization, 1992*, vol. 46, no. 2, p. 545.

52. *See* 'Intervention of Deputy Minister of Foreign Affairs T. Pangalos in the Intergovernmental Conference on Art. 236 of the EEC Treaty (October 1985)', in Perrakis and Gregoriou, *Greece in the Processes of European Integration (1981–1994)*, p. 164 [in Greek].

53. Papandreou argued that his socialist government at least 'sought to endow the concept of convergence with a new meaning'. *See Parliamentary Proceedings*, (Session MH'), 6 December 1985.

than the grave policy endeavour that its implementation entailed; they therefore swiftly moved to secure a transition period for the de-regulation of transport and for the liberalisation of capital.[54]

Taking the road to instability again

The stabilisation programme succeeded in bringing down the rate of inflation from 17.5 per cent in 1986 to 14.3 per cent in 1987, the lowest level in this period. The return of average real wages to their 1980 level led to an improvement of unit labour costs that allowed, in turn, exports to rise from 22 per cent of GDP in 1985 to 29 per cent in 1987; GDP rose to 4.5 per cent in 1988. On the negative side, public consumption was barely reduced, a factor which contributed to the rapid rise in the interest burden. While taxes rose moderately, allowing for an increase in government revenues of 36 per cent in 1987, the tax base was not expanded. The current account deficit was reduced, mainly due to an improvement in the invisibles balance, while the trade balance remained problematic, continuing to reflect the structural deficiencies in the productive base of the economy.[55]

Under the loan's terms, Greece had supposedly undertaken an overhauling of economic policy formation; even the SEA had been used domestically to reinforce the programme's credibility.[56] Rather than adhere to the programme religiously, however, policy makers chose to abandon it altogether, one year before the 1989 elections. The government announced that the austerity period was over, prompting the resignation of the Minister of National Economy. Within the government, the programme had, in any case, lacked the support of ministers; party cadres had also openly and repeatedly asked for a reversal of economic policy.[57] Interestingly, the opposition parties also supported abandoning the programme: an indication of the extent to which the politicisation of the economy had corrupted the party

54. P. Kazakos, 'The internal market programme: content, economic philosophy and problems of implementation', in P. Kazakos (ed.), *1992: The Development of the Internal Market in Europe and Greece,* Athens, Ionian Bank, 1989, p. 43 [in Greek].

55. In comparing Greece's stabilisation programme with the Irish 'Programme for National Recovery', Alogoskoufis adds another insight. He argues that, in the Greek case, the policy mix was inappropriate. The Greek programme rested on revenue increases, rather than reductions in public expenditure. In the Irish case, the programme consolidated public finances through credible reductions in expenditure and extensive tax reform. Credibility in Ireland's counter-inflation efforts was also related to the currency's participation in the EMS. In Greece, it was expressed policy that the nominal exchange rate would accommodate inflation differentials with the rest of the world. *See* G. Alogoskoufis, 'Fiscal policies, devaluations and exchange rate regimes: the stabilisation programmes of Ireland and Greece', *The Economic and Social Review,* April 1992, vol. 23, no. 3, pp. 31–2.

56. K. Lavdas, *The Europeanization of Greece: Interest politics and the crises of integration,* London, Macmillan, 1997, p. 173.

57. P. Liargovas, 'Stabilisation programmes: the experience of Greece and other European countries', *Working Paper No. 19,* Athens, Hellenic Centre of European Studies, 1992 [in Greek] and G. Hadjimatheou, 'Macroeconomic performance and policies: recent past and prospects' in Skouras, *Issues in Contemporary Economics,* p. 52.

system's attitudes towards economic management. The 'possible loss of voters' became the overriding issue in the drafting of the 1988 budget.[58] Following the 1985 experience, an expectation had been formed at the level of political strategy that 'a new electoral-fiscal cycle would win the elections for the governing party. Papandreou waited for the opportune moment'.[59]

In the event, the 1989 elections produced an indecisive outcome. In July 1989, a coalition government was formed (composed of New Democracy and the Left Coalition[60] parties and headed by ND party cadre and former Minister, T. Tzanetakis), which undertook the task of promoting 'catharsis' in political life.[61] After only three months, a 'caretaker' government (12/10/1989–23/11/1989), under the leadership of I. Grivas, then President of the Supreme Court of Greece, led the country to new elections in November 1989. The fact that no party gained an electoral majority led to the formation of the 'ecumenical government' (composed of all the main political parties), with X. Zolotas, the former Central Bank governor, as prime minister. Like its predecessors, the Zolotas government fell victim to the political uncertainty that surrounded its transitory character. Due to the multiple, party-specific calculations of political cost within the government, and ND's pursuit of an electoral majority, policy makers lacked the incentive to provide a stabilisation direction in economic policy. None of the three parties that participated in government were willing to bear the political cost of strict budgetary measures and a tougher incomes policy. In spite of the widening budget deficit and the problems with the balance of payments, their answer to Zolotas's proposed adoption of urgent policy measures was negative.[62]

The country had therefore embarked on a two-year election period, which had coincided, after the abandonment of the stabilisation programme, with a marked deterioration of the economy's overall performance. By 1989, inflation was nearly four times as high as the EC average, rising to 19.9 per cent in early 1990. A steep rise in domestic demand and a deterioration in international competitiveness widened the trade gap, limiting output growth. The current account deficit widened to nearly 5 per cent of GDP (in comparison to an average of 2.85 per cent

---

58. Simitis, then Minister of National Economy, writes that the expansionary fiscal policy and the change in incomes policy were derived from considerations of electoral gain. *See* C. Simitis, *The Policy of Economic Stabilisation*, Athens, Gnosi, 1989, p. 27 [in Greek]. *See also* P. Kazakos, 'Economic policy and elections: the political control of the economy, 1979–89', in Ch. Lyrintzis and E. Nikolakopoulos (eds), *Elections and Parties in the Decade of the '80s: Developments and prospects of the political system*, Athens, Themelio, 1990, p. 151 [in Greek].

59. Interview 2.

60. The Coalition of the Left included the KKE (Communist Party of Greece) and KKE-es (Communist Party of the Interior).

61. The 'catharsis' project was effectively related to the alleged involvement of former Prime Minister Papandreou and other high-ranking PASOK cadres in the Koskotas banking scandal and the subsequent judicial effort to 'purify' the political system from their influence. The charges brought against him by a Special Tribunal were never proven, a factor that affected negatively the credibility of the coalition government.

62. Interview with X. Zolotas, *Economicos Tahydromos*, 26 July 1990, [in Greek].

during the two years of the stabilisation programme). The public sector deficit rose by 16.1 per cent of GDP, in comparison to 14.3 per cent of GDP in 1987. The PSBR shot to 19 per cent in 1989, due to generous tax allowances, higher interest payments, stronger public consumption and reduced efforts to collect taxes during the electoral period.[63]

In April 1990, the state of the Greek economy and the way policy makers handled the EC loan finally became the object of Commission disapproval. President of the Commission Jacques Delors and Henning Christophersen, EC Commissioner for Economic and Financial Affairs, publicly raised grave concerns about the course of the Greek economy in the European environment:

> the serious difference that has been growing between the economic development of Greece and that of the other EC countries embodies the danger of permanently undermining the country's prospect towards the Single Market, Economic and Monetary Union and European Integration.[64]

The formulation and implementation of another long-term programme for the restructuring of the economy was considered the appropriate Greek response. The Zolotas government was promptly dissolved for elections in April 1990. After almost a decade in opposition, ND came to power, with a slim majority in Parliament.

1990–1993: the difficulty of turning the boat around

Endorsing the Delors Report

As the internal struggle to arrive at a majority government further exacerbated the state of the Greek economy, developments at EEC level were gathering pace. The Delors Report had proposed, in April 1989, the establishment of Economic and Monetary Union (EMU) in three stages.[65] Central to the Report were the need for greater co-ordination of economic policies, the design of rules on the size and financing of national budget deficits and, finally, the creation of an independent institution that would be responsible for the Union's monetary policy. Following two intergovernmental conferences, the leaders of the EC member states signed, in December 1991, the Treaty on European Union. The Treaty finalised the three-stage process, which would lead to the adoption of the single currency by January 1st, 1999. Although the construction of EMU necessitated a substantial loss of national policy autonomy, so that the achievement of nominal and real convergence would prove stable and enduring features of the new institutional

---

63. OECD, *Economic Outlook 47*, June 1990.

64. Open Letter of President of the Commission Delors and Commissioner Christophersen to Prime Minister Zolotas, *Economicos Tahydromos*, 15 April 1990.

65. Committee for the Study of Economic and Monetary Union, *Report on Economic and Monetary Union in the European Community*, Luxembourg, Office for Official Publications of the European Communities, 1989.

edifice, EMU participation was quickly becoming the central priority in most member states' policy agendas. Faced with these developments, the new Prime Minister Konstantinos Mitsotakis,[66] was caught between his eagerness to join in the gathering momentum and his awareness that the state of the economy precluded Greece from placing a serious EMU application.

To signal ND's traditional commitment to the EEC,[67] the Greek government had submitted a 'Greek Memorandum on Political Union' to the Commission, a month after its election; its aim was to indicate, to Greece's partners, that 'in spite of the problems of the Greek economy, Greece is playing an active role in Community negotiations, having formulated for this goal the appropriate European policy'.[68] On the relationship between political union and EMU, the Memorandum stated:

> Greece believes that Political Union will have to be the result of a dynamically evolving procedure, that will develop with an accelerating and increasing rate to its final goal, in harmonious conjunction with the implementation of the goals for Economic and Monetary Union and the attainment of a higher degree of internal cohesion and coherence in the Community and the development of a common external and defence policy.[69]

Integrationist rhetoric was welcome in European circles although it could hardly compensate for the country's dire economic situation. While the overall policy stance was tightened in mid-1990, the modification of the wage indexation system failed to arrest the acceleration in the growth of unit labour costs, which rose to 21 per cent in 1990. Sharp rises in administered prices, in an attempt to prevent further increases in public enterprises' deficits, combined with a rise in indirect taxation, pushed the year-on-year consumer price inflation rate to 23 per cent. In spite of the government's publicly proclaimed intentions, the PSBR rose to 21 per cent by the end of 1990.[70]

A programme to set the economic record straight

In February 1991, the government put forward a 'medium-term adjustment' programme, in a renewed attempt to address the large fiscal imbalances and reduce, in the long run, state intervention in the economy.[71] Eager to secure more

---

66. See Appendix A. Biographical Data.

67. Interview 3: 'The fact that K. Karamanlis, ND's founder, had signed the EC Accession Treaty constituted the cornerstone of the party's pro-European stance'.

68. 'Address of the Prime Minister C. Mitsotakis on "Greece's European Policy" in the International Conference of the Hellenic Centre of European Studies on Greece in the European Union', in L. Tsoukalis (ed.), *Greece in the European Community: The challenge of adjustment*, Athens, Papazisis, 1993, p. 37 [in Greek].

69. *See* 'Greek Memorandum on Political Union (15 May 1990)', in Perrakis and Gregoriou (eds), *Greece in the Processes of European Integration (1981–1994)*, p. 370 [in Greek].

70. OECD, *Economic Outlook 48*, December 1990, and OECD, *Economic Outlook 49*, July 1991.

71. The main elements of the programme included: rises in public tariffs, a restrictive budgetary policy, cuts in real wages, measures to increase flexibility in the labour market, increases in interest rates, a not fully accommodating exchange-rate policy, abolition of restrictions on the operation of state-owned banks, privatisation of over-indebted industries, and reform of the public pension

Community funding, policy makers presented the programme to the Commission, in the context of an application for balance-of-payments assistance; the recurring problems which arose from the deterioration in the current account and the need to make substantial repayments of external debt were exacerbated by the economy's serious structural impediments. The programme aimed primarily at fiscal consolidation, with a projected decline of the PSBR to 12.5 per cent of GDP in 1991 and to 6.5 per cent in 1992. Following the abolition of the wage indexation system, and a two-year agreement on wage moderation, inflation was expected to fall to approximately 10 per cent by the end of 1992. Supply-side reforms, such as the privatisation of public sector enterprises, were supposed to strengthen competition and ensure a more efficient functioning of the factor markets. Although projections for GDP growth remained grim, the tightening of macroeconomic policies and the improvement in micro-economic rigidities, which would accrue from less sticky prices and wages, were expected to improve the basic balance of payments.

In March 1991, a loan of 2.2 billion ecus was agreed and a first tranche of 1 billion ecus was disbursed. That Greece managed to obtain another loan was probably a testament to Community solidarity at work; its poor record in the implementation of the 1985 stabilisation programme and the fiscal laxity that had ensued were hardly mentioned in the favourable Council decision. As in the previous EC loan, conditions were attached: the first instalment was to be released once borrowing operations were completed; the next two instalments however, would not be released:

> until the Commission, in consultation with the Council and in the light of an examination made in collaboration with the Monetary Committee of the results obtained in the execution of the programme, is satisfied that the agreed measures have been fully implemented and that the targets of the programme have been achieved or that the necessary additional measures to achieve the targets have been agreed or fully implemented.

Again, the Commission was to examine 'at regular intervals' the evolution of the economic situation and the execution of the economic recovery programme.[72]

Theoretically, implementation of this latest stabilisation programme was supposed to take place in an altogether different policy universe. For the ND party, which had incorporated neo-liberalism[73] in its ideology and had espoused a firm and stable pro-European stance, the twin themes of consolidation and liberalisation offered the principal policy direction. Moreover, the change in government

---

system. See Medium-Term (1991–93) Adjustment Programme of the Greek Economy, Ministry of National Economy, Athens, 4 March 1991 [in Greek], and European Commission, 'Annual Economic Report', European Economy 46, December 1990, p. 46.

72. 'Council Decision of 4 March 1991 concerning a Community loan in favour of the Hellenic Republic' (91/136/EEC), Official Journal of the European Communities, L 66, 12.3.1991.

73. Interview 4: ND's state conservatism of the 1970s was gradually diluted with elements of a Thatcherite neo-liberalism. This can be explained both by the support that the party enjoyed among business and capital, and the re-formulation of the party's ideology under Mitsotakis.

had coincided with a wider debate about the role of the state in the economy.[74] Increased state intervention throughout the 1980s had failed to generate growth or address the economy's structural problems. The government affirmed its concern, time and again, that the country's marginalisation was at stake. Firm implementation would help augment its low policy credibility, while the more active monitoring role envisaged for the Commission and the Monetary Committee would keep the lid on potential deviations.[75]

Progress made with regard to the programme's main goals, however, proved poor, insufficient and reversible.[76] Regarding fiscal adjustment, in particular, there was a large deviation from the targets set. The growth of the PSBR, in conjunction with the increased cost of borrowing and the weakening of economic activity, resulted in the acceleration of the public debt, which rose to 111.8 per cent of GDP in 1993. The government failed to cut total government expenditure, which remained stable, while the shortfall in tax revenues amounted to over 3 per cent of GDP: the recession that hit the urban sector of the economy, the administrative inefficiency of tax-collection and the strong resistance of groups who had traditionally evaded paying taxes all contributed to this development.[77]

In like manner, the implementation of the privatisation programme was painstakingly slow. The proposed transfer of 'ailing companies', public enterprises and state-controlled banks from the public to the private sector was fraught with technical difficulties. Lack of administrative expertise, combined with a constantly evolving legal framework, and the fact that a number of enterprises were added in an *ad hoc* manner affected the credibility and the legitimacy of the transfer procedures. With pressures for fiscal adjustment mounting, Greek policy makers were more concerned with maximising revenues from the sale of public assets than with future effects on efficiency and economic growth;[78] but still, the targeted amount of revenue for 1993, equal to about 2 percentage points of GDP, was not realised. In fact, the outcome of the privatisation programme fell well short of expectations and objectives. While concrete steps were made in certain sectors of the economy, in shipbuilding (with the privatisations of Elefsis and Neorion shipyards), banking (with the privatisation of Bank of Piraeus and Bank of Athens) and industry (with the controversial sale of Aget Heracles Cement to Calcestruzzi), the government failed to cut down on the costly operation of the public enterprise sector.

---

74. 'The elections of June and November 1989, of April 1990, and of October 1993, involved an unresolved debate about a reform of the state's role and operation.' K. Featherstone, 'The challenge of liberalisation: parties and the state in Greece after the 1993 elections', in *Democratization*, 1994, vol. 1, no. 2, p. 281.

75. Prime Minister K. Mitsotakis, *Parliamentary Proceedings* (Session Γ'), 28 July 1992, p. 24.

76. D. Chalikias, 'Economic stabilisation and growth: the case of Greece', in *Greek Economic Review*, 1994, vol. 15, no. 2 [in Greek].

77. European Commission, 'Annual Economic Report 1991–2: strengthening growth and improving convergence', *European Economy 50*, December 1991, p. 47.

78. P. Kazakos, 'The regulatory role of the state in the economy: problems and perspectives of the privatisation policy in Greece', in Tsoukalis, *Greece in the European Community*, p. 150.

The government's commitment was, in any case, progressively weakened as internal divisions erupted in the party[79] and social actors united in powerful policy-opposing coalitions. Exploiting the government's ever-present calculation of political cost and its slim parliamentary majority,[80] 'the parties in opposition, and especially PASOK, utilised the support they traditionally enjoyed among labour unions to disrupt the privatisation of a number of industries, including the Hellenic Telecommunications Organisation (OTE), and the Hellenic Shipyards'.[81] In September 1993, the programme was abandoned and, almost unavoidably, a new electoral cycle – lower in intensity and shorter in duration – got under way. In spite of the affirmed divergence of the Greek economy from European objectives, the supposed ideological shift and the second EC loan that the country had managed to receive, the government failed to make the stabilisation programme 'stick'. It called an election in October 1993, which brought PASOK back to power.

Conclusion: understanding macroeconomic divergence

The 'history' of Greek macroeconomic divergence from the EEC and, subsequently, EMU was rooted in the stability and persistence of a domestic framework that affected both the character of government intervention in the economy and the choice of policy goals. In the 1960s, the country's late and limited industrialisation handed the state a central role in guaranteeing and promoting economic growth. In the 1970s, social pressure for redistribution and social restitution, associated with the restoration of democracy, endowed state intervention with a distinct socio-political dimension. By the 1980s, state intervention in the economy was legitimated by reference to developmental goals and renewed calls for social restitution. This legitimation gradually led, through ever-expanding policies of nationalisation and income redistribution, to the economy's use for social and political goals and eventually to its politicisation. Following EEC accession, the ever-present alternation of expansionary and contractionary macroeconomic policies failed to address the imbalances and structural weaknesses of the economy, the correction of which was a prerequisite for convergence, both nominal and real. If anything, the pursuit of political gain and its flip-side, the avoidance of political cost, became the *real* ideological frames of economic-policy formation. Figure 3.3 points to the public debt trajectory during this period, depicting its dramatic accumulation during the 1980s and early 1990s. Forgoing clear thinking about its future burden on the economy's growth potential, Greek policy makers were content to erect the entitlement state, institutionalising the politics of patronage and solidifying cronyism and rent-seeking.

---

79. Three high-profile MPs publicly asserted that the stabilisation programme could not promote social welfare, as it was based on a reduction in the income of the lower strata. *See* Liargovas, 'Stabilisation programmes', p. 59.

80. Minister of National Economy Christodoulou openly argued in Parliament that the government accepted the costs associated with the programme, 'knowing that, possibly, it has political implications which, in the short-term, are not desirable for a political party'. *See Parliamentary Proceedings*, (Session KZ´), 18 November 1991.

81. Interview 5.

The story presented in this chapter chimes with the institutionalists' insistence that the choice of institutional framework has profound consequences for the efficiency and growth of economies.[82] The persistence of distinctive national patterns of policy-making adversely affected economic performance: annual inflation was, on average, 20 per cent during the 1980s and the beginning of the 1990s; the general government debt-to-GDP ratio shot to 109 per cent by the mid-1990s, up from 25 per cent in 1981, the time of EEC accession; and Greece's general government deficit reached double digits as a share of GDP by the end of the 1980s.

Two major trends in the history of Greece's macroeconomic divergence emerged: first, the politicisation of the economy as an organising principle legitimated the electoral manipulation of the main economic indicators and led to a haphazard and skewed implementation of successive stabilisation programmes. Second, the operation of the institutional framework interfered with the capacity of the economy to adapt to the European economic environment. EEC adjustment proceeded only to the extent that the domestic system's grip on the economy allowed it; it was therefore patchy and asymmetric.

New institutionalism has more difficulty explaining why EEC accession, which could have been interpreted as a force exogenous to the institutional framework, failed to produce a 'critical juncture', during which major policy change would have been feasible.[83] With the exception of the EC-induced liberalisation of financial markets and interest rates, policy makers postponed, sometimes indefinitely, the adoption of measures that would have smoothed transition to a new economic environment. The granting of transitional periods to the Greek side, combined with the institutional inability of the Community to monitor the handling of EEC loans on the ground or to impose sanctions for mishandling, reinforced a domestic policy environment in which the obligations of membership could be bypassed or postponed; policy makers' dissociation of loan disbursements from the implementation of the relevant stabilisation programme was simply another manifestation of this. Substantial EC transfers were wasted on domestic consumption, used to cushion the effects of accession, delay the necessary fiscal and wage adjustment and perpetuate, with supposedly small cost, the electoral fiscal cycle;[84] their developmental impact was therefore limited, while the actual burden of adjustment, resulting from Greece's low structural competitiveness, was not eased.[85] It follows that, with regard to the themes of this book, institutionalists need to rethink their conceptualisation of path-dependent adjustment, particularly in the light of the relationship between the persistence of informal norms and the patent inability (or rather unwillingness) of policy makers to change formal rules.

---

82. *See* P. A. Hall, *Governing the Economy: The politics of state intervention in Britain and France*, Oxford, Oxford University Press, 1986.

83. R. B. Collier. and D. Collier, *Shaping the Political Arena: Critical juncture, the Labor movement and regime dynamics in Latin America*, Princeton, Princeton University Press, 1991.

84. G. Alogoskoufis, 'The Greek Economy and the Euro', in A. Mitsos and E. Mossialos (eds), *Contemporary Greece and Europe*, Aldershot, Ashgate, 2000, pp. 143–4.

85. L. Katseli, 'The internationalization of Southern European economies', in H. Gibson (ed.), *Economic Transformation, Democratization, and Integration into the European Union*, p. 101..

General Government Consolidated Gross Debt
1971–1993

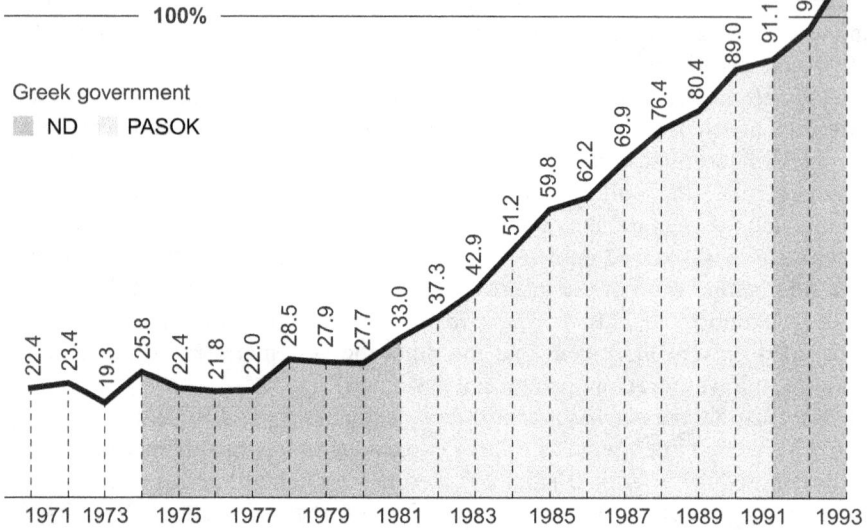

Figure 3.3: Creating the debt burden, general government gross consolidated debt, 1971–93

By setting up an explanation that elucidates how institutional constraints impose on decision-makers, new institutionalism points out the limits of a simple rational-choice framework of economic decision-making. Policy makers knew that they had to formulate a pattern of adjustment yet they repeatedly failed to bring it about; they did not promote fiscal consolidation and price stability, nor did they adopt measures to increase competition in domestic and foreign markets in a way that would stick. They espoused the single market but not the policies of market liberalisation and structural adjustment that lay at its core. The more the domestic institutional context was used as the main reference point, the more policy makers, even newcomers, chose to use it. Interestingly, the 'increasing returns mechanisms' that reinforced policy makers' agency down this path gave rise to policies that aggravated Greece's poor macroeconomic performance and nurtured the multitude of rent-seeking organisations that would prove particularly resistant to the reform of state intervention in the economy. These policies included the survival of inefficient productive structures through the provision of funds from state-controlled banks, the extension of state-guaranteed insurance and pension coverage to large groups of the population without matching contributions to the social security system, the use of public sector employment for the containment of unemployment or for the satisfaction of clientelistic goals and the low pricing policy of public enterprises.

In the process, one thing became certain: European institutions mattered less. Hence, while Greece was already exhibiting, at the time that the EMU project was being formulated, a history of chronic mismanagement, 'Europe', had equally displayed, in the handling of national economies, its own history of careless abandon. Would the EMU regime constrain policy-preferences and goal-setting, if lapses in compliance and supervision at the European level had acquired something of a 'semi-structural' character?

chapter four | EMU negotiations, national strategies and the external constraint

When Greek policy makers walked into the EMU negotiations that led to the Maastricht Treaty, all that they knew was that they wanted Greece 'in'. Ill-equipped and with few cards up their sleeves, they muddled through, hoping that the entry criteria would not prove too stringent. During the actual bargaining, they realised that the Treaty on European Union (TEU) and, in particular, the conditions that it set for EMU membership would constitute, if they were ever to be implemented, nothing short of a catalyst for the reform of domestic processes of planning and implementation. There arose, in their interpretation, a unique opportunity to rationalise the system of economic policy formation and endow the nominal convergence process (geared to fulfilling the convergence criteria on price stability, government budgetary position, exchange rates and long-term interest rates) with the pursuit of wide-scale reform.

This chapter traces both the negotiations that took place in the context of the EMU intergovernmental conferences and the subsequent ratification strategies used at home. The aim is to delineate the way the EMU policy framework was imported to Athens. The national interpretation and the subsequent endeavour to present EMU entry as the only available option – the economy's 'way out' from years of economic mismanagement and instability – were the central elements of the 'external constraint strategy'.[1]

In the Greek case, the government assumed a central role in negotiations, a development that was to be expected. It had to fill in the gaps in weak inter-ministerial co-ordination on the ground; it also had the resources to mould the 'national preference'. Quite predictably, policy makers who operated in two institutional orders had both the power and the opportunity to exploit 'the multiple logics' that national and supranational institutions made available to their advantage[2] and attempt to bind all the relevant non-government actors in credible commitment.[3]

---

1. This strategy was not unique to Greece. *See* K. Dyson, and K. Featherstone, 'Italy and EMU as *vincolo esterno*: empowering the technocrats, transforming the state', *South European Society and Politics*, 1996, vol. 1, no. 2, pp. 272–99.

2. R. Friedland and R. Alford, 'Bringing society back in: symbols, practices, and institutional contradictions', in W. Powell and P. DiMaggio (eds), *The New Institutionalism in Organisational Analysis,* Chicago, University of Chicago Press, 1991, p. 232.

3. *See* A. Moravscik, *The Choice for Europe: Social purpose and state power from Messina to Maastricht*, Ithaca/New York, Cornell University Press, pp. 3–10.

The organisational politics of EMU: setting and negotiating the Greek position

Inter-ministerial co-ordination: formal rules and informal practices

Nine months into the EEC-backed stabilisation programme, Greek policy makers had very little to show for their supposed 'policy overhaul'. When they walked into the intergovernmental conference (IGC) on EMU, therefore, their negotiating strategy suffered from the lack of either a credible narrative or a coherent set of positions. Domestically, the prospect of participating in 'constitution-building' negotiations generated a debate over the role of inter-ministerial co-ordination and the respective roles that the Ministry of National Economy (MNEC) and Ministry of Foreign Affairs (MFA) would be called on to play. The Greek side had placed progress on political union (EPU) at the centre of its strategy, with its 'Memorandum on Political Union'.[4] The MFA, therefore, expected to take precedence in inter-ministerial co-ordination, over-shadowing the MNEC. This was a change of stance; traditionally, its position on 'Europe' was affected by a prevalent diplomatic-service ethos that had defined European affairs as an area of 'low politics' and by a corresponding view that 'working for the General Directorate of the EU, which had under its exclusive jurisdiction the management of Greece's membership of the EU,[5] was a demotion'.[6]

The co-ordination of European policy had, in any case, formal institutional underpinnings: the enactment of Law 1104/80 had created a bi-polar system, whereby the MFA managed all the political aspects of Community membership (institutional issues, enlargement, Treaty revision, political union), the Community's external economic relations, and European political co-operation. It was also responsible for the co-ordination and adjustment of Greek legislation, economy, and administration to the Community status quo.[7] The MNEC had control over Economic and Financial Affairs Council-related matters, structural policy, and the implementation of the internal market.[8]

The system suffered from several problems; for one, multiple hierarchies tended to exist *within* the ministries, as Prime Ministers assigned powers and responsibilities to Alternate and Deputy Ministers, often at the expense of the Minister; 'all too often, Ministers, Alternate Ministers, and Deputy Ministers who subsequently fought for territory, pursued the same agenda in parallel ways, using

---

4. *See* discussion in Chapter Two.

5. Presidential Decree No. 11, *Government Gazette*, 27 January 1992.

6. Interview 6: 'Safeguarding the national interest in Greek-Turkish relations had historically dominated the Ministry's policy agenda; the idea that European affairs were an area of "low politics" defined policy makers' attitudes until the early 1990s'.

7. Art. 3, Law 1104/80 'Regarding the representation of Greece in the European Communities, foundation of Diplomatic and Consular Authorities and the Regulation of other relevant organizational matters', *Government Gazette*, No. 298 A, 29 December 1980, [in Greek].

8. A. Macridimitris and A. Passas, *The Greek Administration and the Co-ordination of European Policy*, Working Paper No. 20, Athens, Hellenic Centre of European Studies, 1993, p. 38 [in Greek].

their own independent staff and resources'.[9] Problems of internal co-ordination were naturally projected on to formal channels of inter-ministerial co-ordination; in the process, those involved opted for looser forms of co-operation, relying more on *ad hoc* arrangements.[10]

Ministers shied away, if they thought that their authority and prestige would be further weakened by sharing functions; preparatory committees were typically attended by high-ranking civil servants who had limited technical knowledge and lacked a firm EEC perspective; those who wanted to have a real input in the process had to bypass committees and build up personal relationships across ministries. Even in Brussels, the Greek Permanent Representation, which constituted the formal mediator between the national and EU levels, had been known to suffer from 'the politicisation of appointments, the consequent lack of technical expertise, the limited degree of networking within the Commission, and more importantly, the uneasy co-ordination relationship between the two Ministries'.[11] Hence, inter-ministerial co-ordination came to depend on the existence of personal channels of consultation and communication, the urgency of a given issue and whether its solution necessitated sharing the responsibility and accountability. In the case of EMU, all three conditions applied.

The Prime Minister as a broker and the role of on-going negotiations

In negotiating the Maastricht Treaty, Prime Minister Mitsotakis sought to insulate the formulation of the Greek strategy from the Cabinet, opting for an inner circle committed to safeguarding Greece's position in European integration. In the context of informal meetings, he gathered around him Efthimios Christodoulou, Minister of National Economy, Antonis Samaras, Minister of Foreign Affairs, and a few select officials. In a symbolic move, the Prime Minister had assumed the office of the Minister of National Economy during most of the IGC period (1 October 1990–8 August 1991). He wanted to signal, particularly to his European partners, that the eventual convergence of the Greek economy was his government's central priority. It was indicative of his intentions that Christodoulou, who replaced Mitsotakis as Minister (8 August 1991–17 February 1992) was previously his Alternate Minister of National Economy (1 October 1990–8 August 1991). As negotiations began, Christodoulou was entrusted with the task of supplying the cabinet with formal reports; the Prime Minister, as well as Yannis Paleokrassas, Minister of Finance, contributed with non-papers (unofficial and off-the-record presentations of government positions), whenever this was deemed necessary. The

---

9. Interview 7.

10. Spanou argues that the general characteristics of the political-administrative system have visibly left their mark; these include, 'a low degree of institutionalisation, a gap between formal rules and informal practices, the fragmentation and importance of personal initiatives and networks, the politicisation of recruitment at the expense of merit, and the lack of continuity'. *See* C. Spanou, 'Greece', in H. Kassim, B. G. Peters and V. Wright, (eds), *The National Co-ordination of EU Policy: The domestic level*, Oxford, Oxford University Press, 2000, p. 174.

11. Interview 6; interview 9; interview 10; interview 11; interview 12.

Cabinet's Economic Policy Committee, which convened weekly, was also kept informed on progress made at IGC level; its input, however, was negligible.

Mitsotakis maintained political control over the entire process, while Christodoulou, a former Governor of the National Bank of Greece, was responsible for the more technical aspects of EMU. This division of labour worked smoothly, as Christodoulou had been a personal choice of the Prime Minister and they both shared the view that, if Greece did not join EMU, it would be marginalised, economically and politically. In addition, the 'spirit' of economic liberalism, which, in their analysis, defined the EMU construction, also defined their guiding philosophy – the stabilisation programme that they tried to implement at home rested, unmistakably, on rolling back the state. Economic liberalism went hand-in-hand with federalism- early on in the parallel EPU negotiations the Prime Minister had signalled his preference for the evolution of European integration along a federal model. Samaras, another personal choice of the Prime Minister, operated from within ND's historical position, which held that the Community constituted a stable framework for the promotion and defence of Greece's national interest.

The Prime Minister's personal involvement in both the IGCs on EMU and EPU enabled him to act as a powerful broker and direct the working relationship between the two ministries. At the level of officials, inter-ministerial co-ordination was kept at a minimum. A nineteen-member committee, headed by Georgios Vlachos, a Secretary-General with the MNEC, had been set up to formulate the Greek positions prior to the start of the negotiations; its main task was to respond to the EC Commission's Draft Treaty of December 1990; Christodoulou forwarded the Greek document, almost equal in length to the Treaty, to the IGC. Once the so-called 'working paper' had been completed, the committee was disbanded.[12] The intensity of the negotiations, the technicality of their content and their separate character, combined with the limited bureaucratic support that respective officials could draw upon, further weakened the *ad hoc* channels of communication and consultation. There would be more casualties down the road. As the institutional creation of EMU began to overshadow EPU, the MFA realised that its strategy of maintaining overall responsibility for both IGCs was not feasible.

National preferences and the Greek negotiating strategy: a story of déjà vu?

From the outset, the government placed Economic and Monetary Union in the context of Greece's affirmed commitment to the *idea* of European integration.[13] In the Greek interpretation, EMU formed part of a wider European project to proceed with a closer union; the centralisation of monetary policy curtailed member states' capabilities in the area of fiscal independence and, more generally,

---

12. K. Featherstone, G. Kazamias, and D. Papadimitriou, 'Greece and the negotiation of economic and monetary union: preferences, strategies, and institutions', *Journal of Modern Greek Studies*, 2000, vol. 18, no. 2, pp. 381–422, p. 400.

13. This section has benefited from a series of interviews conducted with former Prime Minister C. Mitsotakis and former Minister of National Economy, T. Christodoulou, the ministerial head of the IGC delegation.

in the exercise of economic policy. The proposed transfer of instruments and goals pointed towards the creation of a political authority which would counterbalance the centralised power of the newly created monetary authority and would, effectively, compensate for the partial loss of policy autonomy. For the Greek side, grave security considerations were also at work; policy makers assumed that EPU would strengthen the frontiers of Europe, thereby securing Greece's geopolitical interests.

With their credibility at low ebb, Greek negotiators were particularly concerned, in the initial negotiation stages, about the creation of a 'two-speed' monetary Europe. The German, Danish, Dutch and British governments and their central banks, which had adopted an 'economist' approach, suggested that convergence should acquire a variable character, due to the different levels of economic development among member states: EC economies had to demonstrate that they constituted an economic area that functioned in a unified way, before they became one.[14] The proposal did not take off and Greek fear of an effective and permanent exclusion from the projected union was alleviated.

Policy makers nevertheless remained alarmed about the timetable that would lead to EMU. Echoing the negotiation positions of PASOK throughout the 1980s, they called for extended transition periods from one stage to the next, which would enable the adjustment of the weak peripheral economies to the conditions and requirements of EMU. According to the Greek side, the introduction of a 'phased' element in the entire process would constitute both a strong guarantee for the economy's eventual convergence and a strong incentive for Greek policy makers to proceed with the appropriate measures.

Obviously – and this constituted the second pillar of the Greek negotiating strategy – new Community actions would facilitate the economic convergence of the weaker economies. Given that Greek acquiescence to the single market had been accompanied by the doubling in size of the Community's structural funds (between 1987 and 1993), Greek policy makers expected that the path to EMU would be equally well endowed with EC financial support. This expectation was largely based on Council Decision 90/141/EEC of March 1990, wherein the Council undertook the multilateral surveillance of all aspects of member-states' economic policy, both short-term and long-term.[15] In the context of promoting 'a high degree of convergence of economic performances between Member States through greater compatibility and closer coordination of economic policies',[16] Greek policy makers assumed that 'the Economic and Financial Affairs Council (Ecofin) would perceive the necessity of financial assistance measures for the economies which trailed behind and promote them on its own'.[17]

---

14. K. Dyson and K. Featherstone, *The Road to Maastricht: Negotiating Economic and Monetary Union*, Oxford, Oxford University Press, 1999, p. 29.

15. *Official Journal of the European Communities*, 24.03.1990, L 78

16. 'Council Decision of 12 March 1990 on the attainment of progressive convergence of economic policies and performance during stage one of economic and monetary union', *Official Journal of the European Communities*, L 78, 24.03.1990.

17. Interview 13.

As implementation of the stabilisation programme began to falter back home, it became clear that the Greek economy would not be able to recover in the short-to-medium-term. Fears arose that the stringent application of the proposed convergence criteria in the third stage would give the country's current economic marginalisation a more final character; institutional marginalisation would unavoidably follow, barring Greece from participation in the future direction of the new edifice. The Greek position, therefore, was formulated around the idea that a member state should be able to join EMU, even if its performance did not satisfy the requirements of economic convergence. 'Equal and simultaneous participation' became, in fact, the negotiating team's favourite tune. Lacking the credible voice and the sound figures to make this acceptable to its partners, 'a caveat was added; the member-state under consideration should consistently implement a programme of adjustment and structural reform in a framework set by Community procedures and obligations'.[18] Greek negotiators, forgetful of the way previous programmes were mismanaged, did think that, under the EMU umbrella, serious adjustment was feasible and could be brought about at a lower political cost. Greece's EU partners were to prove equally forgetful.

Accepting that some states would be handed 'derogations', Greek policy makers asserted that participation in stage three should incorporate in-built binding procedures that would guarantee fiscal discipline. In an effort to demonstrate their commitment, they even went as far as to support the German proposal for the 'golden rule': a government's deficit should only be designed to serve the financing of investment and not consumption.[19] EMU could not be realised if the fiscal stance of any member state, together with the available policy instruments and the pursuit of national goals, differed considerably from those of the others. Setting up a Community financial mechanism would, in this respect, assist divergent countries in the implementation of their fiscal-reform programmes, as they moved towards fiscal consolidation. The Greek side wanted to avert the introduction of sanctions for profligate member-states. It was careful to state a preference for a flexible set of rules, justified by reference to the subsidiarity principle. Given its history, the country would probably be the prime target of any disciplining mechanism.

The 'small country syndrome'

The influence that 'a small country could exert on the eventual construction of EMU was, in any case, small'.[20] In the build-up to the final text, Greek negotiators did not produce an independent platform, although they had produced the 'Memorandum' in the early stages. They sided with those countries that would best serve Greece's interests or highlight its EMU credentials. They were less concerned to seize the 'big ideas' of price stability and central bank independence, which had already

---

18. Interview 14.

19. Dyson and Featherstone, *The Road to Maastricht*, p. 766.

20. Interview 4.

become tenets of the EMU policy frame, embedded in the IGC structure;[21] they were more eager to promote flexibility in determining entry to stage three and a slower transition period to that stage. Clearly, the Greek economic experience had affected the government's vision of the form that EMU should finally take – 'no one in the negotiating team was to refer to government debt levels and their reduction; for all purposes, they constituted a "non-issue"'.[22]

The real challenge for Greek entrepreneurship, which would make or break the 'success' of the negotiators and determine reception of the deal back home, came down to how much money would end up in the Greek bag. Unable to engage in tactical issue-linkage or obtain any side-payments on its own,[23] Greece joined Ireland, Portugal and Spain in, admittedly, one of the more cohesive issue-based coalitions. In pressuring for convergence-related financial assistance, Spain played the leading role, with Spanish negotiators threatening to veto the entire treaty at the final IGC before Maastricht.[24] A compromise was struck and a Cohesion Fund[25] was established for the provision of financial assistance in the areas of the environment and transport infrastructure. A Protocol attached to the Treaty restricted access to the fund to member states with a *per capita* gross domestic product of less than 90 per cent of the Union average. Although Greece would be one of the beneficiaries, questions were raised over whether the national goals had been entirely achieved. In contrast with European concessions in the past, the fund did not provide a fixed allocation of resources among the four recipients; moreover, provision of the funds was not automatic but was linked to the implementation of convergence programmes for each member state.[26] Table 4.1 presents a summary of Greek positions and the final EMU structure.

---

21. 'The core activity of the IGC is probably as much about the definition of problems and choices as it is about discrete policy decisions', see S. Mazey and J. Richardson, 'Policy framing: interest groups and the lead up to 1996 Inter-Governmental Conference', *West European Politics,* 1997, vol. 20, no. 3, p. 117.

22. Interview 14.

23. Hosli writes that the strategy of 'issue-linkage' provided relatively stronger leverage for smaller states in the negotiation procedures. *See* M. O. Hosli, 'The creation of the European Economic and Monetary Union (EMU): intergovernmental negotiations and two-level games', *Journal of European Public Policy,* 2000, vol. 7, no. 5, pp. 744–66, p. 761.

24. Although a compromise was achieved, 'the coalition had too disparate a stance on other issues to form a more wide-ranging bloc'. *See* Featherstone, Kazamias, and Papadimitriou, 'Greece and the negotiation of Economic and Monetary Union', p. 409.

25. Article 130d, and 'Protocol on Economic and Social Cohesion', TEU.

26. These objections were raised during the ratification period by Leader of PASOK, Papandreou, and Leader of Coalition of the Left and Progress Party, Damanaki. *See Parliamentary Proceedings* (Session Γ'), 28 July 1992.

EMU as a new economic policy framework

The TEU envisaged that Economic and Monetary Union would be introduced in three successive stages by 1 January 1999 at the latest.[27] The first stage began on 1 July 1990. The Council was to assess economic and monetary convergence performance throughout the EC, while member states were to adopt appropriate measures so that they could comply with certain prohibitions laid down by the Treaty (prohibition on restricting capital movements; prohibition on central bank financing of public deficits; prohibition on the granting by central banks of overdraft facilities to public authorities and public undertakings; prohibition on introducing privileged access for the latter to financial institutions). The second stage would be introduced by 1 January 1994.[28] Its purpose was to secure convergence of economic performance among member states, with the aim of preparing their economies for EMU. Progress made with regard to price stability and sound public finances would be monitored and carried out by the Commission. The key institutional development was the formation of the European Monetary Institute (EMI). Its main aims were to strengthen the co-ordination of national monetary policies and make the technical preparations for the introduction of the single currency.[29]

Transition to the third stage would be subject to the attainment of a high degree of sustainable economic convergence. Sustainability would be evaluated against a number of convergence criteria[30] laid down by the Treaty. During this stage, the

---

27. Art. 109j (4) states that if, by the end of 1997, a date for the beginning of the third stage has not been set, it will start on 1 January 1999. In the relevant literature, extensive reference has been made both to the work of the Intergovernmental Conferences which led to the final text of the TEU and to the member-state compromises which made the signing of the treaty possible. *See*, for example, D. R. Cameron, 'Transnational relations and the development of European Economic and Monetary Union', in T. Risse-Kappen (ed.), *Bringing Transnational Relations Back In: Non-state actors, domestic structures and international institutions*, Cambridge, Cambridge University Press, 1995; K. Dyson, *Elusive Union: The process of economic and monetary union in Europe*, London, Longman, 1994; B. Eichengreen and J. Frieden (eds), *The Political Economy of European Monetary Unification*, Boulder, CO, Westview, 1994; P. B. Kenen, *Economic and Monetary Union in Europe: Moving beyond Maastricht*, Cambridge, Cambridge University Press, 1995; T. Padoa-Schioppa, *The Road to Monetary Union in Europe: The Emperor, the Kings, and the Genies*, Oxford, Clarendon, 1994; W. Sandholtz, 'Choosing union: monetary politics and Maastricht', *International Organisation*, 1993, vol. 47, no,1, pp. 1–39; W. Sandholtz, 'Monetary bargains: the treaty on EMU', in A. W. Cafruny and G. G. Rosenthal (eds), *The State of the European Community*, Boulder, CO, Lynne Rienner, 1993.

28. Chapter IV, TEU.

29. 'Protocol on the Statute of the European Monetary Institute', Articles 2–5, TEU.

30. The four criteria, presented in Art. 109j (1) and Protocol 6 of the Treaty are: a) a 'high degree of price stability', apparent from a rate of inflation which is close to and does not exceed by more than 1.5 percentage points that, of at most, the three best performing member states in terms of price stability; b) a 'government budgetary position' that is not subjected to a Council Decision that an 'excessive deficit exists' under Article 104c(6); c) the observance of the 'normal fluctuation margins' provided for by the exchange-rate mechanism of the European System without 'severe tensions' for at least two years prior to the examination and without a 'devaluation' of a currency's

Table 4.1: Comparing notes, Greek aspirations and EMU outcomes

Elements of EMU	Greek Position	Outcome
Single Currency (EMU)	Prefers EMU with no 'opt-out'	EMU with British and Danish opt-out and unilateral German opt-in
Strict Convergence Criteria	Prefers flexible interpretation	Prior to accession, fulfillment of convergence criteria but flexible interpretation
Schedule and Procedure for the Transition	Favours maximum delay and financial resources to aid the transition	If a majority qualify, transition in 1997, otherwise automatic transition in 1999, with QMV to determine membership
ECB autonomy, mandate and voting procedure	Unclear	Politically independent bank, strong anti-inflationary policy stance
Domestic budgetary controls with sanctions	Yes	Yes, decision by QMV
Financial Transfers	Yes	No bail-outs or fiscal federalism but cohesion fund

Source: The structure for this table has been taken from Moravscik, A. *The Choice for Europe* (Cornell: Cornell University Press, 1998)

currencies of the participating member states would be irrevocably fixed against each other and against the euro, which would eventually become the Union's single currency. The task of defining and implementing a single monetary policy would be entrusted to the European System of Central Banks (ESCB), composed of the European Central Bank (ECB) and the national central banks. The primary objective of the new institution would be the maintenance of price stability.[31] Central to its operation would be the guarantee of independence from political interference. On the budgetary front, Stage III ruled out excessive government deficits,[32] the monetary financing of member states' governments by the ESCB,[33]

---

bilateral central rate on its own initiative; d) an 'average nominal long-term interest rate', measured on the basis of long-term government bonds or comparable securities, that does not exceed by more than two percentage points that of, at most, the three best performing member states in terms of price stability. The criteria would not be applied automatically. According to Art. 109j (2) and (3), eligibility decisions would be made by Ecofin and the European Council on the basis of recommendations from the Commission and the EMI and the consultation of the European Parliament.

31. 'Protocol on the Statute of the European System of Central Banks and of the European Central Bank', Chapter II, Art. 2, TEU.

32. Article 104c and 'Protocol on the Excessive Deficit Procedure', TEU.

33. Articles 104 and 104a, TEU.

and the 'bailing out' of indebted member states by the Community.[34] In the case that an excessive deficit persisted (and the member state failed to put in practice the recommendations of the Council), the Council would have the authority to apply a number of measures, including the imposition of fines.[35]

Greek policy makers realised that EMU would amount to a structural break, as price stability and sound public finances, which constituted both criteria for joining and permanent features of EMU, would necessitate better functioning product and labour markets and the fine-tuning of fiscal policies. Now that they had a deadline to meet, Greek policy makers would finally 'find the political will and resources to proceed with this particular adjustment endeavour'.[36] A strict timetable would, it was hoped, mark a break with the politicised logic that had previously permeated macroeconomic decisions.[37] The possibility of modifying five-year and other stabilisation programmes on the basis of 'how they would be regarded by the public was a luxury that could no longer be afforded'.[38] In addition, the externally monitored convergence programmes, combined with the specific timetables for the implementation of goals, were expected to imbue discipline in the behaviour of all relevant policy actors. If the economy had not considerably converged by 1999, or soon thereafter, the country's entry to EMU would be postponed indefinitely. As a result, the Greek economy would remain in Europe's periphery and, in the case of Community enlargement, would face increased competition from new entrants.

In the Greek interpretation, 'the EMU framework would effectively protect the economy from the long-established problems of inflation and balance of payments'.[39] Quite how the goal of price stability and a single monetary policy conducted centrally at ECB level would be compatible with domestic economic conditions, where demand-based growth formed the overriding policy model, never became a serious issue for deliberation;[40] the functioning of EMU was considered secondary, all that mattered was Greece's joining in. The fulfilment of the relevant convergence criteria and the eventual entry of the drachma to the exchange-rate mechanism of the European Monetary System (EMS) would provide the parameters for the conduct of a consistent disinflation policy, a sustained decline in the rate of increase in price levels. Even if disinflation came with its own costs for income distribution – enshrined in lower real wages and high

---

34. Article 104b, TEU.

35. Article 104c, 11–13, TEU.

36. Interview 14.

37. Statements of Minister of National Economy Christodoulou during TEU ratification in Parliament, *Parliamentary Proceedings*, (Session KZ´), 18 November 1991

38. Interview 14.

39. Interview 15; interview 13.

40. The domestic debate on EMU remained within a small group of economists, who hardly constituted an epistemic community. *See*, for example, G. Alogoskoufis, N. Garganas, N. Karamouzis, L. Katseli, T. Kollintzas, M. Xafa, L. Papademos, Y. Stournaras, L. Tsoukalis, N. Christodoulakis, 'Greece and European Monetary Union', *Working Paper No. 9*, Athens, Hellenic Centre of European Studies, 1991 [in Greek]; P. Haas, 'Introduction: knowledge, power and international policy coordination', *International Organisation*, 1992, vol. 46, no. 1, pp. 1–35.

real interest rates – these were never calculated. EMU participation would finally eradicate the established practice of generating inflation-related social benefits and transfers. Moreover, gradual restoration of macroeconomic imbalances, combined with a stable monetary environment, would shield Greece from the occurrence and recurrence of balance of payments crises, which constituted unassailable proof that the country consumed more than it produced. Hence, EMU as a policy framework offered a policy path for the attainment of nominal convergence, credible and effective protection against the damaging effects of financial markets' speculation and, in the medium term, sustained economic growth.

Greek policy makers followed the European trend, setting out 'to link the goal of EMU participation with a programme of fiscal consolidation and structural reorganisation and readjustment';[41] they would now be backed, against potential domestic veto-players, by the procedure of 'multilateral surveillance': member states would submit medium-term convergence programmes to the Council and the Commission with regard to their budgetary position and the economic outlook on which they based their budget plans. The institutionalisation of EU supervision was supposed to alter the incentives faced by all the economic agents involved in programme implementation, ensuring that all aspects of macroeconomic policy cohered credibly around currency stability. Back home, the MNEC used the technical nature and complexities of EMU provisions to consolidate a leading role over its co-ordinating partner, the MFA. Following ratification, 'MFA officials who participated in inter-ministerial committees effectively acquired the status of observer'[42] while 'the MFA was restricted to forwarding papers and dossiers'.[43]

Greek policy makers were certainly not the only ones who interpreted the EMU policy framework for their domestic audience. The distance that had to be covered from rhetoric to execution was so great however, and the fear of losing the country's EU standing so pervasive, that the *national* interpretation and the domestic debate that followed omitted one central question: was the country's economy compatible with the dictates of EMU? Quite a few of Greece's EU partners must have also been asking: is the type of monetary union proposed appropriate for Greece?

The almost unanimous ratification of the Treaty

Prime Minister Mitsotakis, a self-proclaimed 'conscious European', had an ideological commitment to joining EMU;[44] EMU was part of a wider project of political union which would, *pace* Moravscik,[45] safeguard Greece's vital foreign

---

41. Interview 16.
42. Interview 9.
43. Interview 6.
44. Interview 4.
45. In Moravscik's interpretation, national preferences are best explained by reference to structural economic interests rather than European ideology and geopolitical interests. He concedes, however, that in EMU negotiations these were more closely balanced. *See* Moravscik, *The Choice for Europe*, p. 477.

and security interests.[46] Spurred by geopolitical calculations, he suggested that 'Political Union constitutes the primary element. Economic and Monetary Union comes second, as a complement'.[47] Even if EPU's thin structure proved him wrong, Mitsotakis operated from within a party tradition that interpreted the TEU as the latest step in building a politically united Europe. Security considerations and ideology mattered, particularly for a country which, back in 1981, had seen in accession to the EEC, the consolidation of its democracy and affirmation of ideological adherence to the 'West'.

Following the majority of Community governments, the ND government decided not to carry out a referendum on the TEU – 'no risks could be taken'.[48] Ratification followed a four-day, specially convened debate during the Parliament's summer session. Prime Minister Mitsotakis moved the process then, as he did not trust Papandreou, Leader of the Opposition, and was concerned that PASOK would vote against it.[49] In any case, most opposition parties criticised the government for choosing this ratification procedure; Mitsotakis, however, was more concerned to display his government's integrationist credentials and ratify the Treaty with a considerable majority.[50] The vote took place on 31 July 1992. Out of 295 Deputies who voted, 286 voted in favour, 8 voted against (7 Greek Communist Party Deputies and 1 Ecology Party Deputy) and 1 PASOK Deputy sought a present vote to be registered. The 'yes' majority was one of the largest ever recorded in Greece's Parliamentary history.[51] During ratification, the two major political parties, ND and PASOK, sought to highlight the best transition road as well as the most appropriate national strategy *vis-à-vis* EMU entry.

For Prime Minister Mitsotakis, the TEU served Greece's national interest, both politically and economically. TEU was linked with three different, yet inter-related sets of goals: the modernisation and strengthening of the economy, the social development and restructuring of the administrative system and the consolidation of national independence and security. Mitsotakis chose to present the convergence effort for the attainment of Greece's 'equal' participation in EMU, as a 'one-way

---

46. This conception of political union explains why the Greek position differed from that of most of the other member states; the latter linked a possible deepening of political integration with the loss of important sovereign rights. In contrast, Greek policy makers assumed that political union would render Greek borders European, thereby guaranteeing their protection. P. C. Ioakimidis, *European Political Union, Theory-Negotiation, Institutions and Policies: The Maastricht Treaty and Greece*, 2nd edn. Athens, Themelio, 1995, 448–9 [in Greek].

47. *Parliamentary Proceedings* (Session Γ´), 28 July 1992.

48. Interview 4.

49. Interview 4.

50. Interview 4.

51. The constitutional issues raised by the Treaty and the concern with the new type of European power that was being created have been presented in K. Koliopoulos, 'Greece and the ratification of the Maastricht Treaty', in F. Laursen and S. Vanhoonacker (eds), *The Ratification of the Maastricht Treaty: Issues, debates and future implications*, Maastricht, Martinus Nijhoff Publishers, 1994, pp. 114–5.

street'.[52] The government would follow 'the economic policy that is imposed by the way things are, in accordance with numbers';[53] the dilemma of getting on the convergence path or staying at the margins left very little room for creative or idiosyncratic economic policy-making.

Government policy makers were keen to identify EMU participation with the implementation of their chosen policy programme. Fiscal consolidation constituted, as was expected, the primary target; without suitable tightening up, the effort to reduce inflation, cut nominal interest rates and facilitate the drachma's participation in the Exchange Rate Mechanism (ERM) would not be feasible. The effects of the excessive public-debt-to-GDP ratio on private saving, public investment, total factor productivity and long-term nominal and real interest rates offered the greatest cause for immediate policy action. Accompanying the endeavour was an equally ambitious structural adjustment programme: reduction in the size of the public sector through extensive privatisation, reorganisation of public enterprises' financing and liberalisation of goods and factors markets were all expected to overturn the structures that had led to Greece's economic divergence in the first place.

PASOK, the major opposition party, agreed with the general supposition that Greece would be marginalised if it failed to participate in EMU. While the party line dictated a 'yes' vote for the Treaty, its main speakers emphasised the cost of adjustment to Greece's fragile economy.[54] The TEU had failed to address the question of whether unemployment would rise in EMU, as markets adjusted to the new competitive conditions; nor had it instituted relevant EU-wide measures. The convergence criteria, which echoed the concerns of the Bundesbank, hardly constituted a serious guarantee for the attainment of social solidarity and cohesion. Equally, the transfer of monetary policy to the EU level was not accompanied by the evolution of the role of the Community budget. In PASOK's interpretation, this budget should have acquired a fiscal role, carrying out the Community's re-distributive, development, and social policies.

PASOK deputies were also particularly critical of what they perceived as the patent lack of a national negotiating strategy. The government had failed to link its acceptance of EMU provisions with country-specific measures for easing adjustment or with extensive financing from the second CFS. In comparison, when PASOK was in power, it had extracted, from the creation of the Integrated Mediterranean Programmes onwards, considerable Community funding. The ND government had accepted a homogeneous convergence course for all member states, irrespective of their economy's point of departure. By failing to secure a longer transition period for the weaker economies, and in the absence of specific

---

52. *Parliamentary Proceedings* (Session Γ´), 28 July 1992.

53. *Ibid.*

54. Analysis of PASOK's position is based on the speeches of former Prime Minister A. Papandreou and former Minister of National Economy (1982–85) G. Arsenis. *See Parliamentary Proceedings* (Session Γ´), 28 July 1992 and *Parliamentary Proceedings,* (Session B´), 27 July 1992, respectively.

financial assistance, Greece would *de facto* be left out of EMU. For PASOK, the appropriate policy response to pressures for adjustment involved the formation of an internationally competitive manufacturing sector, reorganisation of agricultural production, modernisation and extension of the tertiary sector, a redistributive policy guaranteeing basic social needs and the institutionalisation of a fair and effective tax system.

The Coalition Party voted in favour of ratification. Its strategy was one of critical support for the Treaty.[55] The Community's three basic achievements of pluralist democracy, acceptable standards of living and a relatively high level of social protection formed the basis of the party's principled assent to the creation of a European Union. Greece had also secured the highest *per capita* EC transfers from its membership; it could not afford to stay out of EMU. The party's Leader, Maria Damanaki, expressed concern with the way the government tried to turn the national consent that had been formed around Greece's 'European choice' to its advantage, using it to advance its particular economic policies.

The Greek Communist Party rejected the Treaty and demanded a referendum; ratification went, in the party's interpretation, beyond the parliament's jurisdiction.[56] The party's 'No' vote to Maastricht aimed to highlight a different opportunity, that of attaining independent economic development. The party discarded EMU's conservative character and rejected PASOK's and the Coalition Party's claims that EMU could be achieved in conjunction with the implementation of social policies. The only alternative route was the exploration of new economic, commercial and cultural relationships with Arab, Balkan and other non-EU countries.

The single deputy of the Ecology Party also voted against ratification. The convergence criteria set a particularly high standard of economic stability that only the developed countries could attain. The particular deadlines specified by EMU, combined with the absence of clear social rules, would swiftly put Greece's convergence effort at risk.

Conclusion: conceptualising the 'external constraint' as strategy

EMU negotiations presented Greek policy makers with the opportunity to play a two-level game.[57] In the first version, policy makers seek to use ratification problems or other constraints at the domestic level in order to augment their bargaining power at the European level. Greek negotiators refrained from playing this game; they were 'laggards' within an EU negotiation process that was structured by 'leader' states;[58] the organisation of IGC negotiations, Greece's

55. Analysis of the Coalition's position is based on the speeches of former President of the Coalition, Maria Damanaki. *See Parliamentary Proceedings* (Session Γ'), 28 July 1992.

56. Analysis of the Communist party's position is based on the speeches of former President of the Parliamentary Group, D. Kostopoulos. *See Parliamentary Proceeding* (Session Γ'), 28 July 1992.

57. R. D. Putnam, 'Diplomacy and domestic politics: the logic of two-level games', *International Organisation*, 1998, vol. 42, no. 3, pp. 427–60, p. 440.

58. The notions of 'laggard' and 'leader' are borrowed from K. Dyson, *The Politics of the Euro-Zone:*

limited role in policy coalitions, and its status as a periphery country with a small economy largely affected the government's autonomy and negotiating strategy *vis-à-vis* its partners.

In the second version, policy makers seek to use EU institutional arrangements or policy developments in order to change the nature of constraints at the domestic level. Faced with two difficult and inter-related problems – Greek macroeconomic divergence from the EU average and Greece's questionable capability to join EMU – they saw EMU as the last opportunity for proceeding with the reform and the stabilisation of the Greek economy.[59] This formulated the core of the 'external constraint' strategy.

To sell the *idea* that EMU constituted an external constraint, government policy makers exploited the autonomy which they traditionally enjoyed *vis-à-vis* all other actors: the complex political, technical, and economic facets of EMU, the uncertainty that surrounded the final outcome and the lack of knowledge and information on precisely how EMU would affect domestic business organisations operated as significant disincentives for the reorganisation of Greek economic interests. Obviously, this was not unrelated to the peripheral role that even peak associations held in the decision-making system.[60] The Greek government ensured that power asymmetries, which worked in its favour at domestic level, remained unchanged at EU level; it was no accident that the Bank of Greece's participation in the Committee of Central Bank Governors 'failed to augment its role in the formation of the Greek negotiation stance'.[61]

At EU level, where asymmetrical interdependence counted, as did Greece's economic record, the Greek story was predictably different. Greek policy makers participated in a process that was largely out of their control: in entering the IGCs, they entered a pre-structured world; this took the forms of 'historic inheritance; of institutional rules and policy styles; of the D-Mark as the 'anchor' currency of the ERM; of global financial markets; and of the state of economic and monetary policy knowledge and reigning economic policy ideas'.[62] They were forced to adapt and prepare. 'Whenever the Greek team produced a decent position, in accordance with the set of acceptable positions promoted by the Monetary Committee and the Committee of Central Bank Governors,[63] the other member-states were reluctant

---

Stability or breakdown?, Oxford, Oxford University Press, 2000, p. 115.

59. Interview 14; interview 16; interview 20.

60. *See* discussion in Chapter Four.

61. Interview 17.

62. Dyson and Featherstone, *The Road to Maastricht*, p. 19.

63. For how 'acceptable positions' came to be formed, see A. Verdun, 'Monetary integration in Europe: ideas and evolution', in M. G. Cowles and M. Smith, (eds), *The State of the European Union: Risks, reform, resistance, and revival*, Vol. 5, Oxford, Oxford University Press, 2000, p. 102. *See also*, A. Verdun, 'Governing by committee: the case of the Monetary Committee', in T. Christiansen and E. Kirchner, (ed.), *Administering the New Europe: Inter-institutional relations and comitology in the European Union*, Manchester, Manchester University Press, 2000.

to contradict it in its entirety; its interests would be heard or taken into account'.[64] The presence of Ministers in the various meetings, and the exchange of arguments that took place, induced them 'to take their responsibilities seriously'.[65]

An important finding of this chapter is that the personalisation of leadership trumps government and bureaucratic structures in a domestic setting, where formal rules will allow for this kind of tampering. In a supranational setting, however, where power is reshuffled, personalisation may diminish policy entrepreneurship, as the weakness of domestic infrastructure institutions affects the formulation of the national position and impedes political performance. There is also a trickier issue. Greek political leaders knew, from repeated interactions, that they were constrained both by the particular institutionalisation of EMU and by stronger policy entrepreneurs who enjoyed more power and authority in the negotiation setting. This knowledge and the limits that it imposed on agency challenges rational-choice claims that a final agreement, involving the creation of new rules and procedures, is reached when it is optimal for all parties involved. In the Greek case, in fact, revealed preferences, as recorded in public dialogue and in a series of interviews, suggest that Greek policy makers accepted an outcome that was sup-optimal, in comparison to their declared objectives: they favoured maximum delay – the cut-off point for the transition was 1999 – they expected some form of fiscal federalism – they got the Cohesion Fund – and they wanted political union to evolve in parallel with monetary union – this was hardly on the agenda.

In some of the better analyses, EMU was supposed to offer a real opportunity to institutionalise credible commitment.[66] In return for delegating and pooling sovereignty, governments expected to reap significant gains, measured primarily by more efficient decision-making. Greece was not the only country to demonstrate a great eagerness to take on the obligations that emanated from transition to EMU. The government could not clean up its act alone, nor could it bind domestic actors to an effective adjustment programme, without holding the external constraint 'threat' over their heads. Pre-committing 'to implement or enforce prior agreements'[67] was cheap, however. The rules and the institutions that had been set up glossed over the heterogeneity of the participating economies; hence, it was conveniently assumed that the 'no-bail-out rule' would magically eradicate moral hazard, or that losing control over the money supply would be painless, although the European Central Bank's mandate prohibited the monetary financing of public-debt issuance.

Pierson posited that integrative decisions became 'locked-in', even if institutional designers were not acting instrumentally, politicians heavily discounted long-term effects and the great potential for unanticipated consequences was not

---

64. Interview 18.

65. Interview 19.

66. Moravscik, *The Choice for Europe*, p. 487.

67. *Ibid.*, p. 488.

factored in.[68] The Maastricht 'lock-in', establishing a politically independent European Central Bank and enforcing the political supremacy of price stability, certainly disproved Pierson; institutional designers were well aware that, in opting for this arrangement, 'particular features' would produce 'specific consequences'.[69] The application of one interest-rate instrument to an economic area with different rates of growth, unemployment and inflation in the sub-regions could well trigger asymmetric effects in the member economies;[70] these could, in turn, be intensified by the variety of monetary transmission mechanisms, which followed from differences in the structures of goods, labour and financial markets.[71] Institutional designers were even aware that 'it was necessary to prevent governments from running irresponsible fiscal policies'; hence, they made it 'a legally binding part of the Treaty that no country can have a deficit of more than 3 per cent'.[72] While the problems of long-term horizons and unanticipated effects remained to be solved, there was a yawning gap in the logic of fiscal decision-making under EMU, which was not picked up: on top of economic heterogeneity, the heterogeneity of 'national politics and administrative systems' was bound to affect members' 'ability to abide by the rules set'.[73] How could a government with Greece's history, for example, be expected to make a credible, long-term commitment to fiscal prudence?

In terms of this book's themes, EMU created a new opportunity structure that offered domestic actors additional resources, notably importable institutional constraints, a legitimate framework for action and a set of common ideas, for proceeding with their preferred agenda. The extent to which EMU altered or could alter the context of future decision-making was a non-issue. The government exploited its power in the system, neutralising any 'veto points'[74] that could have arisen during ratification; the national frame, which legitimated the extended

---

68. P. Pierson, 'The limits of design: explaining institutional origins and change', *Governance: An International Journal of Policy and Administration*, 2000, vol. 13, no. 4, pp. 475–99.

69. For Pierson, the link between 'features' and 'consequences' shows instrumental design. *See ibid.*, p. 478.

70. P. Arestis, A. Brown, K. Mouratidis and M. Sawyer, 'The Euro: reflections on the first three years', *International Review of Applied Economics*, 2002, vol.16, no.1, pp. 1–17.

71. E. Hein and A. Truger, 'European Monetary Union: nominal convergence, real divergence and slow growth?', *Structural Change and Economic Dynamics*, 2005, vol. 16, p. 18.

72. 'It was a very strong request by Chancellor Kohl and the finance minister Theo Waigel to create strict criteria to guarantee fiscal soundness. That was the binding legal framework.'. Interview with Jean-Claude Trichet, President of the European Central Bank, Süddeutsche Zeitung, 23 July 2011 (accessed 25 September 2012). Online. Available: http:///www.bis.org/review/r110725a.pdf.

73. K. Featherstone, 'Le choc de la nouvelle? Maastricht, déjà vu and EMU reform', in E. Panagiotarea (ed.), *Greek Review of Political Science*, 2012, no. 39, Special Issue on 'The Politics of the Eurozone Crisis: Balancing between National Independence and Supranational Interdependence'.

74. Veto points 'refer to all stages in the decision-making process on which agreement is legally required for a policy change'. *See* M. Haverland, 'National adaptation to European integration: the importance of institutional veto points', *Journal of Public Policy*, 2000, vol. 20, no. 1, p. 85.

and extensive role of the state in the economy, had cracked;[75] the serious macroeconomic imbalances effectively jeopardised Greece's position in the new institutional edifice, while the transformation of economic conditions at the global level had already rendered notions of national monetary policy autonomy obsolete.

While 'the equal and simultaneous participation' in EMU was not guaranteed, EMU could at least be the 'external constraint' that would trigger domestic reform. In the process, the most obvious question, namely how a country with an industrial structure or trade patterns markedly different from those of the monetary union as a whole could withstand asymmetric shocks, having lost monetary and exchange-rate autonomy, was never really considered. Similar concerns that were raised for Ireland, Portugal and Spain[76] were equally disregarded or, at best, confined to academic circles. In the end, Greek policy makers accepted an EMU agreement into which their input had been small; their power to interpret it for the domestic audience, according to *their* revised, post-Maastricht, position, however, remained intact. In promoting the external-constraint strategy, they finally had the opportunity to map out a logical plan: put forward a viable convergence programme and use externally-induced discipline to make it stick.

---

75. Cracks occur with the growing incapacity of a given paradigm to offer satisfying and/or legitimate public-policy solutions. *See* Y. Surel, 'The role of cognitive and normative frames in policy-making', *Journal of European Public Policy*, 2000, vol. 7, no. 4, p. 505.

76. J. Pisani-Ferri, 'Monetary Union with variable geometry' in J. Frieden, D. Gros, and E. Jones (eds), *The New Political Economy of EMU*, Lanham, MD, Rowman and Littlefield, 1998, p. 156.

chapter five | nominal convergence and macroeconomic policy

Agreeing to EMU was one thing, embarking on a nominal convergence effort was another; the stop–go policies that were typical of Greece's macroeconomic management up to 1993 proved that Greek policy makers would not or could not stick to a single stabilisation programme. This was an unfortunate state of affairs – the long and winding road to EMU required the formulation *and* implementation of a series of convergence programmes; outcome failures could no longer be assumed away or whitewashed because results had to be delivered within a fixed timetable, if the Maastricht criteria were to be met. However, at least, EMU presented the sort of sustainable adjustment path that policy makers had not been able to create for themselves. 'If EMU did not exist, it would have to be invented' was the consensus view among the policy-making elite; therein lay, in fact, the essence of EMU as an external-constraint strategy.

Employing the strategy, Greek policy makers expected to resolve the commitment problems that had resulted from the country's institutional and policy lack of fit, to enhance the efficiency of rule-making by transferring responsibility and implementation to credible institutions and to proceed with unpopular policies without having to calculate the political cost. Even if the government surrendered some of its power in the process, by delegating policy competence to the EU level and by inadvertently accepting weaker mechanisms of control,[1] it finally had an opportunity to impose economic discipline from above. The fact that the Greek economy's more differentiated structure would require painful structural reforms, or that its debt dynamics would stand in the way of fiscal consolidation, never really became a serious issue. All that mattered was that Greece was about to embark on an ambitious macroeconomic stabilisation policy that would reverse the negative trends of high inflation, high unemployment and growing fiscal deficits.

Fighting inflation amidst fiscal imbalance

From the 'crawling peg' to the hard Drachma

Throughout the 1980s, Greece's inflation rate had galloped at an average of almost 20 per cent, while real growth was stagnant at less than 1 per cent. The 'crawling peg' exchange-rate policy (which involved adjusting the currency gradually, in response to changes in selective quantitative indicators) had failed to generate the

---

1. According to the argument by Thatcher and Stone Sweet, the more powers are delegated to an agent, the weaker will be *ex-post* mechanisms of control. *See* M. Thatcher and A. Stone Sweet, 'Theory and practice of delegation to non-majoritarian institutions', *West European Politics*, vol. 25, no. 1, January 2002, pp. 5–6.

expected economic growth and development, undermined by the expansionary fiscal policy and loose monetary policy of the period. The fight against high inflation was, in fact, unstable and haphazard, with the exception of the brief application of the 'hard-Drachma policy' during 1986 and 1987.[2] Following the 1985 balance of payments crisis, monetary authorities began to pursue a policy of limited depreciation that did not fully offset the inflation differential between Greece and its major trading partners. In any case, it was abandoned soon enough because the re-emergence of expansionary fiscal and monetary policies from 1987 onwards was, ultimately, inconsistent with the exchange-rate rule.

In the early 1990s, however, the Maastricht criterion imposed a serious rethinking of the inflation problem and how it could be tackled; an inflation rate of 10.8 per cent simply stood in the way of EMU membership. The ND government, which replaced the 'Medium Term Adjustment Programme' [MTAP] 1991–1993 with the '1993–1998 Convergence Programme' [CP] resuscitated the use of the exchange-rate policy, in a renewed attempt to contain inflationary pressures. Progress was limited, circumscribed by the large fiscal deficits that the government was unable to control. Moreover, one-off measures, such as the indirect-tax increases of 1992–3, had the effect of interrupting the downward path of inflation. Lack of political will to implement 'difficult' measures, absence of a coherent implementation plan and the EMS crisis of 1992–3 (which caused disturbance in the financial markets and recession in Europe), all threw the programme off track.

Following the 1993 elections, the new PASOK government announced its intention to revise the 1993–1998 CP, which had only been implemented for eight months. Rather than addressing head-on the fiscal crisis that was brewing, the government chose to initiate a public dialogue with trade unions, producers and certain other social groups, with the aim of creating a climate of consent for the adoption of stabilisation measures.[3] In the post-Maastricht policy environment, however, wasting precious time came at a considerable cost. As the country's anti-inflationary credibility hit a low point, the government finally decided to 'harden' the Drachma: in 1993–4, the rate of the Drachma's depreciation was reduced in stages, while 'from 1995 onwards the stability of the exchange rate became the central policy concern'.[4]

Consistent implementation was partly related to the final de-regulation of the credit system and the liberalisation of interest rates, which were completed during

---

2.   The hard-Drachma policy first surfaced with the 1986–7 stabilisation programme. The disinflationary exchange-rate policy aimed to offset the differential in unit wage costs rather than the differential in retail prices. *See* Commission of the European Communities, 'Annual Economic Report 1986–7', *European Economy*, November 1986, no. 30. Interview 15: 'With the policy, the government sought to signal its prioritisation of price stability'. Interview 17: 'In adopting intermediate targets, and in particular the exchange rate parity, the BoG steadily sought, in the aftermath of the 1986 balance of payments crisis, to pursue a tighter monetary policy; it raised interest rates against the government's preference of fully accommodating the inflation differential'.

3.   N. Christodoulakis, *The New Setting of Development*, Athens, Kastaniotis Editions, 1998, p. 43 [in Greek].

4.   Interview 20.

1993 and over the early months of 1994. After years of 'gradual de-regulation' and 'a strategy of critical acquiescence'[5] to the Bank of Greece's pressure,[6] the government had to expedite procedures. Stage one of EMU ended in January 1994 with the rules being applied universally: Greece could no longer afford to be an exception. The lifting of administrative controls on interest rates was completed with the abolition of the administrative setting of minimum interest rates on savings-account deposits. The requirement for commercial banks to invest part of their deposits in Treasury bills was abolished. In July 1993, the requirement for commercial banks to earmark a percentage of their new deposits for the financing of small and medium-sized manufacturing firms was also abolished. In January 1994, the Bank of Greece (BoG) proceeded with the de-regulation of consumer credit. Following the abolition of all foreign-exchange controls and restrictions on current transactions in 1992, the full liberalisation of capital movements was also under way by 1993. This was effected by Presidential Decree 96/1993, which harmonised Greek law with the provisions of Council Directives 88/361/EEC and 92/122/EEC. Subsequently, restrictions on medium- and long-term capital movements between Greece and the rest of the EU were lifted, while short-term capital movements were freed in May 1994.[7]

The government's grip on monetary policy loosened, as it had to stick to the sequence of stages imposed by the EMU timetable. From stage two, the Treaty prohibited the direct financing of deficits by national central banks (Art. 101), as well as the public sector's privileged access to financial institutions (Art. 102). Until the mid 1980s, the Bank of Greece financed a substantial part of the Public

5.   Interview 21: 'The government only signalled a minimum commitment to the deregulation process with the Report of the Committee for the Reformation and the Modernisation of the Banking System (the Karatzas Committee). While the report was merely a blueprint for policy-making, its importance lay in the fact that it had originated in the Ministry of National Economy. De-regulation was placed alongside the 1986 stabilisation programme, which constituted the government's policy response to the balance of payments crisis of 1986. Fearing that the dramatic rise in real interest rates – associated with the abolition of administrative controls – could destabilise the debt-accumulation process, the government wanted the completion of deregulation to coincide with the stabilisation of the economy. In any case, the implementation of de-regulation did not follow in the orderly way that the report had envisaged. This was related to the abandonment of the stabilisation programme in 1987 and, with the elections of 1988, the prevalence of political calculations in the management of the economy'.

6.   For the BoG, de-regulation would trigger the efficient operation of the monetary framework, which had been distorted by the system of specialised credit rules and controls. The conduct of monetary policy had long been impeded by the significant increases in the domestic money supply, the underdeveloped nature of the money and credit markets and the over-financing of certain traditional sectors at the expense of more dynamic ones. *See* D. Chalikias, 'Financial reform and problems of monetary policy', *Bank of Greece: Papers and Lectures, 59*, Athens, Bank of Greece, 1987 [in Greek] and G. Hadjimatheou, 'Macroeconomic performance and policies: recent past and prospects' in T. Skouras (ed.), *Issues in Contemporary Economics, Vol. 5, The Greek Economy: Economic policy for the 1990s*, London, Macmillan, in association with the International Economic Association, 1992.

7.   The account of the completion of de-regulation which follows is based on the Bank of Greece, *Report of the Governor for the Year 1992*, Athens, Bank of Greece, 1993; *Report of the Governor for the Year 1993*, Athens, Bank of Greece,1994; *Report of the Governor for the Year 1994*, Athens, Bank of Greece, 1995 [in Greek].

Sector Borrowing Requirement (PSBR);[8] the rise of the PSBR from 8.4 per cent of GDP in 1980 to 16.0 per cent in 1988 had led, in fact, to the monetisation of the public debt and to the acceleration of the money supply (M3). While the large fiscal deficits of this period influenced the setting of interest rates, commercial banks were required to invest a proportion of their funds in treasury bills. In addition, the specialised credit institutions (namely, the Agricultural Bank, the mortgage banks and the investment banks) depended for their operation on central-bank financing. As a result, the BoG could not effectively control the monetary base. It did act, however, as a constraint on the government's wildest political demands,[9] utilising the reputation that it had acquired as 'an agent of stability' in the system of economic-policy formation.[10] Governors shared 'a common monetary ideology, often the result of their educational background and their career advancement through the BoG's hierarchy; they were to project a continuity in the pursuit of the BoG's policy goals which gave them an advantage *vis-à-vis* regularly alternating Ministers and their policy advisors'.[11]

Backed by the Treaty provisions and the relevant secondary legislation, the BoG adopted market-oriented, indirect means of monetary control and gradually developed the framework that would strengthen their effectiveness. Critical to the BoG's strategy was the activation, from mid-1993, of the bills and notes rediscount mechanism and the introduction of a new type of central-bank lending to commercial banks, using government paper as collateral. The availability of market-intervention mechanisms depended on the full operation of money and capital markets. The BoG played a decisive role in their development by accepting more categories of securities for open-market operations, creating a secondary market for government securities and improving selling methods.[12] As a result, it increased its intervention capacity for the purpose of monetary control and facilitated the management of public debt.

How to further harden the Drachma?

During this stage, the 'hard Drachma' policy provided Greece with a relatively loose nominal anchor: the currency continued to depreciate at rates ranging from 11.5 per cent to 7.2 per cent, both relative to the ECU and in nominal effective

---

8. The 1986 OECD Report held that, in spite of this rise in the PSBR, GDP rose by only 4 per cent in the two years to 1985. This was related to how 'lack of competitiveness, market rigidities and the associated misallocation of resources have weakened the response of the Greek economy to domestic and external stimulus'. *See* OECD, *OECD Economic Surveys Greece 1986*, Paris, OECD, 1986, p. 65.

9. Interview 17: 'At the time of the June 1989 election, the Finance Minister tried to persuade the BoG to breach the law which prohibited the outstanding amount of central bank credit to the government from exceeding 10 per cent of budgeted expenditure. We suggested, instead, that the Minister raised the rate on government securities, a proposal that was adopted'.

10. Interview 24.

11. Interview 17.

12. Y. Boutos, 'Economic developments and policy orientations', *Bank of Greece: Papers and Lectures, 78*, Athens, Bank of Greece, 1994, p. 23 [in Greek].

terms. Inflation began to fall but progress was slow and inconsistent. This had to do both with breaks in implementation[13] – typical of the Greek approach – and with the half-hearted application of the fiscal consolidation measures, which were supposed to solidify the exchange-rate commitment. In 1994, the inflation differential *vis-à-vis* a basket of industrial countries stood at 8.5 per cent while the real effective exchange rate (CPI-based) had risen by 4.4 per cent; the weaker currency peg mitigated stronger real appreciation.[14]

Exploiting the proposed institutionalisation of price stability, the BoG sought to voice and act on its corporate interests.[15] Against a background of increased government and market watchfulness, it calculated that the diversification of supervision strategies would enable it to monitor the inflation target in a discretionary manner; even the Bundesbank, which religiously adhered to the money stock M3 as the key reference variable for its monetary policy, broadened its view after a second wave of M3 overshooting occurred in 1996.[16] De-regulation had, in any case, brought about changes in the operation of financial markets that had affected the effectiveness of traditional monetary policy, altering the relationship between intermediate targets, such as M3, and final objectives.

Endorsing the 'eclectic' approach followed by other central banks, the BoG subscribed to the view that, 'the Banks that performed their tasks efficiently, aimed at a multiple assessment of monetary conditions in their exercise of monetary policy'.[17] While interest-rate policy was primarily linked to the exchange rate, its conduct was also influenced by the course of monetary and credit aggregates and by progress attained in reducing inflation – the final target. Hence, the setting of interest rates took into consideration the course of the Drachma's parity with the ecus in foreign markets and the development of the rate of inflation, current and future. In this respect, the Greek approach borrowed some elements from the strategy of inflation targeting; if the expected development of inflation, based on a forecast for a six- and an eighteen-month period, did not follow the target set for inflation, interest rates were adjusted in order to achieve this target. In determining the appropriate level of interest rates, however, monetary authorities

---

13. The first occurred in the beginning of 1994, when the relaxation of monetary policy caused a sustained rise in short-term interest rates, triggering a Drachma crisis throughout the summer of 1994. Inflation also rose in the pre-1996 election period, due to high wage increases in the public sector that affected, in turn, wages in the private sector. *See* G. Alogoskoufis, 'The Greek Economy and the Euro', in A. Mitsos and E. Mossialos (eds), *Contemporary Greece and Europe*, Aldershot, Ashgate, 2000, p. 150.

14. *See* E. Detragiarche. and A. J. Hamman, 'Exchange rate-based stabilization in Western Europe: Greece, Ireland, Italy and Portugal', *Contemporary Economic Policy*, July 1999, vol. 17, no. 3, pp. 358–69.

15. In this way, central bankers across Europe were able to reclaim, in a way, the power they were losing to globalised markets and the regional process of EMU. *See* K. Dyson, K. Featherstone and G. Michalopoulos, 'Strapped to the mast: EC central bankers between global financial markets and regional integration', *Journal of European Public Policy*, 1995, vol. 2, no. 3, p. 486.

16. F. Giordano and S. Persaud, *The Political Economy of Monetary Union: Towards the Euro*, London/New York, Routledge, 1998, p. 78.

17. Interview 22.

also monitored developments in the money supply, particularly credit expansion. In 1998, for example, when, prior to the Drachma's entry to the ERM, the currency was placed under speculative pressure, it was primarily credit expansion that caused the setting of high interest rates (three-month Treasury bill rates rose by over 4 percentage points, reaching 12.8 per cent in March 1998) rather than the maintenance of the parity.[18] For the monetary authorities, deceleration in credit expansion would indirectly support the exchange-rate parity and render it more credible to the markets.

Monetary convergence and fiscal divergence?

A new convergence programme

In the early 1990s, the serious problem with the Greek strategy, in view of the targeted EMU membership, was the fact that fiscal consolidation continued to fall behind monetary stabilisation; repeating the pattern of the mid-1980s, the precarious policy of combating inflation without prioritising the reduction of public deficits and the stabilisation of total debt resurfaced. The failure of this policy mix was evident in the way that the BoG pursued its intermediate targets – exchange rate stability and limited money supply growth – with one policy instrument, the interest rate.[19]

Pursuant to the new procedures of the Treaty on the European Union (Art. 104c) regarding policy co-ordination and budgetary discipline, however, Greece's fiscal mess was no longer solely its own problem. In September 1994, the Council decided that an excessive deficit existed in Greece.[20] With a sense of urgency, authorities formulated a new convergence programme covering the period 1994–9. Central to the programme was the recognition that 'the chief factor standing in the way of economic stabilisation and exploitation of the favourable prospects for growth is the fiscal problem'.[21] Approved by the Council, the programme – which aimed to achieve 'the necessary adjustment of the Greek economy and establishment of the conditions necessary' for participation by Greece in the European Economic and Monetary Union – advanced an ambitious set of goals: the fiscal deficit would be reduced to 3 per cent of GDP by 1998, while public debt as a percentage of GDP would be stabilised by 1996. In 1997, inflation and interest rates would be very close to the convergence criteria. With the nominal convergence process completed by 1998, Greece would join EMU on 1 January 1999.[22]

---

18. Interview 22.

19. M. Arghyrou, 'EMU and Greek macroeconomic policy in the 1990s', in Mitsos and Mossialos, *Contemporary Greece and Europe*, p. 168.

20. The Council Decision asserted the existence of excessive deficits in ten member states (Belgium, Denmark, France, Germany, Greece, Italy, Netherlands, Portugal, Spain and United Kingdom). *See EU Bulletin No 9-1994*, p. 12.

21. Ministry of the National Economy, Directorate of Economic Policy, *Revised Convergence Programme for the Greek Economy, 1994–1999*, Athens, June 1996, p. 2 [in Greek].

22. *Ibid.*

Average Inflation Rate (HICP) and the Reference Value
1996–March 2000
*Unweighted arithmetic average of the three best performers in the terms of inflation plus 1.5%

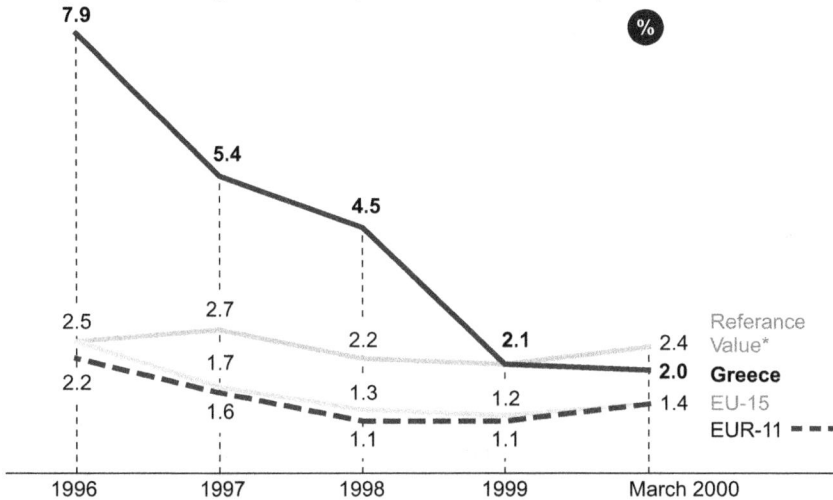

Figure 5.1: Attaining disinflation: Greece's inflation rate (HICP), 1996–2000

Rushing to jump on the EMU bandwagon

In 1996 PASOK won the national elections; the new Prime Minister and PASOK leader Costas Simitis[23] was determined to push forward with the nominal convergence endeavour. On the fiscal front, the government's strategy was based on four types of measures; the enactment of taxation laws; changes in the budgetary drafting procedure; cut-backs in non-investment expenditure; and an increase in state revenues from the stock-market flotation of shares in public enterprises. Rationalisation of the budgetary process constituted 'the key to curbing primary expenditure and, subsequently, to promoting fiscal consolidation'.[24] Firmer adherence did begin to produce results: while the budget deficit stood at 13.8 per cent in 1993, it fell to 4.0 per cent of GDP in 1997. Moreover, by 1997, the primary surplus of the ordinary budget (5.6 per cent of GDP), the rate of GDP growth (3.5 per cent) and the fall in the interest payments on the public debt led to a stabilisation of the public debt as a percentage of GDP; after a peak of 111.6 per cent of GDP in 1996, it fell to 108.7 per cent in 1997.

This improvement in fiscal performance, however, could hardly constitute fiscal consolidation. The latter would have required both a change in the size of government and a substantial reduction of state involvement in the public sector. Any adjustment that was achieved resulted largely from lower interest payments

---

23. *See* Appendix A. Bibliographical Data.

24. Interview 23.

on the debt and a decrease in capital expenditures. Moreover, while the percentage of public spending was reduced, traditional areas of slippage – such as the wage bill – were not eradicated. To take an example from individual categories of primary expenditure, public sector personnel outlays rose by 15.2 per cent in 1997 (and by 55.2 per cent since 1992) in a period of supposed tight fiscal and incomes policy. Worse, the government unceremoniously shelved an independent report on pension reform when it emerged that 'the changes proposed to the system of ludicrously privileged arrangements' could seriously affect its electoral prospects.[25]

On the revenue front, the enactment of a series of tax-reform laws between 1994 and 1998 did trigger a steady revenue increase; in comparison to average EU performance, however, revenues fell short by 7 per cent. Authorities, while continually referring to the need to curb tax evasion and expand the tax base, passed a law containing regulations to that effect only in February 1998. Over-optimistic expectations also stymied structural adjustment reform; the pace at which 'rationalisation' of the operation of the social security system and of the funding of public enterprises proceeded was sufficiently slow as to impede a more favourable course for the reduction of the ratio of public debt to GDP.[26]

Central bank independence, at last

The projected entry of the Drachma into the ERM, combined with the completion of liberalisation, allowed the BoG to tighten monetary policy further. Inflation fell from 14.2 per cent in 1993 to 5.4 per cent in 1997. Figure 5.1 shows how the 12-month average inflation rate had a sustained downward trend from the end of 1996, reflecting this new phase in the application of the strategy; it reached 2.0 per cent in March 2000, against a reference value of 2.4 per cent.

The decline in the inflation differential and the relative stability of the Drachma's exchange rate also led to a fall in long-term interest rates. In September 1997, the average long-term interest rate fell to 9.5 per cent (with an EU reference value of 7.8 per cent).[27] In what seemed like a last-minute effort to boost its EMU credentials, the government finally decided to pass, in line with the Treaty and Statute requirements for EMU stage three, the legislation for central bank independence in November 1997; it became legally effective a month later, in December 1997. The BoG had first raised the issue during the IGC negotiation period:

---

25. Interview 31.

26. Bank of Greece, Annual Report of the Governor for the Year 1997, Athens, Bank of Greece, 1998–9 [in Greek].

27. The interest-rate data for Greece, which referred, until May 1997, to bonds with original maturity of less than 10 years, were not strictly comparable with those of other member states. See European Commission, 'Commission's recommendation concerning the third stage of economic and monetary union', 'Convergence report 1998', 'Growth and employment in the stability-oriented framework of EMU', European Economy, No. 65, 1998, p. 21.

The main changes required in the legal and institutional framework of the Bank of Greece, in order to enhance the effectiveness of monetary policy and make the Bank's statutes compatible with the Maastricht Treaty, relate to the adoption of institutional provisions which safeguard its independence while ensuring democratic accountability.[28]

In 1993, the BoG even proposed a first draft for its enactment, which never reached parliamentary stage.[29] The government had refused to budge, while the method of appointment and term of office of successive governors continued to signal acute political interference: in 1993, the Governor was swiftly dismissed with the change of government, while the former Minister of National Economy who replaced him held the post for less than a year. Even when the position stabilised, with the appointment of Governor Papademos in 1994, the government effectively waited until the stage-three 'deadline' to pass the relevant legislation. In the BoG's interpretation, this 'delay' was not related either to the government's lack of understanding of its obligations or the lack of technical preparation.[30]

The new law 2609 introduced two important amendments to the goals and operation of the BoG. According to Article 4,

> the primary objective of the Bank is to ensure price stability. Without prejudice to this objective, the Bank shall support the general economic policy of the government.

And according to Article 5a,

> neither the Bank of Greece nor any member of its decision-making bodies shall seek or take instructions from the government or any organisation. Neither the government nor any other political authority shall seek to influence the decision-making organs of the Bank.[31]

For monetary authorities, this long-awaited change in the monetary framework would enhance the credibility of the chosen monetary policy and facilitate the achievement of a rate of inflation in line with the goals set in the nominal convergence process. They were, nevertheless, careful not to draw a direct link between granting central bank independence and a further fall in the inflation rate;[32] they

---

28. Bank of Greece, *Annual Report of the Governor for the Year 1991*, Athens, Bank of Greece, 1992 [in Greek].

29. Interview 22.

30. Interview 24.

31. Law 2609/1997, 'Validation of certain provisions of the Statute of the Bank of Greece and other provisions', *Government Gazette*, No. 101A, 11 May 1998 [in Greek]. See also Law 2548/97 'Regulations for the Bank of Greece' [in Greek], Government Gazette, No 259A, 19 December 1997.

32. Interview 22. For different views on whether central bank independence can affect the course of disinflation, *see* V. Grilli, D. Masciandaro and G. Tabellini, 'Political and monetary institutions and public financial policies in the industrial countries', *Economic Policy*, 1991, vol. 13, pp. 342–92; D. Gros and N. Thygesen, *European Monetary Integration: From the European Monetary System to Economic and Monetary Union*, 2nd edition, London, Longman, 1998; K. C.

were concerned that, if they failed to conform to explicit performance criteria, the BoG's credibility would suffer. The 'closed circle' character of the policy process ensured, in any case, that policy decisions were rarely challenged by interest groups or other non-state actors.[33]

The Drachma in the ERM

The timing of the decision

The Greek authorities decided to apply for the Drachma's entry to the ERM in March 1998.[34] At that stage, the stabilisation of the Drachma's parity, primarily based on setting interest rates at high levels, was proving too costly to maintain. According to official estimates, the loss in competitiveness, which had cumulatively reached 10 per cent, could only be recovered, prior to Greece's entry to EMU, by 'adjustment'– that is, devaluation – of the parity; without ERM entry, however, such a prospect would prove politically and economically unpalatable. In the wake of the Asian financial crisis, the perception that the Drachma was overvalued had already generated, in late October 1997, speculative pressures. Another speculative episode could not be ruled out; the markets were already anticipating that the Greek authorities would apply in May, when the European Council of Heads of State and Government would deliver its final decision on the member states that would meet the EMU criteria. The Greek authorities calculated that 'if the Greek Drachma's entry (GRD) was, in fact, delayed *until* May, it would have triggered a new round of attacks, which would have become increasingly impossible to fend off'.[35] Concerned with the reaction of financial markets, the Greek authorities decided to expedite the application.

In the negotiations that took place in the Monetary Committee, a number of items were on the agenda: the appropriate parity at which the Drachma was to enter the ERM; additional measures of fiscal consolidation together with the tight incomes policy that was to accompany the new parity; and, finally, careful reduction of basic interest rates of intervention of the Central Bank. ERM members pressed for the formulation of an accompanying programme of structural adjustment; they wanted 'specific guarantees that the Drachma's entry would be firmly placed in the broader nominal convergence effort and that it would not endanger the operation

---

Kaltenthaler, and C. J. Anderson, 'The changing political economy of inflation', *Journal of Public Policy*, 2000, vol. 20, no. 3, part 2, pp. 109–31.

33. Interview 25; *see also*, M. Xafa, 'Greece and EMU', in E. Jones, J. A. Frieden and F. S. Torres, (eds), *Joining Europe's Monetary Club: The challenges for smaller member states*, Basingstoke, Macmillan, 1998, p. 111.

34. In the relevant interviews, there was a consensus of views among officials at the Bank of Greece, the Ministry of National Economy and the Prime Minister's Office about the reasons and the timing for the GRD's entry in the ERM.

35. Interview 19.

of the mechanism as a whole'.[36] The initial Greek proposal for a three-year implementation schedule was swiftly dismissed. The Greek side was forced to accept an implementation period of 18 months.

The Drachma entered the ERM at a central rate of 357 Drachma to the ECU; this amounted to a nominal devaluation of 13.8 per cent. In the new policy environment, the hard-Drachma policy would retain its relevance, with the stability of the exchange-rate parity – vis-à-vis other currencies participating in the ERM and, beginning in 1999, the euro – constituting an intermediate target for the further reduction of inflation. A stable exchange rate was defined by the BoG as an average annual exchange rate within 2.5 per cent of the central rate (the formal range of fluctuation allowed was 15 per cent). If, however, a policy dilemma was to arise between the objectives of disinflation and exchange-rate stability, the Bank of Greece would adhere to the inflation target, allowing the exchange rate to appreciate by more than 2.5 per cent.[37] Following entry to the ERM, the currency appreciated by more than 5.5 per cent, due to increased market confidence and the positive rate differential on Drachma-denominated financial instruments. By the end of December 1998, when a co-ordinated reduction of short-term interest rates took place among the euro countries, except for Italy, this appreciation reached 7–8.5 per cent.[38]

A first test for the convergence effort

The Greek monetary authorities were eager to use the EMS as a constraint and the Greek government, searching for political cover and an opportunity to defer reform fatigue, was content to play along; by 'tying their own hands' and fixing the value of their currency to that of a low-inflation country, they limited their policy autonomy in exchange for a smoother transition to the final goal, price stability.[39]

---

36. In this section, any reference to the Greek stance during the negotiations has profited from interviews with the two negotiators, N. Garganas, then Deputy Governor of the Bank of Greece, and Professor Y. Stournaras, then President of the Council of Economic Advisors.

37. Interview 15.

38. Bank of Greece, *Report for Monetary Policy 1998–99* (submitted to the Parliament and the Ministerial Council), Athens, March 1999, p. 18 [in Greek].

39. In the standard interpretation of the EMS as a constraint, Giavazzi and Pagano suggest that 'joining the EMS can be seen precisely as a way of changing the set of incentives faced by the monetary authority'. The trend was evident in the smaller European countries. See F. Giavazzi and M. Pagano, 'The advantage of tying one's hands: EMS discipline and central bank credibility', *European Economic Review*, 1998, vol. 32, no. 5, pp. 1055–82. The empirical resonance of this argument has often been questioned. Dornbusch, for one, writes that a substantial body of research has not demonstrated conclusively that a shift in expectations or in credibility has occurred as a result of EMS membership. He suggests that countries outside the EMS have had a similar disinflation experience to those in the EMS group. Even the countries that joined the EMS were, in any case, predisposed to bring about disinflation, particularly after the late 1970s. See R. Dornbusch, 'Problems of European monetary integration' in A. Giovannini and C. Mayer, (eds), *European Financial Integration*, Cambridge, Cambridge University Press, 1991, pp. 3089.

The EMS was more than a self-imposed constraint that operated politically,[40] however. The authorities' newly acquired ability to adhere to a binding strategy was undoubtedly linked to the system's and in particular the ERM's institutional characteristics. Entry provided a stable anchor for the use of the exchange rate and EU guarantees that the currency would be safeguarded against external turbulence. It was also expected to dampen the attraction of large capital inflows. Monetary authorities now had no option but to play by the system's rules, in the same way that the government had no option but to respect them. As a result of the financial crisis in Russia and the turbulence in international markets that occurred in August 1998, the BoG intervened extensively in the currency market in order to avoid large fluctuations that would have disrupted the Drachma's parity. In this way, it gave a transparent and clear signal of its commitment to the disinflation process.[41]

Operating with prudence within the mechanism was, in fact, a 'test' for the Greek side. The policy makers who handled Greek negotiations considered that it worked in two inter-related ways. At the domestic level, it bound all the major policy actors to the goal of a stable Drachma; at the EU level, it signalled both to the markets and to the other member states the Greek commitment to maintaining the parity. The components of this strategy were 'rational' in that they were consistent with the broader strategy of using EMU as an external constraint. While Greece could not and would not meet the Maastricht nominal criteria by 1998 – the programme's central tenet – ERM entry provided a stable anchor for the entire convergence effort; the government could therefore 'legitimately' affirm its revised commitment to bringing the economy into the euro area in January 2001.[42]

In their reading, Greek policy makers had finally acquired the ability to invest their policy choices with credibility. Entry to the mechanism was a 'public act'[43] that signalled an end to the haphazard and unstable attachment to price stability manifested in the adoption and abandonment of previous stabilisation programmes. It also offered a stable framework for the reduction of long-term inflation and long-term interest rates which, generally, required a lengthier timescale than establishing tight monetary and exchange-rate stability.[44] 'The ERM was considered credible in itself; the Drachma's entry constituted, therefore, visible proof that the Greek nominal convergence endeavour that had been undertaken so

---

40. *See* A. Menon and J. Forder, 'Conclusion: states, the European Union and macroeconomic policy', in J. Forder, and A. Menon (eds), *The European Union and National Macroeconomic Policy*, London, Routledge, 1998, pp. 177–8.

41. Bank of Greece, *Report for Monetary Policy 1998–99*, p. 18 [in Greek].

42. Interview 26.

43. For Dornbusch, credibility follows the removal of a critical element of instability by a drastic public act. This is immediately recognised as such, triggering a rapid response in the markets. *See* R. Dornbusch, 'Credibility, debt and unemployment: Ireland's failed stabilisation', *Economic Policy*, 1989, vol. 8, p. 175.

44. P. De Grauwe, *The Economics of Monetary Integration*, 3rd edition, Oxford, Oxford University Press, 1997, p. 145.

far was credible'.[45] A different interpretation, namely that the EMS did not possess any inherent credibility but rested on the political commitment of governments willing to maintain their currency within specific bands and bear political costs, never took off in public debate.[46] All that mattered was that 'Greece had acquired its 'passport' to eventual EMU entry'[47]. On 25 March 1998, the time of the convergence examination, Greece did not meet any of the convergence criteria mentioned in the four indents of Article 109j(1) of the Treaty; it did not therefore 'fulfil the necessary conditions for the adoption of the single currency' and had, according to Article 109k, a 'derogation'.[48] With the start of EMU, Greece joined the Exchange Rate Mechanism II.

A programme setting out 'the entire adjustment path'

Securing ERM participation meant that one of the bigger hurdles on the convergence path was cleared: at the end of 1998, long-term interest rates fell to 6.9 per cent, from 11 per cent in January 1998; key to their reduction was market optimism about Greece's eventual entry to EMU. Responding to the new conditions imposed by the Drachma's devaluation and the operating framework of the ERM, the government proceeded to formulate 'The 1998 Update of the Hellenic Convergence Programme', which lay down 'the entire adjustment path of the Greek economy towards EMU until 2001';[49] the Stability and Growth Pact adopted in 1997 required, in any case, 'non-participating' states to formulate programmes, describing the policies that would aim at 'a high degree of sustainable convergence'.[50]

The programme was to promote adjustment on four fronts: wage and labour market flexibility; privatisation; social security reform; and restructuring of loss-

---

45. Interview 15.

46. For this argument, *see* J. T. Woolley, 'Policy credibility and European monetary institutions', in A. Sbragia, (ed.), *Euro-Politics: Institutions and policymaking in the 'new' European Community*, Washington DC, Brookings Institution, 1992, p. 166. The credibility of institutions is not automatic; the policy commitment, which helped establish the credibility of the system, preceded any EMS capability to provide a binding constraint on domestic policy makers. *See also* J. Frieden, and E. Jones, 'The political economy of European Monetary Union: a conceptual overview', in J. Frieden, D. Gros, and E. Jones, (eds), *The New Political Economy of EMU*, Lanham MD: Rowman & Littlefield, 1998. Theoretically, it was not really proved why 'a government's commitment to monetary integration should be more 'credible' than its commitment to an exchange rate, monetary, or inflation rate target'. Empirically, various countries' attempts at purchasing credibility using a fixed exchange rate collapsed, together with the credibility of the government 'purchaser'.

47. Interview 26.

48. Council Decision of 3 May 1998 in accordance with Article 109j(4) of the Treaty (98/317/EC), *Official Journal of the European Communities*, L 139, 11.5.1998.

49. Ministry of National Economy and Finance, 'The 1998 Update of the Hellenic Convergence Programme: 1998–2001', Athens, June 1998, pp. 1–18 [in Greek].

50. 'Council Regulation (EC) No. 1466/97 of July 1997 on the strengthening of the surveillance of budgetary positions and the surveillance and co-ordination of economic policies', *Official Journal of the European Communities*, L 209, 2.8.1997.

making public operations.[51] To accompany the programme, the government pursued a self-binding strategy of 'locking' the Greek economy unilaterally into a programme of strict fiscal measures, equivalent to those that would be operative for the Stability Pact countries.[52] It based its medium-term strategy on the performance of public debt, as this was considered critical to evaluating the credibility of the entire convergence effort. Regarding fiscal consolidation, the general government deficit was to be brought in line with the Treaty criterion, while the ratio of general government debt to GDP was to decline for a second consecutive year; the large primary surplus and privatisation revenue were expected to outweigh the effects on public debt of the Drachma devaluation and the interest-rate rise in the first three months of 1998. Government guidelines on private-sector wage moderation and limited wage increases in the public sector would further strengthen the disinflation process. Rapid progress in structural reform would promote real convergence with other member states of the European Union.[53]

In its opinion of a convergence programme that was consistent both with the BEPGs defining the economic policies of the member states and of the Union, and the objective of full participation in the euro area from 1 January 2001, the Council raised sound criticisms: wage moderation should extend beyond the programme to secure durable progress in disinflation; an *ex ante* and binding norm for the control of primary expenditure would have been welcome; the reduction of the deficit should be reflected to a larger extent in the reduction of the debt; greater use should be made of privatisation receipts to reduce debt; structural reforms should be implemented as scheduled.[54] The Council's underlying tone – that these reforms should become a permanent feature of the policy framework and not be seen as one-off measures – was missed on the Greek side. After all, enthusiasm over budget consolidation was probably justified. In November 1999, the decision that an excessive deficit existed in Greece was abrogated, while a budget surplus of 0.2 per cent of GDP was projected for 2002. With lower long-term interest rates, interest payments on public debt fell from 12 per cent of GDP in 1996 to 9 per cent in 1999. The combination of higher real growth, lower deficit and privatisation revenues from the sale of state enterprises led to a reduction of the debt to GDP ratio.[55]

51. Ministry of National Economy and Finance, 'The 1998 Update of the Hellenic Convergence Programme', pp. 1–18 [in Greek].

52. Interview 19.

53. Ministry of National Economy and Finance, 'The 1998 Update of the Hellenic Convergence Programme', pp. 1–18 [in Greek].

54. 'Council Opinion of 12 October 1998 on the Convergence Programme of Greece, 1998–2001', *Official Journal of the European Communities*, C 372, 2.12.1998; in reality, progress in programme implementation was more pronounced on the privatisation front with the sale of the Bank of Crete and the Bank of Central Greece; the Ionian Bank was finally sold in April 1999. At the same time, by the end of 1998, the privatisation of a number of organisations (the Duty Free Shops, Olympic Catering and the Corinth Canal) had to be postponed to a future, unspecified date. The rationalisation of the social security system was postponed until the year 2000, while labour market flexibility was effectively removed from the agenda. National Bank of Greece, *Annual Economic Review: Greece 1998–99*, No. 2, April 1999 [in Greek].

55. European Commission, *European Economy*, No. 67, 1999, p. 79.

The government declared its intention to apply for EMU entry in March 2000; its latest programme, 'The Updated Convergence Programme of Greece, 1999 to 2002', formulated in compliance with the 1999 BEPGs and the medium-term objective of the Stability and Growth Pact, asserted: 'Greece is ready to accept the euro and share the benefits and responsibilities that the common currency entails. Following euro-zone participation, efforts will concentrate on further pursuing real convergence.'[56] A convergence trend was by now noticeable and, everyone hoped, irreversible; its underlying factors included the significant decline in the inflation differential – Greek monetary policy had a favourable influence on Greek inflation and inflation expectations – as well as improvement in the country's fiscal position. The substantial decline in long-term interest rates stimulated the Greek economy, while their eventual convergence towards euro area levels was expected to exert an expansionary influence. The rate of inflation fell from 20.4 per cent in 1990 to 2.6 per cent in 1999; the increase in compensation per employee decelerated from 12.2. per cent in 1995 to 4.8 per cent in 1999 while growth in unit labour costs declined from 11.6 per cent to 2.5 per cent. These wage reductions were supported by strong productivity growth and a two-year national general collective agreement reached by the social partners in May 1998. Temporary factors – a round of consumption-tax reductions (on petrol, heating oil and cars), a reduction in electricity prices, and a series of gentlemen's agreements with commercial and industrial enterprises and service providers to keep retail prices for goods and services stable or at least restrain their growth – were critical to disinflation, as the government did not wish to take any risks with the inflation criterion.[57] Increased government revenues and reduced interest payments led to a fall in the general government deficit to 1.6 per cent of GDP. The debt ratio declined for a third consecutive year, to 104.4 per cent, mainly due to the rise in the primary surplus, from 6.4 per cent of GDP in 1998 to 7 per cent of GDP in 1999, and to privatisation proceeds that reached 2.5 per cent of GDP in 1999.

There was no shortage of guidelines for Greece when the Council gave its formal opinion. Progress made towards disinflation should acquire a lasting character, particularly as monetary conditions in Greece would converge with those prevailing in the euro-zone, affecting demand and prices; incomes policies, including wage agreements and the co-operation of all social partners, should further secure an environment of low inflation. Greek authorities should achieve better budgetary outcomes than the bare minimum that had been planned; the stance of fiscal policy should be tightened from 2001, if inflationary pressures were to be contained. Structural reforms should enhance competitive conditions and the adequate operation of labour, goods and capital markets in order to enhance the productive potential of the economy.[58] The Greek government was, for all intentions and purposes, warned.

---

56. Ministry of National Economy and Finance, 'The 1999 Update of the Hellenic Convergence Programme: 1999–2002', Athens, December 1999, p. 1 [in Greek].

57. Interview 27.

58. 'Council Opinion of 31 January 2000 on the updated Convergence Programme of Greece, 1999 to 2002', *Official Journal of the European Communities*, C 060, 2.3.2000.

Greece joins the 'club'

In March 2000, Greece submitted its application for EMU entry. The government's formal position, voiced by Prime Minister Simitis, was that 'the efforts and sacrifices of the Greek people have borne fruit' and that Greece would join 'by virtue of its achievements'.[59] With the application, 'a 25-year cycle of economic, social and political developments' was closed, while 'the Greek economy has a prospect of long-term stability because foreign exchange risks are fading, interest rates are falling and the business environment becomes more stable'.[60] Minister of National Economy and Finance, Yannos Papantoniou, asserted that 'Greece was joining EMU on its own merits, with no political conditions or commitments, following the fulfillment of all EMU convergence criteria'.[61] In a joint statement, European Commission President Romano Prodi and Commissioner for Economic And Monetary Affairs Pedro Solbes welcomed the formal submission: 'An enlarged area will be positive both for the Eurozone area and for the countries joining.'[62]

Greece was well on its way to becoming the Eurozone's twelfth member. In May 2000, in accordance with the procedure for the abrogation of derogations of Article 122(2), the government requested the Commission and the ECB to prepare a report that would communicate to the Council whether Greece had fulfilled the conditions for adopting the single currency. The reports by the Commission and the ECB, based on the 1999 data, stated that Greek legislation, including the statute of the national central bank, was compatible with Articles 108 and 109 of the Treaty and the Statute of the ESCB. The reports also concluded that Greece had achieved a high degree of sustainable convergence, as evaluated by reference to the convergence criteria. The average inflation rate in the year ending March 2000 stood at 2.0 per cent: below the reference value of 2.4 per cent. The 17 December 1999 Council Decision had abrogated its decision on the existence of an excessive deficit in Greece. Greece had been a member of the ERM from 1998 and, subsequently, of ERM II. The Greek Drachma's bilateral central rate against any other member state's currency had not been subject to severe tensions nor had Greece devalued. Figure 5.2 shows the path of exchange-rate stability, by tracking the movements of the Drachma *vis-à-vis* the median ERM currency and, from 1 January 1999, the euro. Finally, in the year ending March 2000, the long-term interest rate was, on average 6.4 per cent, below the reference value of 7.2 per cent. It followed that Greece fulfilled the necessary conditions for joining the single currency. On the basis of the reports, the Commission adopted a proposal for a Council decision to abrogate, with effect from January 2001, the derogation

---

59. 'Statement by Prime Minister Costas Simitis', *Athens News Agency*, 10 March 2000.
60. *Ibid.*
61. *Ibid.*
62. 'Joint Statement by European Commission President Romano Prodi and Commissioner for Economic And Monetary Affairs Pedro Solbes', Brussels, 10 March 2000.

Exchange Rate of GRD against EUR, 1998-2000 %

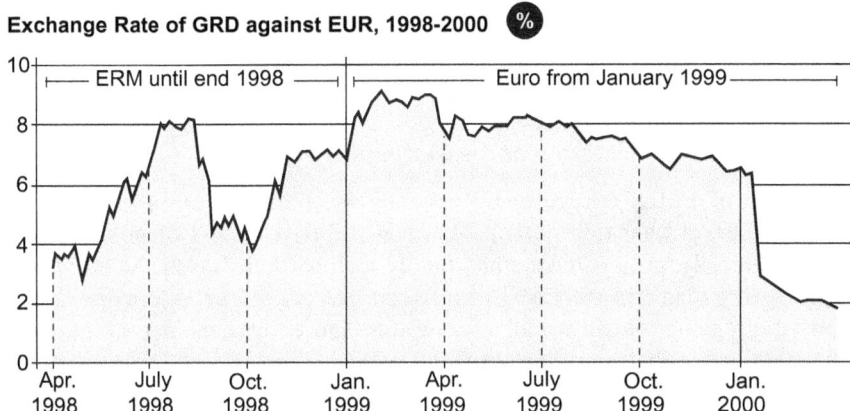

Figure 5.2: Exchange-rate stability achieved: spread of GRD vis-à-vis the ERM and ERM II

of Greece. The derogation was abrogated when Greece formally joined EMU.[63]

In fact, the country 'joined without negotiations and without conditions, but with praise'.[64] In June 2000, the Feira European Council *unanimously* approved Greece's entry to the EMU, on the first day of the summit. Prime Minister Simitis subsequently referred to an 'historic day'; 'Greece's course towards unified Europe, which started in 1981, is being completed with today's decision'. After joining the euro, 'Greece is not lagging behind in any sector and is stronger at present than it was in the past'.[65] Amidst the celebrations, the difficult questions that were raised in some quarters regarding the path that Greece should take as a member of the Eurozone were quickly silenced or made to seem irrelevant. The self-censoring optimism that enveloped the nation was unavoidable after a long nominal convergence endeavour that had paid off. EMU accession would permit Greek policy makers to 'better exploit possibilities provided by European unification and constitutes a qualitative change since it promotes Greece to a higher level'.[66] Greek enthusiasm seemed to be matched with that of its soon-to-be partners: 'The European Council congratulates Greece on the convergence achieved over recent years, based on sound economic and financial policies, and welcomes the decision that Greece will join the Euro area on 1 January 2001, which constitutes an additional positive step in the monetary integration of the

---

63. 'Council Decision of 19 June 2000 in accordance with Article 122(2) of the Treaty on the adoption by Greece of the single currency on 1 January 2001 (2000/427/EC)', *Official Journal of the European Communities*, L 167, 7.7.2000, pp. 19–21.

64. 'Statement by Minister of National Economy and Finance Yannos Papantoniou', *Athens News Agency*, 20 June 2000.

65. 'Statement by Prime Minister Costas Simitis', *Athens News Agency*, 21 June 2000.

66. *Ibid.*

Union'.[67] Following the recommendation of the Finance Ministers of Austria, Spain, and France, Greece was invited to attend Eurogroup meetings in July, a full five months prior to Greece's formal entry.

Conclusion: EMU accession and sustainability

In the case of EMU, Greece could not play the reluctant European card; nor could it secure a transition period. This was a different kind of political game and, theoretically, policy makers had finally learned their lesson. At the time of accession, the idea that the EMU framework had created an externally induced stabilisation path, which would ensure the future implementation of sound macroeconomic policies, had acquired the status of conventional wisdom: or was it wishful thinking? Joining the club was certainly the most tangible indication that the Greek *nominal* convergence effort had paid off. Difficult structural reforms had yet to be implemented and, following stage three, national economic-policy formation would be left with fewer policy instruments to respond to real asymmetric shocks. Greek policy makers, however, never really questioned the economics of EMU: the broad societal consensus that had formed around the necessity of EMU spurred them on.

What was so special about EMU that forced the 'adjustment' that had been postponed for most of Greece's Community membership? In terms of this book's themes, EMU institutions and instruments provided a real constraining framework which, at pre-entry stage, goaded the convergence effort forward. If anything the fixed deadline made for a strict implementation schedule. In addition, the Drachma's entry to the ERM provided a stable anchor for the disinflation process, and an 'elite socialisation mechanism', through which sound-money ideas were diffused.[68] Severing direct institutional ties to elected officials – with the implementation of the EMU provision for central bank independence – appeared to create an apolitical environment for monetary policy-making.[69] Monetary authorities had to abide by the ERM 'code of conduct'[70] while government policy makers, operating in the environment of 'mutual tolerance' prevalent at the Ecofin meetings, realised that 'the credibility of the policy of price stability would

---

67. 'Presidency Conclusions, Santa Maria da Feira European Council 19 and 20 June 2000' (accessed 5 February 2012) Online. Available: http://eeep.pspa.uoa.gr/fileadmin/eeep.pspa.uoa.gr/uploads/RUT_Presidency_Conclusions_02/Feira_19–20.Jun.2000.pdf

68. *See* K. Dyson, *The Politics of the Euro-Zone: Stability or breakdown?*, Oxford, Oxford University Press, 2000, p. 128.

69. K. McNamara, 'Rational fictions: central bank independence and the social logic of delegation', *West European Politics*, 2002, vol. 25, no. 1, pp. 47–76, p. 53.

70. De Macedo suggests that the ERM code of conduct enabled both Portugal and Spain to gain external credibility and fend off the recession that threatened to hit their domestic economies in the early 1990s. *See* J. B. de Macedo, 'Portugal's European integration: the good student with a bad fiscal constitution', in R. Sebastián and P. C. Manuel, *South European Society and Politics*, 2003, vol. 8, nos. 1–2, Special Issue: 'Spain and Portugal in the European Union, The First Fifteen Years', p. 179.

constitute the key to Greece's EMU entry'.[71] The quest for 'credibility' indicated that the EMU frame had acquired the power to legitimise or, alternatively, penalise governments' policy choices.

The important question that arises in this chapter is whether, following completion of the nominal convergence process, policy makers would be able to 'break' the domestic path of the politicised economy? Would the actors that mattered, the government, the central bank and the unions controlling wage settlements, acquire a new set of preferences? The government, for one, which had retained control over taxing and (deficit) spending, had no real incentive to be bound by EMU fiscal commitments. While the Excessive Deficit Procedure and the Stability and Growth Pact represented the EU's concrete answers to the problem of fiscal deficit reductions,[72] they allowed a considerable degree of flexibility in choosing medium-term objectives. Effective implementation, therefore, would depend on the type of self-commitment for which Greek political authorities had not previously displayed enthusiasm. After all, Greece had brought its budget deficit down just three months prior to its renewed application for EMU entry; the Council had first decided that an excessive deficit existed in Greece on 26 September 1994. With a view to 'bringing the deficit situation to an end',[73] there were, in fact, five recommendations (on 7 November 1994, 24 July 1995, 16 September 1996, 15 September 1997 and 29 May 1998), yet no formal Ecofin sanction; the Council abrogated the decision of an excessive deficit in December 1999. If neither Council sanctions nor the intention to impose them were fully credible,[74] however, a member state with Greece's history could very well be expected to dodge the rules and not adhere, once in EMU, to the medium-term budgetary objective of maintaining a position close to balance or in surplus. This was never taken as a serious issue by EMU institutions and actors.

In the absence of fiscal institutional arrangements of an ECB type therefore, which lengthened actors' time horizons, removed certain policy options from the agenda and isolated electoral calculations, the government's preferences could remain politically sensitive to the electorate and to election returns. This was not

71. Interview 19.

72. M. Buti and A. Sapir, (eds), *Economic Policy in EMU: A study by the European Commission Services*, Oxford, Clarendon Press, 1998, p. 15.

73. 'Council Decision of 17 December 1999, abrogating the Decision on the excessive deficit in Greece', *Official Journal of the European Communities*, C 077, 09.03.2001.

74. According to Gros and Thygesen, the Stability Pact did not solve the problem of delivering a formal Ecofin Council sanction against a recalcitrant member state. Governments could choose not to vote against a country that accumulated excessive deficits under unfavourable economic circumstances for fear that, in the future, they would be in a similar position themselves. Their argument was based on the fact that sanctions were never imposed under the EDP. *See* D. Gros, and N. Thygesen, *European Monetary Integration: From the European Monetary System to Economic and Monetary Union*, 2nd edition, London, Longman, 1998, p. 345. For an analysis of situations in which sanctions are fully credible, *see* M. J. Artis, and M. Buti, 'Close to balance or in surplus: a policy-maker's guide to the implementation of the Stability and Growth Pact', 2000, *Journal of Common Market Studies*, vol. 38, no. 4, p. 565.

the case with the BoG; its preference for price stability was aligned with that of the ECB, with the BoG welcoming the transfer of power over determining interest rates and the money supply. Following accession, its single policy option was to implement 'the common monetary policy of the Euro-system', whose primary goal was 'price stability in the medium-term'.[75] The main unions (the General Confederation of Greek Workers, GSEE and the Civil Servants' Confederation, ADEDY), enveloped in their symbiotic relationship with government ministers, formulated their preferences quasi-automatically; their commonly applied strategy, across sectors, was that 'we make demands and we subsequently negotiate on the basis of these demands':[76] the national general collective agreement specified the salary *increases* that would be given every year, which were 'usually the expected inflation rate plus the growth rate of GDP'.[77] EMU membership was not expected to affect this; during the convergence effort, when the government followed a 'tight' fiscal policy and theoretically froze salaries in the public sector, budget expenditure on salaries increased by about 14 per cent each year, 'due to subsidies and the application of new payroll systems'.[78] In like manner, trade unions in the major public enterprises assumed that part of the revenues from stock-market flotations undertaken to reduce public debt should be channelled, through a rise in wages, to their members.[79] The strategy of extracting exemptions and benefits was simple: 'after the powerful unions negotiated an advantageous settlement or exemption, the less powerful would ask for the same treatment or concessions'.[80] Even if the bail-out option of exchange-rate devaluation would no longer be available after EMU entry, therefore, trade unions were not expected to associate better functioning markets with any adjustment in their preferences regarding wage settlements: after all, labour and product 'adjustment' was not really anchored in *new* EMU institutions or instruments.

While rational-choice theorists and historical institutionalists have long battled over the formation of preferences, they have recently, Katznelson and Weingast argue, converged on the importance of the institutional setting, in which power and problem-solving meet.[81] The above discussion confirms this, allowing, however, for considerable variation in the *relevant* institutional setting, that is, the institutional setting in which preferences can be acted on. EMU was a regime

75. Bank of Greece, *Report for Monetary Policy 2001–2002*, Athens, March 2002, p. 11 [in Greek].

76. Interview 30.

77. European Parliament, 'Briefing 22: EMU and Greece', *Task Force on Economic and Monetary Union*, 28 April 1998, p. 15.

78. *Ibid*.

79. Interview 32.

80. Interview 40.

81. I. Katznelson and B. R. Weingast, 'Intersections between historical and rational choice institutionalism', in I. Katznelson and B. R. Weingast, (eds), *Preferences and Situations: Points of intersection between historical and rational choice institutionalism*, New York, Russell Sage Foundation, 2005, p. 16.

change which did not – with the exception of monetary policy – significantly constrain the power of actors to carry on with 'business as usual': they had, of course, to rise to the twin challenges of retaining fiscal policy on a consolidation path and promoting further disinflation. With the external-constraint strategy rendered irrelevant, however what was required, following EMU membership, was the political will to promote politically costly, deep-cutting interventions in the operation of the economy: the public sector wage bill had to be reined in; tax administration and collection improved; and wider public sector liabilities reduced via bold privatisation steps. In addition, the future burden of population ageing had to be tackled via extensive reform of the pension and social security systems. A speedy transposition of Single Market legislation into national law, further progress with regard to the liberalisation of network industries and increased flexibility in the labour market would have further eased the transition of the Greek economy into the Eurozone.

The idea that EMU was an institutional edifice whose chances of success rested, according to Issing 'on the ability of each country to undertake its own reforms' was not taken seriously.[82] 'Institutional complementarities',[83] as promoted by Hall and Soskice, were, at the time of accession, absent both between the national economy and EMU and within the Greek political economy. Even if, at that point, national differences in economic performance theoretically, did not matter, Greece's Mediterranean capitalism was a poor match for the coordinated and liberal capitalism of other members – attention only had to be paid to the productivity gap and labour participation deficit. Moreover, the 'coalitions of social or political actors that provide the support for a change in regulations or policy regime'[84] had still not formed and nor could it be safely assumed, *pace* Hall and Thelen, that they would be formed. Policy entrepreneurship had proved, in this respect, rather thin on the ground.

The fly in the ointment of Greece's EMU entry was always going to be its government debt to GDP ratio. Unless additional and lasting measures on the expenditure side were undertaken, the high level of debt – 104.4 per cent at the moment of accession – would impose a continuous and heavy burden on fiscal policy and the economy as a whole.[85] Despite high primary surpluses and

---

82. O. Issing, 'Economic and Monetary Union in Europe: political priority versus economic integration?', paper presented at the European Society for the History of Economic Thought Conference, February 2001 (accessed 6 June 2012) Online. Available: http://www.ecb.int/press/key/date/2001/html/sp010223.en.html.

83. P. A. Hall, and D. Soskice, 'An introduction to varieties of capitalism', in P. A. Hall and D. Soskice, (eds), *Varieties of Capitalism: The institutional foundations of comparative advantage*, Oxford, Oxford University Press, 2001, p. 18.

84. P. A. Hall and K. Thelen, 'Institutional change in varieties of capitalism' in B. Hancké, (ed.), *Debating Varieties of Capitalism*, Oxford, Oxford University Press, 2009, p. 264.

85. The discussion that follows, including the figures used, is based on the European Central Bank's Convergence Report 2000; *European Central Bank, Convergence Report 2000*, Frankfurt-am-Main, ECB, 2000. Use has also been made of Commission of the European Communities, 'Report from the Commission: Convergence Report 2000 (prepared in accordance with Article 122 (2) of

substantial privatisation receipts, in the order of 3 per cent of GDP per year in 1998 and 1999, the reduction in Greece's public debt was slow. Deficit-debt adjustments amounted, in the period between 1995 and 1999, to GRD 5.4 trillion, or 14 per cent of GDP in 1999: these came mainly from the revaluation effects of government debt denominated in foreign currency following the devaluation of the Greek Drachma and from transactions in financial assets. In addition, in the early 1990s, the government, in compliance with Articles 101 and 102 of the Treaty, assumed the debt obligations of the Bank of Greece, including accumulated foreign-exchange valuation losses, previously recorded under miscellaneous accounts. In the context of the abolition of its overdraft facility with the central bank, in January 1994, the government also issued securities in order to build up a reserve for liquidity purposes. From the mid-1990s, equity injections in a number of public enterprises and banks and the government assumption of public-enterprise debt further resulted in the upward increase of public debt. Due to this wide exposure to debt-increasing adjustments, fiscal balances were sensitive to exchange-rate volatility: in 1998, the proportion of debt denominated in foreign currency was still high at 31.8 per cent; it increased to 33 per cent in 1999, of which more than half was denominated in non-euro area currencies. Officials at the European Commission and the European Central Bank calculated that continued levels of high debt could lead to vulnerability, if slippages in Greece's fiscal performance were to raise the perceived credit risk of public debt. The production of independent and reliable statistical data would provide the best safeguard against adverse fiscal developments.

With the fulfilment of the convergence criteria secured, the pace, extent and depth of *real* convergence that lay ahead remained a moot point. The most 'visible' measure of convergence, convergence in *per capita* income level, suggested that Greece was, after almost twenty years of membership, still catching up with the EU. In 2000, gross domestic product at current market prices per head of population was 67.1 for Greece, 82.1 for Spain, 75.7 for Portugal, and 114.3 for Ireland. Among the four so-called cohesion countries, Greece was the under-performer: the considerable income divergence which had begun in the second half of the 1970s continued well into the 1990s.[86]

Entry to the 'strong' EMU club constituted a significant opportunity, *if* the government proceeded with the necessary reforms to 'enhance the potential of the economy, strengthen its competitiveness and improve the conditions for sustainable growth and employment creation'.[87] Not that EMU was a panacea to all ills: it rested on a monetary union without a fiscal budget; a central bank without a legitimating political authority; limited and largely unsupervised co-ordination of budgetary policies; and the absence of a framework for creating competitive

---

the Treaty', COM (2000) 277 final, Brussels, 3 May 2000.

86. European Commission, 'EU Economy: 2000 Review', *European Economy,* No. 71, 2000.

87. 'Council Opinion of 12 February 2001 on the stability programme of Greece, 2000–2004', *Official Journal of the European Communities,* C 077, 09.03.2001.

and flexible markets. Moreover, its long-term operation was bound to generate distributional outcomes which, given the continuing diversity of economic and political structures among participating member-states, could well produce an inequitable sharing of burdens.

chapter six | the 'good' EMU years

With the nominal convergence process out of the way, Greek policy makers were intoxicated with the 'real convergence' prospects that lay ahead. Institutional weaknesses of the EMU edifice were casually brushed aside:[1] this was convenient for both Greece and its partners, who were, theoretically, reaping the benefits of a stable monetary union. The Eurozone was not an optimal currency area and no one pretended that it was or that it could be. Greek policy makers acquiesced; giving up monetary sovereignty for price stability was not such a bad deal. Comfortable with the idea that the single monetary policy would cater to the interests of the *entire* euro area – even if the 'benefits' of high labour mobility or a single fiscal policy were not available – they failed to ask some important questions. For one, how the central monetary authority would respond to asymmetries in financial shocks experienced by individual member states, or to asymmetries in the transmission process of symmetric shocks,[2] was unknown; yet either possibility could, given Greece's particular economic structure, trigger significant effects on the policy targets and on welfare. On the fiscal front, EMU included 'in-built guarantees that economic rules would be respected';[3] in the event of a liquidity crisis and in the absence of a fiscal stabilisation mechanism, however, the ECB could not act as a lender of last resort, nor could participating members infringe the 'no-bail out clause'. The fundamental issue, namely, that the country could not really afford to relax its fiscal consolidation effort or give in to adjustment fatigue, was swept under the carpet. If Greek policy makers added the absence of a fiscal stabilisation mechanism to the EMU equation, they should have begun setting up an adequate safety margin for cyclical downturns or asymmetric shocks that might lie ahead.

EMU institutions and actors entrusted with an incomplete system, *still* had a responsibility to see both that the procedures put in place worked – especially the Stability and Growth Pact – and that the stability programmes, ensuring rigorous budgetary discipline through surveillance and co-ordination, were adhered to. Obviously, the better the outcomes that were produced for the Eurozone as a whole, the more its constituent parts would benefit. This was, in any case, the argument made against the sobering voices that drew attention to known

---

1. *See* C. A. Goodhart, 'The political economy of monetary union' in P. B. Kenen, (ed.) *Understanding Interdependence: The macroeconomics of the open economy*, Princeton, Princeton University Press, 1995, p. 467.

2. P. De Grauwe, 'Monetary policies in the presence of asymmetries', *Journal of Common Market Studies* 2000, vol. 38, no. 4, p. 609.

3. L. Jonung, 'EMU and the euro – the first 10 years: Challenges to the sustainability and price stability of the euro area – what does history tell us?', *Economic Papers No. 165*, European Commission Directorate-General for Economic and Financial Affairs, February 2002.

macroeconomic and competitive imbalances among participating economies. In the Greek case, trade integration with the rest of the euro area was lower than in any other country, increasing the likelihood of high costs in the incidence of cyclical divergence or asymmetric shocks; the large size of the Greek agricultural sector and Greek's different financial-market structure further pointed to the economy's vulnerability.[4]

The first years

How to turn a surplus into a deficit

When the country adopted the single currency, at least one simple question was left unanswered; could positive developments in macroeconomic performance be sustained? In a union that prized price stability above all, it was a fact well known to the Greeks, the European Commission and the European Central Bank that the reduction in Greek inflation was partly attributable to temporary factors.[5] Following entry to the Eurozone, the sustainability of inflation performance would critically depend on continued efforts to support price stability; moreover, the resulting monetary stimulus from the alignment of Greek interest rates with those of the euro area and the remaining depreciation of the Drachma towards its conversion rate were expected to exert upward pressure on prices.[6]

On the fiscal front, the policy endeavour that was required was even larger. The high public debt level could adversely affect the country's growth prospects, while restricting the ambit of tax and expenditure policies. A restructuring of public expenditure at the level both of the central government and the broader public sector would require an unprecedented level of discipline in the conduct of fiscal policy. Greece's weak institutional system, however, lacked procedures for close internal audit or processes of setting quantifiable targets and expenditure assessments that would render budget-control effective; moreover, a long-term strategy, including the setting of multi-annual fiscal rules, was simply not available.[7]

At the time, such unpleasant considerations were ignored amidst the climate of general exuberance: in the coming years, GDP was expected to be amongst the highest in the EU and certainly higher than the European average, 'contributing, thus, to the real convergence of *per capita* income'.[8] In December 2001, Greece boasted, for 'the first time in the last two decades', a general government surplus; this was 0.1 per cent of GDP, rather than the targeted 0.5 per cent, but a surplus

4.   OECD, OECD Economic Surveys Greece 2000–2001, Paris, OECD, 2001, p. 44.
5.   These included gentlemen's agreements with a series of business interests and cuts in indirect taxes in 1998–1999. *See European Central Bank, Convergence Report 2000,* Frankfurt-am-Main, ECB, 2000.
6.   *Ibid.*
7.   Interview 10.
8.   Ministry of Economy and Finance, 'The 2001 Update of the Hellenic Stability and Growth Programme: 2001–2004', Athens, December 2001, p. 2.

nevertheless. Future projections indicated a surplus of 0.8 per cent of GDP for 2002 and 1.0 and 1.2 per cent for 2003 and 2004 respectively. General government consolidated gross debt had fallen to 102.7 per cent of GDP in 2000 and was expected to be reduced to 99.6 per cent in 2001.

The picture was so rosy that the PASOK government disregarded Council warnings that, following accession, the potential for overheating in the economy would require a tight fiscal stance to prevent it, with restraint on current expenditure and wage moderation.[9] Having acquired a fresh mandate following the 2000 national elections, the government opted, instead, for an incomes policy that would ensure 'not only improvements in competitiveness but also convergence of the real compensation of employees with the rest of the EU'.[10] The annual growth of real compensation per employee was projected to remain between 2.3 per cent and 2.5 per cent, *twice* as high as the corresponding European average. From 1 January 2002, a catch-up clause contained in the collective bargaining agreement concluded between the General Confederation of Employees and the employers' organisations in 2000 provided for an automatic increase in the minimum wage by almost 1 per cent.

At the same time, the government announced an overall tax reform to simplify the system, promote a more equitable distribution of the tax burden, enhance the competitiveness of the Greek firms and reduce tax evasion. This was partly related to a shortfall on revenues; a recurring slippage had been well evidenced prior to EMU accession, even during the 1996–9 convergence 'drive'. The Council found the proposed measures wanting, urging Greek authorities to adopt a 'clear binding norm for current primary expenditure';[11] with high public debt standing in the way of better results for targeted primary balances, Greek policy makers should 'take advantage of the current favourable macroeconomic situation to reduce the government debt as fast as possible'.[12]

A first rude awakening came with the 'update' of Greek figures in 2002. While the government's efforts in the field of public finances had yielded good results, 'a significant methodological revision in the statistical treatment of a number of operations took place in the course of 2002';[13] these included the reclassification of some categories of expenditures, like capital injections to public enterprises and debt assumptions, together with a change in the treatment of privatisation

---

9.   'Council Opinion of 12 February 2002 on the updated stability programme of Greece, 2001–2004' (2002/C 51/04), *Official Journal of the European Communities*, C 51/5, 26 February 2002.

10. Ministry of Economy and Finance, 'The 2001 Update of the Hellenic Stability and Growth Programme', p. 13.

11. *See* 'Council Opinion of 12 February 2002 on the updated stability programme of Greece'. This had already been suggested in 'Council Opinion of 31 January 2000 on the updated Convergence Programme of Greece, 1999 to 2002', *Official Journal of the European Communities*, C 060, 2 March 2000.

12. 'Council Opinion of 12 February 2002 on the updated stability programme of Greece'.

13. Ministry of Economy and Finance, The 2002 Update of the Hellenic Stability and Growth Programme: 2002–2006, Athens, December 2002, p. 6.

certificates and convertible bonds. Hence, the general government accounts were *now* in deficit, compared with a surplus reported previously, while the debt ratio reached 107 per cent of GDP in 2001 against a projected 99.7 per cent. After consultations with the Eurostat and the Greek authorities, the surpluses of 2000 and 2001 were recorded as deficits of 1.8. and 1.2 per cent of GDP.[14]

The Commission's response to the revised Greek government accounts was tempered: officially, no mention was made of the fact that Greece had joined EMU on the basis of the 1999, non-revised, data. The reclassification and the correction in the treatment of a number of operations, however, did change 'significantly the starting point of the medium term budgetary projections'. The fiscal developments, as they stood 'corrected' in line with ESA national accounting rules, along with the slow pace of reduction in the government debt ratio during a period when the Greek economy was posting high growth rates, had now become 'a matter of serious concern'.[15] This was also the view adopted by the Council: improvement in the government balance would have to come from reduction in interest payments and retrenchment in current primary expenditure: the latter was, however, 'difficult to achieve', particularly as the programme did not include 'clear binding norms'. The government was urged by the Council to 'take advantage of the current favourable macroeconomic situation to undertake determined effort in order to implement a durable budgetary adjustment leading to an improvement in the underlying budgetary position and a satisfactory pace of debt reduction'.[16]

Back to stability

Following the statistical revision, the government was to continue its efforts to achieve 'real convergence' *and* 'stability', the latter re-entering the equation as an economic goal. Facing increased pressure to proceed with its structural-adjustment programme, the government placed social security reform at the top of the agenda: in theory, the enactment of Law 3029/2002 would promote the rationalisation and homogenisation of the pension system and ensure the financial sustainability of IKA (the pension fund for most private-sector employees) up to 2030. In reality, this was a 'velvet' intervention that left key problems unaddressed: it failed to ease the fiscal burden which was, in fact, projected to increase; it upheld major inequities in provision and, in the end, it retained the system's fragmented institutional structure.[17] On the privatisation front, a more 'proactive

---

14. *See* European Commission, 'Eurostat News Release, No 35', 21 March 2002 and European Commission, 'Eurostat News Release No 116', 30 September 2002.

15. European Commission, 'Update of the Convergence Programme of Greece (2002–2006): An Assessment', ECFIN/5/03-EN, Brussels, 8 January 2003, p. 3.

16. *See* 'Council Opinion of 21 January 2003 on the updated stability programme of Greece, 2002 to 2006' (2003/C 26/03), *Official Journal of the European Communities*, 4.2.2003. It is worth noting that the Council had used the same wording in its previous Opinion, *see* 'Council Opinion of 12 February 2002 on the updated stability programme of Greece, 2001–2004'.

17. K. Featherstone, 'The politics of pension reform in Greece: modernization defeated by gridlock',

approach' was introduced, which included new procedures; it also lifted the upper privatisation limit for some companies – the government proceeded with the sale of an additional 67 per cent of the Hellenic Industrial Bank, the assignment of 49 per cent of the Hellenic Casino of 'Mont Parnes' to a strategic partner and additional offerings of the Football Prognostics Organisation (OPAP) and Hellenic Telecommunications Organization S. A (OTE).

Given the renewed drive to contain spending pressures, the government tabled a draft law to enhance transparency and improve auditing procedures at all levels of public expenditure. A code for fiscal stability would adopt a kind of 'golden rule', according to which the only categories of expenditures financed through borrowing would be public investment and the acquisition of military equipment.[18] The major tax reform announced the previous year materialised, with a bill in July 2002 on extensive simplifications of tax administration procedures and one in November that simplified, again, the collection system for enterprises and households. In spite of the projected 'clean up' on the revenue front, the extraordinary expenses that the organisation of the Athens Olympic Games required for the years 2002, 2003 and 2004 were expected to overshoot public expenditure by almost 1 per cent of GDP.

The fact that government consumption was proving a rather inelastic category of expenditure was not unrelated to the short-term influence of the political cycle: general elections were to take place in April 2004 at the latest. Unsurprisingly, the adjustment effort in 2003 was strongly back-loaded, postponing harsh measures to the years beyond 2004, when the costs of the Olympic Games would, allegedly, have been borne out. Recurring slippages in fiscal and inflation targets aside, the government announced, in early September 2003, a 'social package', benefitting low-income pensioners and some other social groups,[19] along with an increase in civil servants' wages. Generous cuts were announced in the areas of personal and corporate income tax, while the government submitted to Parliament, yet again, a new draft law for the simplification of the tax system. A draft law on auditing and evaluation procedures for all categories of public expenditure was also submitted. The code of fiscal stability, first announced in 2002 and welcomed by the Council in January 2003, was reintroduced as part of a broader draft law 'expected to be approved early next year'.[20] In simple words, it had yet to be adopted.

This relaxed approach to fiscal consolidation coincided with a debt-to-GDP ratio which remained above 100 per cent at the end of 2003, one of the highest in the European Union. Once more, the Council picked up on this:

paper presented at the Modern Greek Studies Association Conference, Toronto,16–18 October 2003.

18. Ministry of Economy and Finance, 'The 2002 Update of the Hellenic Stability and Growth Programme: 2002–2006', Athens, December 2002, p. 16.

19. Ministry of Economy and Finance, 'The 2003 Update of the Hellenic Stability and Growth Programme: 2003–2006', Athens, December 2003, p. 6.

20. *Ibid.*, p. 12.

In the light of the debt ratio, the overall proposed adjustment is limited while a more balanced 'policy mix' would call for a stricter stance of fiscal policy and an effective use of the opportunity provided by favourable growth prospects.[21]

A new body, the Public Debt Management Office, was expected to rationalise the maturity structure of public debt, as the high deficit-debt adjustments continued to haunt Greece's debt-management.

The notorious fiscal audit: cleaning up the act?

In March 2004, leader of New Democracy Party Kostas Karamanlis[22] won the national elections. The new government's first major initiative was to embark on 'a far reaching fiscal audit, aimed at achieving clarity and transparency in the fiscal balances of the Greek economy'.[23] Triggering intense and sustained political controversy about its goals – ND was even accused of 'selling out' to the Europeans – this audit was to disprove, once and for all, the idea that Greece had joined the euro club on 'its own merits', on the basis of macroeconomic stabilisation *achieved*. It served to show that all was not well, nor had it been for a while. The Commission had already asked for a full and comprehensive analysis of the state of the Greek economy in the beginning of 2003, which the Simitis government had promised to deliver after the 2004 elections. Apparently, the Commission suspected what the real story with Greece's fiscal deficits was: it just wanted public confirmation from Athens that the rather alarming situation was going to be addressed, sooner rather than later. When the new Minister of Economy and Finance took office, pressures to proceed intensified.[24]

Once the audit results became public, anger in Brussels and Frankfurt could hardly be contained. Athens had broken the Pact's deficit limit every year since 2001. With a revised deficit figure for 2004 calculated at 5.3 per cent of GDP, the Commission announced that it would consider the possibility of suspending the country's cohesion funds.[25] Based on the revised data for 2003 – a general government deficit of 3.2 per cent of GDP and government debt of 103 per cent of GDP – the Commission initiated the Excessive Deficit Procedure (EDP) for Greece on 19 May 2004.[26] On 5 July 2004, the Council concurred with the

---

21. 'Council Opinion of 10 February 2004 on the updated stability programme of Greece, 2003–2006' (2004/C 43/06), *Official Journal of the European Communities*, 19 February 2004.

22. *See* Appendix A. Bibliographical Data.

23. Ministry of Economy and Finance, 'The 2004 Update of the Hellenic Stability and Growth Programme: 2004–2007', Athens, December 2004, p. 2.

24. Interview 28.

25. The threat had already been used successfully against Portugal, which had swiftly lowered its deficit; fear that the new members in Eastern Europe would follow the Greek 'example' also played a part. *See* G. Parker, 'Greece vows to halve deficit amid threats from Commission', *Financial Times*, 30 September 2004.

26. The Commission formulated its Report in accordance with Article 104(3) of the Treaty and subsequently its opinion on the existence of an excessive deficit based on the 3.2 per cent deficit

Commission's recommendation. Under Article 104(7) of the Treaty, the Council established the deadline of 5 November 2004 for the Greek government to take effective action, with a view to bringing the excessive-deficit situation to an end by 2005.[27] Regarding the quality of the statistical methods that had been employed by Greece, the Council opted for a brief factual assessment rather than public condemnation: 'at present, the quality of public finance data remains uncertain'.[28]

In October 2004, a Eurostat mission was sent to check with the Greek authorities the debt and deficit data for the years before 2000. Following the substantial revisions for 2000–3, the notion that Greek 'creative accounting' had wreaked havoc was gaining significant ground in Eurostat, the Commission and Greece's partners in the Eurogroup. When formally approached, the Greek authorities could not provide data regarding the transactions that had been undertaken in the period 1997–9. The official explanation was that, 'after five years, the pre-2000 data were no longer available'.[29] Apparently, significant Greek lobbying in France, Germany and the Netherlands, which held the Presidency of the Council, also took place. The Greek side was only willing to accept that there were 'problems' with the data, not problems dating back to the pre-EMU period. Greece was able to get away lightly, as questions relevant to the 1997–9 data never appeared in any formal texts, either of the Council or the Commission. In private, the Finance Ministers of France, Germany and the Netherlands were fuming; the Dutch Finance Minister, in particular, insisted that, due to the size of Greece's deficits, the country ought to have appealed to the International Monetary Fund for financial assistance.[30]

Eurostat published a scathing report in November 2004, which covered the entire period from 1997 to 2003. 'While revisions in government deficit data were not unusual – allowing for new information or the detection of errors – the revision of the Greek budgetary data was exceptional.' The general government deficit initially reported at 1.7 per cent of GDP in 2003 stood at 4.6 per cent of GDP after the September 2004 notification; public debt rose to 109.9 per cent of GDP, 8.2 percentage points higher than projected. Figures for 2004 revealed a general government deficit of 5.3 per cent and general government debt at 112.1 per cent of GDP. Data revisions of this magnitude gave rise to 'questions about the

---

figure, expecting, however, that this could be revised upwards. *See* Commission of the European Communities, 'Report from the Commission, Greece: report prepared in accordance with Article 104(3) of the Treaty', SEC(2004) 623 final, Brussels, 19.5.2004, pp. 1–10, p. 2. *See also*, Commission of the European Communities, 'Commission Opinion on the existence of an excessive deficit in Greece-Application of Article 104(5) of the Treaty establishing the European Community', Brussels, SEC(2004) 813 final, 24 June 2004, pp. 1–6, p. 2.

27. Council of the European Union, 'Council Recommendation to Greece of 5 July 2004 with a view to bringing an end to the situation of an excessive government deficit', 14554/04, Brussels 22 November 2004, pp. 1–6, p. 4.

28. 'Council Decision of 5 July 2004 on the existence of an excessive deficit in Greece' (2004/917/EC), *Official Journal of the European Union*, L 389/25, 30 December 2004, pp. 1–2.

29. Interview 28.

30. Interview with G. Alogoskoufis, former Minister of Economy and Finance, in *To Vima*, 7 April 2011.

reliability of the Greek statistics on public finances', with Eurostat officials debating statistical discrepancies with Greek statistical authorities 'far more frequently than with any other member state';[31] under-recording of military expenditure, over-estimation of the surplus of social security funds and downward revision of tax-revenue estimates (mainly VAT) accounted for approximately 90 per cent of the total revisions.[32]

Preempting accusations of gross negligence or even incompetence, Eurostat asserted that, in checking the accounting treatment of the data, it did not have audit powers. 'All these verifications do not lead to genuine audit operations for which a legal basis is lacking'. For the quality of the public accounts produced, which depended on the 'administrative ability, good will, good faith and co-operative spirit of member states', Eurostat had to rely on the national statistical institutes; theoretically, they acted in full scientific independence, with a strict respect of the accounting standards defined in Regulations 3605/93 and ESA 95. Hence, the 'verification' of the accounts by Eurostat did not mean that the member states were exonerated from their own responsibility.

The road to real convergence

'Gradual' adjustment, Greek style

With the clean slate provided by the 'final settlement'[33] of long-standing open questions on budgetary statistics, the government was about to implement a responsible, transparent and effective fiscal policy; its aim was to bring the excessive-deficit situation to an end in 2005, in compliance with the Council recommendations under Article 104(7) of 6 July 2004, and proceed toward a significant reduction of the debt-to-GDP ratio. Maintaining high primary surpluses, consistent with the reduction of the expenditure ratio and the increase in current revenues, was part and parcel of the government's intention to proceed

---

31. Eurostat, *Report by Eurostat on the Revision of the Greek Government Deficit and Debt Figures*, 22 November 2004, p. 2.

32. In the Greek case, revisions of data were significant even between the March and September 2004 notifications; these were related to a stricter application of ESA 95 and the availability of new data. In the framework of the EDP, member states were expected, from the beginning of 1994, to report to the Commission (acting as statistical authority) their planned and actual government deficits and levels of government debt twice a year, before end of March and end of September. *See* 'Council Regulation No 3605/93 of 22 November 1993 on the application of the Protocol on the excessive deficit procedure annexed to the Treaty establishing the European Community', *Official Journal of the European Communities*, L 332, 31.12.93, pp. 1–3. This was subsequently reaffirmed with 'Council Regulation No 479/2009 of 25 May 2009 on the application of the Protocol on the excessive deficit procedure annexed to the Treaty establishing the European Community (codified version)', *Official Journal of the European Communities*, L 145, 10 June 2009, pp. 1–9.

33. This was the view formally presented in the Ministry of Economy and Finance, 'The 2004 Update of the Hellenic Stability and Growth Programme', which was not shared by Eurostat in its November 2004 report.

with 'gradual adjustment'; the notion of 'gradual' was not accidental, it was meant to accentuate the contrast with so-called 'shock-therapy' solutions tried elsewhere. As Greece had never undergone shock treatment, the mere idea of drastic restructuring produced negative attitudes among the public, generating social and political opposition.[34]

A number of measures were announced; Law 3259/2004 provided for a tax settlement (including delinquent obligations to the state, repatriation of capital and unsettled tax accounts for professionals and enterprises), whose expected impact on receipts was estimated at 0.2 per cent of GDP for 2004 and 0.70 per cent for 2005, while the tax rate for corporate income was to remain on a downward trend until 2007. Plans to implement a more effective fiscal auditing system were introduced once again, with the creation of an Independent Body of Fiscal Inspectors, as well as internal auditing services in every ministry, local authority or other public entity, with a budget exceeding €3 million.[35] Major privatisations, of Hellenic Petroleum (ELPE) and the National Bank of Greece, were on track, while Public Enterprises and Entities (DEKO) were called to operate under a 'new' framework, based on the strict implementation of business plans, wage moderation and control of borrowing requirements.

Social security reform was still struggling with the implementation of Law 3029/2002; two years after its enactment, steps were taken to distinguish auxiliary from primary pensions, with the consolidation of various funds remaining a major priority. Although many measures 'had yet to be implemented and evaluated before new elements are brought to the system', interestingly, new legislation, Law 3232/2004, was introduced, with the aim of 'amending various aspects of existing legislation, particularly as far as persons with disabilities, farmers, professionals and civil servants are concerned'.[36]

In 18 January 2005, the Council decided, according to Article 104(8) and on the basis of a Commission recommendation, that Greece had not taken effective action in response to the recommendation made under Article 104(7).[37] A month later, on February 2005, the Council proceeded, in accordance with Article 104(9), to give notice to Greece to take the measures for deficit reduction judged necessary to bring the situation of an excessive government deficit to an end, extending the deadline for the correction by one year, to 2006.[38] Exasperated with the Greek

---

34. G. Alogoskoufis, *Greece After the Crisis*, Athens, Kastaniotis Editions, 2009, p. 153 [in Greek].

35. Ministry of Economy and Finance, 'The 2004 Update of the Hellenic Stability and Growth Programme', p. 25.

36. *Ibid.*, p. 21.

37. 'Council Decision of 18 January 2005 establishing, in accordance with Article 104(8) of the Treaty establishing the European Community, whether effective action has been taken by the Hellenic Republic in response to recommendations of the Council in accordance with Article 104(7) of that Treaty' (2005/334/EC), *Official Journal of the European Union*, L 107/24, 28 April 2005, p. 24.

38. 'Council Decision of 17 February 2005 giving notice to Greece, in accordance with Article 104(9) of the EC Treaty, to take measures for the deficit reduction judged necessary in order to remedy the situation of excessive deficit' (2005/441/EC), *Official Journal of the European Union*, L

authorities' continued lack of transparency in their fiscal management, the Council required them to 'identify and control factors other than net borrowing which contribute to the change in debt levels and to improve the collection and processing of general government data'.[39] This preceded a move by Eurostat, on 18 March, not to validate the government deficit figures 'because of an inconsistent recording of flows between Greece and the EU budget'.[40] The Council set a deadline of 21 March 2005 for Greece to produce a report outlining how it would comply with these recommendations.

The Greek government, which affirmed the independence of the National Statistical Service of Greece and 'the transparent and effective reporting of fiscal accounts',[41] promised to proceed with an additional fiscal package of permanent measures. An increase of the average VAT rate by 1 percentage point in 2005 would be accompanied by, among other measures, savings on travel expenses of civil servants, which amounted to the sum of €45 million, and a reduction in subsidies to urban transport companies to the order of €50 million. On 29 March, the government made a public commitment that, conditional on growth, cuts in primary expenditures, especially in the areas of military procurement, state contributions to social security funds, local administration and public investment, would help bring the deficit below the 3 per cent threshold by 2006.[42] Hopeful that this time the pressure would pay off, the Commission adopted, on 6 April, a Communication to the Council,[43] concluding that the measures taken by Greece were consistent with the Council Decision and that no further steps under the EDP were necessary at that stage. The Council concurred with this assessment in its meeting of 12 April 2005.

A new model for growth

The time had come for 'an overhaul of the model upon which Greece's economic growth' was based.[44] Fiscal consolidation, combined with better quality of public finances, would be realised through the productive use of government spending; with a series of structural reforms in key markets and the more efficient operation

---

153/29, 16 June 2005, p. 29.

39. 'Council Opinion of 12 April 2005 on the updated stability programme of Greece, 2004–2007' (2005/C 189/01), *Official Journal of the European Communities*, 3 August 2005.

40. *See* European Commission, 'Eurostat News Release No 39', 18 March 2005.

41. Ministry of Economy and Finance, 'The 2004 Update of the Hellenic Stability and Growth Programme: 2004–2007 (revised)', Athens, March 2005, p. 12.

42. *Ibid.* p. 12.

43. Commission of the European Communities, 'Communication from the Commission to the Council: The action taken by Greece in response to the Council decision of 17 February 2005 in accordance to Article 104(9) of the Treaty for the deficit reduction judged necessary in order to remedy the situation of excessive deficit', SEC (2005) 443 final, Brussels, 6 April 2005.

44. Ministry of Economy and Finance, 'The 2005 Update of the Hellenic Stability and Growth Programme: 2005–2008', Athens, December 2005, p. 3.

of the public sector, an improvement in the business environment would allow for private-sector-led growth. Finally, integration of the Greek economy globally would expand Greece's trade ties, attract foreign investment and promote growth objectives. Although this threefold strategy required time to bear fruit, it was expected to improve multifactor productivity and increase employment rates.

For all the rhetoric, the 'overhauling' of the old model did not seem to introduce a *new* approach: it was more of a rehash. Echoing PASOK sensitivities if not the wording behind its 'social package', the ND government promised to pursue a social agenda, ensuring that 'consolidation does not come at the expense of social welfare'. With savings planned from the wage bill and public consumption-expenditure items, authorities reassured the public that the 2006 Draft Budget Bill would 'remedy injustices to several social groups done in the past',[45] including a refund to pensioners of past contributions on behalf of the Solidarity Account of Social Security Funds (LAFKA), increases in farmers' pensions (OGA, Farmers' Insurance Fund), and in EKAS (Pensioners' Social Solidarity Allowance). Throughout the public sector, salaries and pensions were expected to increase by 6.6 per cent in 2006, while authorities affirmed that they would proceed with 'the much needed personnel hiring, primarily in hospitals, education and security forces'.[46] Elections were obviously around the corner.

Once more, 'new' legislation was introduced: Law 3402/06 would create a General Directorate of Fiscal Audits with a mission to audit all public entities of the general government. On top of tighter control over ministries, local government and public sector enterprises, efficiency gains were expected to accrue from public-debt management, which would re-focus on the cost and risk of borrowing over the long term. The government expected that the new measures would help bring the debt to GDP ratio down to 96.8 per cent of GDP by 2008. An important ally of the consolidation effort was, the authorities claimed, the National Statistical Service of Greece; it continued improving its data-compiling and -reporting processes, in close co-operation with Eurostat.

Fiscal adjustment amounted, at the end of 2005, to 2.3 percentage points of GDP; this was accompanied by an initial list of structural reforms, including the tax reform reducing corporate tax rate to 25 per cent by 2007, the establishment of a legal framework for public-private partnerships, pension reform in the banking sector and the introduction of flexibility in working hours and the reduction in overtime pay. A complete list was contained in the National Reform Programme, submitted on 15 October 2005 in the context of the renewed Lisbon strategy for growth and jobs. Prior to setting out its goals for enhancing employment, growth and social cohesion, the programme included a bold assessment:

---

45. *Ibid.*, p. 11.
46. *Ibid.*, p. 17.

The fiscal expansion following the accession of Greece to the EMU was justified only to a certain extent by the preparations for the Olympic Games and not only was it not accurately recorded in the official data, but it also led to a dead-end and cannot be pursued any further. At the same time, important delays in the implementation of structural reforms placed Greece low in ranking in many areas, with particularly severe consequences on productivity and competitiveness.[47]

Greece and EMU: a mismatch made in Brussels and Frankfurt, part 1

Talk of a new model for growth implicitly suggested the end of an era. Within five years of EMU entry, a notable U-turn of previous 'performance' had been evidenced. Allowing for an average GDP growth of 3.5 per cent, one of the highest in the Eurozone, Greece still managed to be an underachiever; the rate of inflation persisted well above the EU average, while external imbalances continued to rise. Even accounting for the slippages related to the Olympic Games, the general government deficit remained on average 5 per cent of GDP, reaching 6.6 per cent in 2004; together with large below-the-line operations, this contributed to the accumulation of public debt, which remained close to or above 110 per cent of GDP. Greece had been placed in an EDP in 2004 and had promised to correct it by 2006, receiving Council notice upon notice in between. Questions about the sustainability of Greece's public finances, given the projected budgetary costs of its ageing population and its debt ratio, were raised time and again.[48]

Greece was, in fact, repeatedly invited to implement 'permanent measures' to 'correct' its excessive deficit, ensure a 'faster debt reduction path', implement pension reforms to ensure the 'sustainability of public finances', and 'improve the collection and processing of general government data'. The 'invitation', however, lacked credibility. The discipline of the Stability and Growth Pact was already proving ineffective, particularly after the way Germany and France had been let off the hook back in 2003.[49] Only a year after the Pact's ill-fated March 2005

---

47. Ministry of Economy and Finance, *National Reform Programme for Growth and Jobs 2005–2008*, Athens, October 2005, p. 1.

48. 'Council Opinion of 14 March 2006 on the updated stability programme of Greece, 2005–2008' (2006/C 82/01), *Official Journal of the European Union*, 5 April 2006, p. 3.

49. *See* European Court of Justice, 'Press Release No 57/04: Judgment of the Court of Justice in Case C-27/04 Commission of the European Communities v Council of the European Union', 13 July 2004. The Court did not accept the Commission's claim that it should annul the Council's failure to adopt decisions to give notice to France and Germany. On the other hand, the Court annulled the conclusions adopted by the Council, in which the Council held the excessive-deficit procedures in abeyance and modified the recommendations previously made by it to each of those member states for correction of their excessive deficit. *See also* Commission of the European Communities, 'Communication from the Commission to the Council: The situation of Germany and France in relation to their obligations under the EDF following the judgement of the Court of Justice', COM (2004) 813, Brussels, 14 December 2004. For the way the collapse of state stabilisation policies in France and Germany led to the Pact's reform, *see* S. Donnelly, 'Explaining EMU reform', *Journal of Common Market Studies* 2005, vol. 43, no. 5, pp. 947–68.

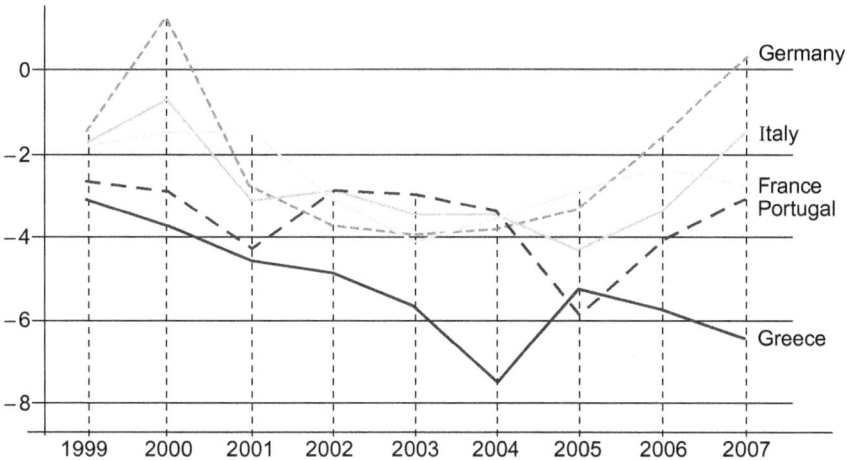

Figure 6.1: Discipline in short supply: budget deficits after the launch of the euro

reform, which accented its highly political nature,[50] the debt ratio in the EU increased from 62.4 per cent of GDP in 2004 to 63.4 per cent of GDP in 2005.[51] Germany, which had broken the pact every year since 2002, was again 'invited' to correct its excessive deficit by 2007 at the latest.[52] Figure 6.1 shows that even the big economies broke the rules, almost immediately after the launch of the euro.

The pattern of fiscal profligacy that was beginning to emerge across the Eurozone, with the budget deficits of the three big economies above the EMU ceiling of 3 per cent of GDP, prompted the ECB to announce, as a matter of clarification, that it would not accept sovereign debt from fiscal 'offenders', that is, countries whose credit ratings had slipped. Backed by an increasingly frustrated Commission, the ECB expected that a dose of market discipline would have a salutary effect on countries with high levels of debt and high deficits, primarily, but not exclusively, Greece and Italy. Greek policy makers, of course, shrugged at this: 'Greece would have to drop two notches in the ratings to be affected. From the latest rating agency reports it seems that Greece is more likely to be upgraded rather than downgraded.'[53]

---

50. M. Segers and M. van Esch, 'Behind the veil of budgetary discipline: the political logic of the budgetary rules in EMU and the SGP', *Journal of Common Market Studies* 2007, vol. 45, no. 5, pp. 1089–1109.

51. Commission of the European Communities, Communication from the Commission to the Council and the European Parliament, 'Public Finances in EMU 2006 – the first year of the revised Stability and Growth Pact', COM (2006) 304 final, Brussels, 13.6.2006.

52. Commission of the European Communities, 'Recommendation for a Council Decision giving notice to Germany, in accordance with Article 104(9) of the EC Treaty, to take measures for the deficit reduction judged necessary in order to remedy the situation of excessive deficit', SEC(2006) 285 final, Brussels, 1 March 2006.

53. Quote by senior Greek official, in G. Parker, R. Atkins, and K. Hope, 'Eurozone ministers step up drive for fiscal discipline', *Financial Times*, November 9, 2005. Jean-Claude Trichet, ECB

Landing an abrogation: fiscal adjustment works

Evidently empowered by progress made on 'supply-side development, investment in productive capacity and job creation',[54] Greece proposed a gigantic upward revision of its GDP statistics in October 2006, without previously notifying the Commission or other finance ministers. Revisions typically ranged between 1 and 2 per cent, although Greece and Italy did occasionally break this 'rule'. The proposed 25 per cent revision of annual gross domestic product for the 2000–2006 period raised a few eyebrows in Brussels, as the National Statistical Service had now included parts of the black economy in the revised national accounts.[55] Commissioner Almunia took the initiative to write to George Alogoskoufis, Greek Finance Minister, pointing out the country's 'particular history on statistical data revisions'.[56] Waiting for verification from Eurostat, the Commission proposed to review Greece's economic performance based on the old data. Unperturbed, the Finance Minister planned to submit the budget for 2007, using both the old and the new figures.[57] The Ministry's position was that Greece had merely updated its national accounts and, if Eurostat proceeded to revise the 'revised' data, all that would change would be the 'denominator', that is the size of GDP. This was not as 'innocent' as the Greek authorities made it out to be; the revision, some suspected, was designed to make the budget deficit, measured as a ratio of GDP, look smaller.

At least, fiscal tightening seemed to be paying off. The official figure for the general government deficit in 2006 was 2.6 per cent of GDP,[58] 3.5 percentage points lower than in 2003, the year that was the basis for opening the EDP. With revenues and expenditure contributing almost equally to this reduction, the excessive deficit stood corrected. In addition, general government gross debt had declined from 108.5 per cent of GDP in 2004 to 104.5 per cent in 2006, a ratio that could be considered as 'sufficiently diminishing towards the 60 per cent of GDP reference value'. The Commission suggested that, in the case of Greece, sizeable revisions in government accounts since 2004 were the outcome of measures taken to improve the collection and processing of government finance statistics, in line

---

president, confirmed that the Bank would only accept bonds with at least a single A-rating in its financial-market activities.

54. Ministry of Economy and Finance, 'The 2006 Update of the Hellenic Stability and Growth Programme: 2006–2009', Athens, December 2006, p. 3.

55. K. Hope, and G. Parker, 'Oldest profession boosts Greek output', *Financial Times*, September 28, 2006.

56. G. Parker, 'EU finance ministers clash over cheap loans', *Financial Times*, October 10 2006.

57. *Naftemporiki*, October 12, 2006 [in Greek].

58. GDP in this instance referred to the unrevised GDP series provided by the Greek authorities as an annex to the EDP notification of April 2007 and not to the 'revised' GDP data reported by the Greek authorities in October 2006, which could lead to an upward revision of nominal GDP by around 26 per cent per year since 2000. Given the magnitude and complexity of this revision, it was subject to examination by Eurostat. *See* Commission of the European Communities, 'Recommendation for a Council Decision abrogating Decision 2004/917/EC on the existence of an excessive deficit in Greece', SEC (2007) 620 final, Brussels, 16 May 2007, p. 4.

with the Council Recommendation of 5 July 2004 and Decision of 17 February 2005. Eurostat had subsequently validated the Greek government deficit and debt figures reported in October 2006 and April 2007. In the Commission interpretation:

> Although one cannot exclude future revisions in the Greek government deficit, given the distance between the currently reported deficit and the deficit reference value, there is a relatively low probability that any future revision of government accounts raises the 2006 deficit ratio in excess of 3 per cent of GDP. Such a probability will be even lower, in case the revised GDP series reported by Greece in October 2006 and April 2007 [suggesting a growth of 26 per cent per year since 2000] are validated by Eurostat later in the year.[59]

On 5 June 2007, the Council abrogated Decision 2004/917/EC on the existence of an excessive deficit;[60] the successful outcome could not have come about 'without the good rapport' that the Greek authorities had cultivated with their Eurozone counterparts.[61] The country's partners were initially hard to please and appease; there was no doubt that, in their estimate, the measures that had been implemented were 'too light'. Greek policy makers had taken the notion of 'gradual' far more seriously than would have been desirable or acceptable.[62] Still, there was a certain optimism that the Greek exit from the EDP, rubber-stamped by the Council's decision, would finally introduce a more dynamic phase of fiscal consolidation.

Taking stock of Greek adjustment

Fiscal consolidation, stage two

The ND government called elections six months prior to the end of its first term, in October 2007, and won with a reduced margin. An electoral cycle had, once again, been at work: on top of various one-off measures, including emergency assistance for the victims of the wildfires that had broken during the summer and had caused unprecedented and disastrous damage,[63] expenditure on social security

---

59. *Ibid.*, p. 5.
60. 'Council Decision of 5 June 2007 abrogating Decision 2004/917/EC on the existence of an excessive deficit in Greece' (2007/465/EC), L 176, *Official Journal of the European Communities*, 6 July 2007.
61. Interview 28.
62. Interview 29.
63. Skouras and Christodoulakis actually report striking increases of Greek wildfires and tax evasion around elections, complementing it with evidence that 'these increases are caused by government decisions on matters such as the intensity with which transactions are audited'. The cost of these effects has cumulatively risen to 8 per cent of GDP in recent years. While tax evasion is caused by looser auditing of transactions for businesses which may or may not be specifically targeted as special-interest groups, wildfire spikes in election years are caused by looser procedures for granting building permits. *See* S. Skouras and N. Christodoulakis, 'Electoral misgovernance cycles: evidence from wildfires and tax evasion in Greece and elsewhere', *GreeSE Paper No 47*, Hellenic Observatory Papers on Greece and Southeast Europe, London, 2011, p. 29.

Greek government ■ ND ▨ PASOK

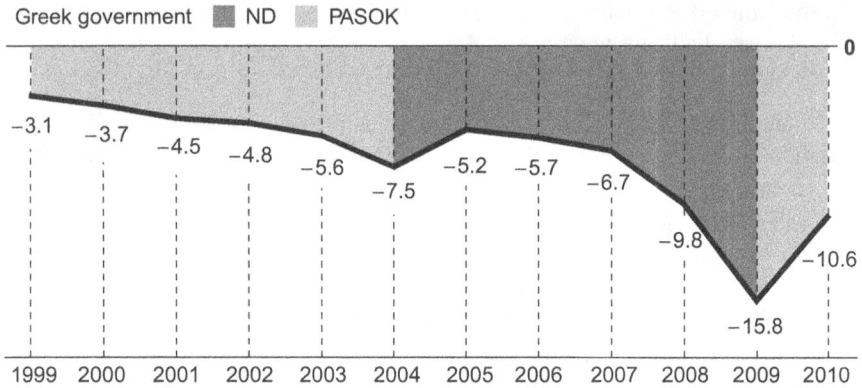

Figure 6.2: Elections and general government budget deficit, 1999–2010 (% of GDP)

and health care had grown by 14.9 per cent in 2007.[64] The general government deficit rose to 2.7 per cent of GDP in 2007, compared to the targeted 2.2 per cent, while public debt stood at 93.4 per cent. With the 'clean slate' provided by the exit from the EDP pertinently used both to reinforce the credibility of the economic policy that had been followed and to justify the controversial fiscal audit, it was about time to achieve a balanced budget, a goal set for 2010. Figure 6.2 presents the deterioration of budget-deficit figures, with election years constituting well defined points.

The government's strategy rested on the implementation of discretionary measures in indirect taxes and real-estate taxation and renewed efforts to combat tax evasion. To signal commitment, a new law aimed at enhancing the effectiveness and objectiveness of tax audits and increasing tax-payers' contributions was approved in Parliament in November. New institutions were to be created: a National Committee to tackle tax evasion, with the participation of all social partners; and a tax-analysis unit at the Ministry of Economy and Finance to monitor debts in tax offices and revenues and debts in customs offices.

No mention was made of the 'new' economic model, announced only a year ago. With elections out of the way, a new mandate assured and PASOK, the main opposition party, caught up in a leadership crisis, the government could, theoretically, have proceeded with difficult reforms, including the restructuring of the pension system, whose impact on the sustainability of public finances was considered 'rather acute'.[65] Interestingly, long-term projections of pension expenditure were not available in the Greek case, the 'latest' information having

---

64. Ministry of Economy and Finance, 'The 2007 update of the Hellenic Stability and Growth Programme: 2007–2010', Athens, December 2007, p. 19.

65. 'Council Opinion of 4 March 2008 on the updated stability programme of Greece, 2007–2010' (2008/C 74/08), *Official Journal of the European Union*, 20 March 2008, p.3.

been recorded in the 2002 stability programme update.[66] Rather than tackling the budgetary implications head on, however, the government chose to stick to what it knew best: searching for the maximum possible consensus, through an ongoing process of public consultation, and waiting for the technical report an 'Experts Committee' would prepare. The adoption of measures was postponed for yet another year.[67]

Once more, blatant procrastination was replacing adjustment. Prime Minister Karamanlis had calculated that, with his slim majority of two MPs and with presidential elections scheduled for 2010, 'he only had two years to govern; if painful fiscal measures were to be undertaken, public discontent would ruin his chances for re-election'.[68] Eschewing fiscal consolidation and foregoing important structural adjustment was a small price to pay, as the 'needy' gripped the government's attention. A draft law was submitted to Parliament regarding the establishment of a National Fund for Social Cohesion, which would reduce the poverty rate to 15 per cent within the next five years. The fund would finally ameliorate the basic deficiency of social-transfer schemes in Greece, namely that they were 'not well targeted to those who are really in need'.[69] In a government-spending bonanza, increased expenditure was allocated for higher salaries and pensions for military staff, while extra benefits were handed out to the judiciary and families with three children. Expenditure for salaries and pensions was expected to rise to 9.2 per cent of GDP in 2008.

The strong Greek economy had nothing to fear. At the end of 2007, in fact, the Commission approved the upward revision of GDP by around 9.6 per cent (*vis-à-vis* the proposed 25.6 per cent); as a result, the government had to make an increased contribution to the EU budget which amounted to €1.110 million. More importantly, political authorities confidently asserted that the financial crisis that had originated in the sub-prime mortgage market of the United States in 2007 did not appear to affect Greece's issuance policy: the financing of its borrowing requirements continued without impediment, at a weighted average cost of 4.4 per cent for an average duration of 15.1 years (for new borrowing) and with an oversubscription ratio of 3.83.

Lessons not learned

Desperate times call for desperate measures

As the financial crisis intensified in the autumn of 2008, the Greek economy began to feel the pinch. Following the mid-October 2008 European Council Agreement,

---

66. *Ibid.*
67. Ministry of Economy and Finance, 'The 2007 Update of the Hellenic Stability and Growth Programme', p. 4.
68. Interview 28.
69. Ministry of Economy and Finance, 'The 2007 Update of the Hellenic Stability and Growth Programme', p. 20.

member states that 'took advantage of the good times to achieve more sustainable public finance positions and improve their competitive positions'[70] were to adopt a Commission-approved fiscal stimulus package. Greece did not have this option; its budgetary policy was finally having to own up to the significant imbalances that were becoming visible. Fearful that the crisis would shake investor confidence in the Greek financial system, however, policy makers proceeded to announce a number of measures, including a deposit- guarantee scheme and borrowers' protection from foreclosure requirements, alongside a rescue plan designed to ensure adequate financing for consumers and enterprises, especially SMEs.

Following the country's exit from the EDP, fiscal policy results were, once more, disappointing: the government deficit rose to 3.7 per cent of GDP in 2008 against the targeted figure of 2.5 per cent; expenditure overruns contributed to this outcome, as the financing of pensions, social security funds and social-solidarity benefits increased. On the revenue side, the mechanism for the new property tax was not fully operative, while tax collection had 'not been working at full steam for some time'.[71] To tighten up the process, a new system of programme budgeting for the preparation, implementation, and monitoring of the state budget was announced; with full implementation scheduled for 2012, however, Greece's partners were not too impressed. Worse, there were no detailed plans for how fiscal consolidation would proceed in 2009 or any concrete measures backing the planned adjustment from 2010 onwards. The Council invited Greece to 'strengthen significantly the fiscal consolidation path already in 2009, through well-specified permanent measures curbing current expenditure, including a prudent public sector wage policy, thereby contributing to necessary reduction in the debt-to-GDP ratio'.[72]

Drawing a line under the unsatisfactory practices of the past, Law 3697/2008 on the 'transparency of the state budget' was supposed to contain the expenditure of general government entities and enhance the accuracy of data reported to Eurostat; in like manner, a central authority for public sector wages would rationalise the payments system. Efforts to consolidate the financial conditions of Public Enterprises and Entities (DEKO), which were finally to adopt international accounting practices, would continue, while the announced Hellenic Railways Organisation restructuring would proceed as planned. With the long-term sustainability of public finances now 'being at high risk', social security system reform finally took off the ground with Law 3655/2008; savings and the more efficient management of reserves would accrue from the merging of 133 social security organisations into thirteen.[73]

---

70. Commission of the European Communities, Communication from the Commission to the European Council, 'A European Economic Recovery Plan', COM 800 final, Brussels, 26 November 2008 p. 7.

71. Ministry of Economy and Finance, 'The 2008 Update of the Hellenic Stability and Growth Programme 2008–2011', Athens, January 2009, p. 15.

72. 'Council Opinion of 10 March 2009 on the updated stability programme of Greece, 2008–2011' (2009/C 64/02), *Official Journal of the European Union*, 19 March 2009, p. 4.

73. At the end of 2008, there were still no updated figures on the projected development of pension

Policy discipline in short supply

At this point, the risks of Greece's high public debt were being re-evaluated. In spite of favourable conditions, a strong growth performance, a substantial fall in interest rates up to 2005 and privatisation proceeds, Greek policy makers had failed to reduce debt to a sustainable level; high budget deficits, which consistently exceeded the 3 per cent of GDP ceiling, combined with significant deficit-debt adjustments, accounted for this. By 2008, the Bank of Greece was warning that the country's debt-to-GDP ratio, the second-highest in the EU, had become a 'major source of vulnerability for the economy' and the underlying factor behind 'the large widening of the yield spread between Greek and German government bonds'.[74]

Policy discipline proved to have been in short supply. Greece's average inflation rate consistently exceeded that of the euro area by 1.1–1.2 per cent, while other developments, including wage growth, which ran at around 5 per cent per annum, led to increases in average nominal earnings: between 2001 and 2009, they cumulatively reached 63 per cent, against 25.6 per cent for the euro area[75] partners. Competitiveness shrank, with Greek export volumes growing at just 3.8 per cent per annum, compared to double the weighted rate of growth of imports for the country's major trading partners. A combination of high domestic-demand growth, persistent fiscal imbalances and an inability to enhance, through structural reforms, the economy's production base or to increase productivity worsened the external balance of the Greek economy: the current account deficit peaked at 14.9 per cent of GDP in 2008, from a close-to-balance position in the mid-1990s.[76]

The negative developments in the current account noted during this period, partly fuelled by serious competitiveness losses, further reflected the significant shortfall of national saving relative to domestic investment.[77] As in other peripheral countries, the financial liberalisation that took place in Greece in the

expenditure. The National Actuarial Authority, in co-operation with the International Labour Office, put forward a set of macroeconomic and demographic assumptions, which, in January 2009, awaited formal approval. *See* Ministry of Economy and Finance, 'The 2008 Update of the Hellenic Stability and Growth Programme 2008–2011', p. 31.

74. Bank of Greece, *Annual Report 2008*, Athens, Bank of Greece, April 2009, p. 28.
75. Bank of Greece, *Annual Report 2009*, Athens, Bank of Greece, April 2010, p. 28.
76. M. Arghyrou and G. Chortareas, 'Current account imbalances and real exchange rates in the euro area', *Review of International Economics* 2008, vol. 16, pp. 747–64. The deteriorating pattern indicated that the current account deficit, which had historically operated as a binding constraint on policy makers, no longer had this effect. In the first part of the 1980s, when the average deficit value was equal to 5.3 per cent of GDP, the Greek Drachma experienced two substantial discrete devaluations against the USD dollar (in 1983 and 1985), whereas discrete devaluations also occurred every year (or the year immediately after) the Greek current account deficit surpassed the threshold of 4 per cent of GDP, namely in 1974, 1983, 1985 and 1998. Within EMU, the option of devaluation was obviously not available. *See* M. Arghyrou, 'The accession of Greece to the EMU: initial estimates and lessons for the new EU countries', *Liverpool Quarterly Economic Bulletin* 2006, vol. 27, no. 4, p. 7.
77. Bank of Greece, *Annual Report 2007*, Athens, Bank of Greece, April 2008, p. 26.

1990s and the process of monetary convergence that led to the adoption of the euro in 2001 resulted in considerable credit expansion and a sharp fall in the national saving rate.[78] However, in the Greek case, this savings decline continued dramatically, dropping from 18.5 per cent in the five-year period 1992–6 down to 14.0 per cent in 1997–2001, 10.5 per cent in 2002–2006, 7.6 per cent in 2007 and 7.1 per cent in 2008.[79] Even worse, the net national saving rate, after adjusting for capital consumption, was negative in the period 2000–2009 (-5.1 per cent of GDP in 2008 against a positive ratio of 5.8 per cent for the euro area), with the exception of the years 2001 and 2004, when it turned positive (0.2 per cent of GDP).[80] Greece and Portugal were, in fact, the only two countries for which the net national saving rate turned negative under the euro: no other countries relied on foreign capital to such a large extent. Large fiscal deficits, combined with the growth of private consumption (between 1996 and 2008 it posted an average of 72 per cent of GDP against 57 per cent in the euro area as a whole[81]) accounted for this shortfall.

The check, please

The fact that Greece persistently failed to deliver on the targets agreed with the Commission and the Council reflected the *non-binding* character that the implementation of national budget aims had acquired. 'We never abided by the stability programmes. Why should we? We could not really implement our budget';[82] this stunning admission summed up both the prevailing attitude and the extent of policy incompetence. At the heart of Greece's fiscal vulnerabilities lay the domestic budgetary framework, both in the preparation of the budget and in its execution.[83] Year after year, national Budget Laws progressively became empty promises, as annual budgetary targets were consistently and systematically missed. Expenditure control supposedly lay at the heart of all 'reform' efforts; each new plan to strengthen the budgetary process, however, particularly the control of primary expenditure, was ineffective; when instituted, it was either negated in practice or set for implementation only at some future date.

Hallberg, Strauch and von Hagen offer a systematic explanation of the extent of compliance with EMU's fiscal framework on the basis of national

78. *See* S. N. Brissimis, G. Hondroyiannis, G. C. Papazoglou, N. T. Tsaveas and M. A. Vasardani, 'Current account determinants and external sustainability in periods of structural change', *ECB Working Paper Series No 1243*, September 2010, p. 10. Some widening of the current account deficit was to be expected, 'but not necessarily of that magnitude and speed'.

79. European Commission, 'European economic forecast Autumn 2009', in *European Economy 10*, 2009, p. 209.

80. Bank of Greece, *Annual Report 2009*, p. 27.

81. *Ibid.*, p. 23.

82. Interview 28.

83. Commission of the European Communities, 'Report from the Commission, Greece: Report prepared in accordance with Article 104(3) of the Treaty', Brussels, 18 February 2009, p. 8.

budgetary institutions.[84] The degree of fiscal discipline is dependent on whether a country's budget process is shaped by the 'delegation' or 'contract' approach: the differences between the two boil down to basic political characteristics, such as party and electoral systems. Single-party majority governments or closely aligned coalitions, in which ideological distance among parties is low, delegate control to strong ministers of finance who can co-ordinate the government; countries with dispersed coalition governments, where ideological dispersion is high, rely on numerical budgetary targets negotiated among key policy makers. It follows that the Stability and Growth Pact may be less effective in countries whose budget process is shaped by the delegation approach.

Greece appears to be a straightforward delegation case and it certainly has had an appalling record of not avoiding excessive deficits. At variance with the 'strong minister' supposition and the minister's central place in agenda-setting, formulation and implementation of the budget, however, Greek ministers of finance evoked the image of working with a gun on their temple at the end of every fiscal year: they succumbed to all sorts of last-minute demands, often in the form of other ministers' explicit threats, to pay for pensions and other items.[85] This tradition of intimidation and capitulation went back to the significant strengthening of the Prime Minister's institutional position in the 1980s. Using his control over PASOK, Papandreou redefined the Prime Minister's Office as a supervisory body over all government activity, reinforced party discipline in parliament and used periodic cabinet reshuffles as a means of keeping his ministers in check.[86] This style of leadership, combined with a party-dominated parliament, enhanced the zero-sum quality of executive power and enabled the Prime Minister to play a game of divide and rule. Sixteen Ministers of National Economy alternated between 1981 and 1994;[87] these served alongside eight Alternate and sixteen Deputy Ministers, who took office over the same period. If one considers the division of the economic policy process between the Ministry of National Economy and the Ministry of Finance (between 1981 and 1984[88] and 1985 and 1996[89]) and

---

84. M. Hallerberg, R. Strauch and J. von Hagen, *Fiscal Governance: Evidence from Europe,* Cambridge, Cambridge University Press, 2009.

85. Interview 23; interview 28.

86. By enacting and subsequently applying Law 1558/1985, Papandreou expanded and contracted the cabinet according to his own will. It is indicative of the way that Papandreou's personality dominated the government that protesting or dissenting ministers would bring their cases to the prime minister's private residence rather than to a collective body. D. Sotiropoulos, 'Administering the summit: the Greek case', in B. G. Peters, R. A. W. Rhodes and V. Wright, (eds), *Administering the Summit: Administration of the core executive in developed countries,* Basingstoke, Macmillan Press, 2000, pp. 180–1.

87. Former Minister Y. Papantoniou is the only minister who remained at his post between 1994 and 2001.

88. G. Arsenis, Minister of National Economy between 5 July 1982 and 26 July 1985, also took the post of Minister of Finance between 27 March 1984 and 26 July 1985.

89. Papantoniou, Minister of National Economy from 6 May 1994, also took the post of Minister of Finance from 25 July 1996 to 24 October 2001.

the number of Finance Ministers (twelve), Alternate (three) and Deputy Ministers (eighteen) that also alternated, the implications for monitoring and co-ordinating budget policies are not difficult to gauge.

The institutional position of the Finance Minister stabilised in 1994, with the same Minister presiding over the convergence period up to 2001; in 1996, the Ministries of National Economy and Finance were finally amalgamated. Even then, however, policy actors opted to exhaust the external-constraint strategy rather than create a 'stabilisation state';[90] the fact that monetary policy bore the brunt of the nominal convergence effort, combined with the postponement of politically costly structural reforms and the preference for the stock-market flotation of public sector enterprises, all pointed to Ministers' unwillingness to 'overcome the deficit bias in public budgeting'.[91]

Following accession, the Greek case seems to confirm Dodson's claim that 'finance ministers in delegation states that breached the pact somehow lack the institutional conditions to make delegation work'.[92] There is a further point that needs to be made, however; policy makers chose either not to create the necessary institutional conditions, or, once they had created them, chose to undermine them. Engaged in law-making and the design of new rules and agencies throughout the 2001–8 period, Greek policy makers pretended that they could save the day or save face. As one law came after another, the credibility of such devices progressively and predictably plummeted. Without a coherent plan or organising principle, auditing procedures were replaced by 'golden rules', in turn replaced by bodies of inspectors, then traded for directorates of fiscal audits, or followed by programme budgeting; the real problem, that of creating binding norms for cutting down public expenditure, was forever elusive for policy makers. The hazy alternation of procedures – hazy because there were instances of overlap and co-existence – effectively clogged implementation; rather than improving accountability and effectiveness, therefore, 'laws' and 'rules' became a breeding ground for a lack of accountability and transparency. The end result was the *de facto* abandonment of any real effort at putting the country's fiscal house in order.

90. 'A stabilisation state will seek to rely on market allocation and to diminish state interventions under the premise that interventions would create longer-term disequilibria by distorting market signals and resource allocation.' G. Pagoulatos, 'Economic adjustment and financial reform: Greece's Europeanisation and the emergence of a stabilisation state', *South European Society and Politics* 2000, vol. 5, no. 2, p. 207.

91. M. Hallerberg, 'The importance of domestic political institutions: why and how Belgium and Italy qualified for EMU', *ZEI Working paper No. B10*, 2000 (accessed 18 March 2012) Online. Available: http://hdl.handle.net/10419/39489.

92. D. Hodson, *Governing the Euro Area in Good Times and Bad*, Oxford, Oxford University Press, 2011, p. 65.

Greece and EMU: a mismatch made in Brussels and in Frankfurt, part 2

Following EMU entry, was the single monetary policy *incompatible* with the requirements of the Greek economy? In the 2001–5 period, when Greece posted higher-than-EMU-average growth, nominal interest rates should have been set higher, the argument goes, so that inflationary pressures would not have given rise to higher inflation. The ECB's low interest rates over-stimulated Greek domestic demand, fuelled inflationary pressures, increased real exchange-rate overvaluation and, ultimately, led to excessively high current account deficit levels. This development, unwelcome as it was, was theoretically consistent with the short-term credibility effects of Greece's accession, which were nevertheless supposed to dissipate in the medium term.[93]

The 'medium-term' scenario was never borne out for Greece, or the 'periphery', however. The external imbalances between 'north' and 'south', already present in the creation of EMU, produced, following the adoption of the single currency, an asymmetry that was almost structural in character.[94] Greece, Portugal and Spain ran ever-growing current account deficits, which were conveniently explained away: they reflected higher investment needs in lower-income countries in Southern Europe, as they were 'catching up'; or they were the demand-driven effects of large fiscal deficits, which, in the Greek case, at least, fuelled public consumption. If only the 'surplus' countries such as Germany could pursue policies to promote consumption and increase personal-income growth, then all would be well. In reality, although surpluses were the mirror image of deficits, the large economies were fiercely reluctant to shoulder part of the burden of adjustment, leaving the 'south' and Ireland to be 'penalised'. In 2008, when foreign capital-flows fell sharply in these countries, triggering recessionary effects, it became apparent that the wage and price run-ups of the boom days had amounted to very little; unable to cut interest rates or devalue their currencies, Greece, Portugal and Ireland would soon have to pay the price for reckless borrowing, public and private.

Conclusion: 'Ostrichism' won the day

What happened to 'real' convergence? EMU accession was supposed to be the beginning of a serious shake-up of the Greek economy, not its substitute. Against a background of continuous economic growth, policy makers failed to generate a clear fiscal-consolidation path – which would have reduced the public-debt ratio – or to proceed with the opening-up of major markets; the effects of this failure are depicted in Figure 6.3. Wild wage increases, accompanied by firms' arbitrary

---

93. M. Arghyrou, 'Monetary policy before and after the euro: evidence from Greece', *Cardiff Economics Working Papers*, E2006/26, November 2006, pp. 19–20.

94. N. Christodoulakis, 'How is Europe coping with the present state of the crisis? North-South asymmetry in the Eurozone', paper presented in the ELIAMEP seminar on Economic Governance and the EU: Drawing Lessons from the Crisis, Athens, June 2010 (accessed 10 January 2012) Online. Available: http://europeanseminars.eliamep.gr/wp-content/uploads/2010/07/Nikos-Christodoulakis-North-South-Asymmetry.pdf.

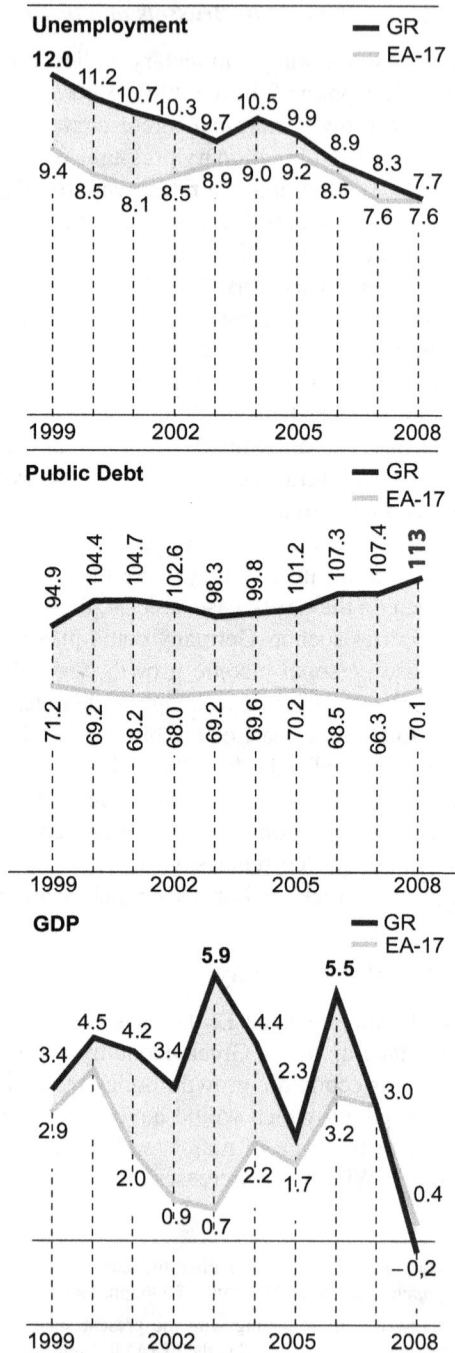

Unemployment — GR, EA-17

12.0, 11.2, 10.7, 10.3, 9.7, 10.5, 9.9, 8.9, 8.3, 7.7
9.4, 8.5, 8.1, 8.5, 8.9, 9.0, 9.2, 8.5, 7.6, 7.6

1999 2002 2005 2008

Public Debt — GR, EA-17

94.9, 104.4, 104.7, 102.6, 98.3, 99.8, 101.2, 107.3, 107.4, 113
71.2, 69.2, 68.2, 68.0, 69.2, 69.6, 70.2, 68.5, 66.3, 70.1

1999 2002 2005 2008

GDP — GR, EA-17

3.4, 4.5, 4.2, 3.4, 5.9, 4.4, 2.3, 5.5, 3.0
2.9, 2.0, 0.9, 0.7, 2.2, 1.7, 3.2, 0.4, −0,2

1999 2002 2005 2008

Figure 6.3: Joblessness and debt-led growth, 1999–2008

pricing policies, disrupted the environment of price stability and ate away at Greece's competitiveness; measures to correct distortions in the social security system and the product and labour markets remained mostly on paper, further heightening the country's structural weaknesses. By 2008, the high deficits that had led to one of the highest debt ratios in the EU suggested that even 'nominal' convergence had become all but 'convergence' in name. The good years had been squandered.

Even acknowledging the significant economic divergences that played out across the Eurozone, Greece was truly 'in a league of its own', with its combination of persistent fiscal imbalances and protracted losses of competitiveness.[95] At the bottom of this was a peculiar form of ostrichism, an ostrich-like behaviour, eagerly adopted by Greek policy makers; in fact, they buried their heads in the ground, almost uninterrupted, until well into 2009. Routine deviation from targets, over-optimistic assessment of planned procedures and missed timetables quickly came to define the Greek approach to its obligations under the Stability and Growth Pact. Theoretically, the preparation and assessment of the Stability and Growth Programmes formed the core of the preventive work under the Pact; theoretically, the programmes would anchor the expectations of the markets and all participants in the euro area. In reality, however, 'no one took the programmes seriously – not even the markets'.[96] With economic surveillance typically exhausted in an *ex-post* assessment of pre-cooked programme targets, all that member states were required to do was present economic policies that *appeared* compatible with the rules of the SGP and the BEPGs.

Obviously, ostrichism would have not reigned supreme if the SGP did not give ample scope for rule-breaking. The idea that the Pact would prove a sufficient deterrent for fiscally lax members was naïve; its ill-fated reform in March 2005, following successful resistance to sanctions by Germany and France, effectively opened a free-for-all. The German and French stance, confirming rationalist-institutionalist assumptions that when 'a decisive player wants to play according to different rules', then 'the rules are not in equilibrium and the 'institution' is fragile'[97], made the Pact, which the two countries had previously championed, unenforceable. As the game proceeds, revealing the 'complexity of the rule structure', there is, in any case, ample scope 'for individual skill or creativity'.[98] The emerging informal norm of defying Excessive Deficit Procedure obligations, mirrored in Ecofin's relaxed approach to closing-down procedures, combined with

95. European Commission, 'Special issue: the impact of the global crisis on competitiveness and current account divergences in the euro area', *Quarterly Report on the Euro Area*, vol. 9, no. 1, 2010, p. 5.

96. Interview 28.

97. K. A. Shepsle, 'Rational choice institutionalism', in S. Binder, R. Rhodes and B. Rockman (eds), *Oxford Handbook of Political Institutions*, Oxford, Oxford University Press, 2006, p. 26.

98. A. Scheingate, 'Rethinking rules: creativity and constraint in the U.S. House of Representatives', in J. Mahoney and K. Thelen (eds), *Explaining Institutional Change: Ambiguity, agency, and power*, Cambridge, Cambridge University Press, 2010, p. 169.

reluctance to engage in effective multilateral budgetary surveillance, meant that some governments did not want to take control over their fiscal policy – or perhaps took too much control, playing up to their electorates.

A second theme emerges: considerable asymmetry of power and authority arose between the Ecofin and the Eurogroup as well as between both these institutions and the Commission which, theoretically, had not been in the original design. In an edifice that was created *ab initio*, those who *took* the power to interpret and re-interpret the rules for others confirmed their own freedom and established important precedents for action. Vis-à-vis a Council of strong member states – some stronger than others – the Commission lacked both the independent power and the legitimacy to employ sanctions effectively against transgressors. The (informally) *revised* rules, which were validated by collective deviant behaviour, combined with the tranquil behaviour of the markets, prompted Greek policy makers to calculate that Greece was not likely to be punished for its excessive deficits. Even when, under the Excessive Deficit Procedure, the country was moved to Article 104(9), one step before paragraph 11, which would require the member state in question to make a non-interest-bearing deposit of an appropriate size with the Community, or risk the European Investment Bank reconsider its lending policy, or having to pay fines of an appropriate size, Greek policy makers assured themselves that 'this would never happen'.[99]

In defending their status, including their ability to unilaterally shape and interpret commonly agreed rules, Eurozone members failed to defend an edifice that depended, for its orderly operation, on fiscal and financial stability. After the Greek misreporting of the EDP data in 2004, for example, the Commission wanted wider powers for Eurostat, including the examination of national figures. EMU governments were reluctant to confer them, turning the issue into whether Eurostat should be made more independent. In the end, Council Regulation 2103/2005[100] strengthened Eurostat's control powers, but in a much weaker version than initially requested. With strict constraints on their exercise – methodological visits were 'exceptional'; member states had no obligation to provide the information requested; the institutional setting was out of Eurostat's scope of action – Eurostat hardly had the authority or the means to enforce stricter adherence.

For better or worse, Eurozone authorities who failed to follow *their own* rules, subscribed to their own version of ostrichism. At Eurogroup and Ecofin meetings, peer *review* of national developments and economic policies often succumbed to peer *pressure*: 'the governments did not carry out the strict peer surveillance of behaviour that was called for by the Pact'.[101] With sanctions

99. Interview 28.

100. 'Council Regulation No 2103/2005 of 12 December 2005 amending Regulation No 3605/93 as regards the quality of statistical data in the context of the excessive deficit procedure', *Official Journal of the European Union*, L 337, 22.12.2005, pp. 1–6.

101. Interview with Jean-Claude Trichet, President of the European Central Bank, *Süddeutsche Zeitung*, 23 July 2011, accessed 25 September 2012, http:///www.bis.org/review/r110725a.pdf

being a no-go area, however, the worst that could happen was harsh criticism of a 'naming and shaming' variety.[102] If any proof was required, Eurozone members knew, since 2006, that the Greek economy 'had been steadily losing ground in terms of competitiveness, and that Greek public finances were deteriorating at an alarming pace'.[103] When he was President of the Eurogroup Finance Ministers, Jean-Claude Juncker wrote of having 'many discussions with the Greek Prime Minister and the Finance Minister' in which he 'repeatedly warned them that their situation was by no means sustainable'. Even when Greece emerged from the EDP, Greece's partners expressed worries 'that the state of Greece's public finances was unsatisfactory'. The Council's opinions on successive updates of the Greek stability programme were indeed 'a matter of record' but so was its inability to institute credible enforcement and compliance mechanisms.

In their theory of gradual institutional change, Mahoney and Thelen make a bold attempt to create a typology of change agents, together with the institutional matrix, including context and institutions, that shapes them. Applied to the operation of EMU, there appears to emerge no perfect fit between particular kinds of actors and modes of change, although one category, the symbionts of the parasitic variety, can flourish 'where expectations about institutional conformity are high, but the actual capacity to enforce those expectations is limited'.[104] In the case of EMU, the actors, somewhat paradoxically, sought 'to preserve the existing institutional rules' but, at the same time, did not 'abide by the institutional rules',[105] a possibility that the theory does not seem to capture. To make sense of this, one must turn again to the ostrichism displayed, this time by Eurozone members.

For years, they acted as if prudent budgetary policies were being followed across the Eurozone, as if greater economic convergence would result from the smooth operation of the single currency. The convenient assumption that Greece would simply embark on an uninterrupted path of fiscal discipline, its history forgotten, was unwarranted. Among EMU institutions, the ECB had warned, back in its 2000 Convergence Report, of potential pitfalls; it could not have calculated, however, and nor could have the Commission, the cost of non-reform. Worse, little attention was paid to Greece's current account deficit, which, by 2009, had become unsustainable; productivity in the economy was negatively affected by 'a number of problems at the institutional level': corruption; the poor quality

102. Successive ministers of finance conceded that Eurozone authorities did not have any other 'weapons' at their disposal.

103. All citations have been taken from J.-C. Juncker, 'The Eurozone enters adulthood' (accessed 28 August 2011). Online. Available: http://www.europesworld.org/NewEnglish/Home_old/Article/tabid/191/ArticleType/ArticleView/ArticleID/21830/language/en-US/Theeurozoneentersadulthood.aspx

104. J. Mahoney and K. Thelen, 'A theory of gradual institutional change', in Mahoney and Thelen, *Explaining Institutional Change: Ambiguity, agency, and power*, p. 24. The mismatch occurs because symbionts rely on institutions that are not of their own making.

105. *Ibid.*, p. 23: these are the two criteria by which Mahoney and Thelen define their typology of actors.

of the legal framework, in particular, the plethora of laws; product and labour market rigidities; the shortcomings of the educational system; and the inadequacy of infrastructures.[106] Structural reforms, supposedly the 'cornerstone' of Greece's strategy for 'real convergence', together with repeated shake-ups of the fiscal policy framework, were presented, year after year, to Greece's Eurozone's partners, the Commission and the Council. The fact that the Greeks were not called on these indicated how multilateral surveillance and supervision worked in practice.

While Mahoney and Thelen engage with the significant fine-tuning that takes place between actors and their environment, their analysis fails to bring into focus the relationship between a weak institutional environment and actors' near-institutionalised belief that the rules, even the formal ones will not be followed. As EMU unfolded and ostrichism prevailed, the two fed off each other, with the actors making the first move in order to weaken their institutional environment. Accepting that both veto-capabilities and discretion-levels in interpretation/enforcement are useful devices for tracking gradual change, it is the 'political relationships' that lie beneath the creation of and support for institutional arrangements that need to be brought into focus.[107]

Politics usurped the domestic level, as well. In the Greek case, actors' systematic non-enforcement of EMU's fiscal framework became, *pace* Mahoney and Thelen, an important source of institutional stability. In line with the ostrich approach, some window-dressing, that is 'auditing', regarding the budget process, did take place: it concerned the legitimacy and regularity of budget expenditure, however, not its control. Equally, although revenue projections were consistently over-optimistic, no correcting measures were ever administered, nor were laws against tax evasion adhered to. Credibility plummeted, together with the accurate recording of Greek government accounts. Eurostat paid a number of methodological visits to Greece – the only member state to have had this honour – but was still 'unable to detect the level of (hidden) interference in the Greek EDP data'.[108] Faced with a 'spoiled' electorate, conditioned by a spoils system which had permeated the entire party system and political class, government policy makers did what they knew best: set targets that would not be met; avoided reform until it was absolutely necessary and then implemented 'measures' in a haphazard and partial way, typically through laws, rules, and instruments that would not be enforced or adhered to. Lacking clear binding norms, the requisite level of commitment and the technical know-how to rationalise the economic-policy formation process was, in fact, the best way to sustain a resistance-to-adjustment model that had survived for thirty years.

106. Bank of Greece, *Annual Report 2009*, Athens, April 2010, p. 28.

107. S. Haggard, 'Institutions and growth in East Asia', *Studies in Comparative International Development*, 2004, vol. 38, no. 4, p. 74.

108. European Commission, 'Report on Greek Government deficit and debt statistics', January 2010, Brussels, COM(2010) 1 final, 8.1.2010, p. 10.

chapter seven | salvation does not come cheap

When the financial crisis that hit the global economy in the summer of 2007 arrived in Europe in 2008, it was assumed that the European economies would weather it well. Although EU real GDP was projected to shrink by approximately 4 per cent in 2009, the 'sharpest contraction in its history', the lessons had apparently been learned: 'large-scale bank runs have been avoided, monetary policy has been eased aggressively, and governments have released substantial fiscal stimulus'.[1] In 2009, there was already talk of an 'orderly exit strategy from expansionary macroeconomic policies' as an 'essential part of crisis resolution'.[2] Creating a co-ordinated crisis-management framework for the *future* was the next logical step. This kind of naïve optimism, overlooked a core feature of the single currency: it was a supranational agreement that had tied its members to a regime of mutual dependence and interconnectedness.

Eurozone governments could not avoid the constraints that came with sharing one currency *ad infinitum*. The recession, 'the most serious worldwide economic recession for many decades',[3] hit Eurozone budget deficits hard, as government overspending was accompanied by a sharp fall in revenue. Debt sustainability came to be questioned, as the markets began to assess growth prospects and reassess national debt ratios. In Greece, for example, gross government debt had reached 115 per cent of GDP in 2009, up from 103 per cent of GDP in 2000, while net external debt had risen to almost 100 per cent of GDP, up from 45 per cent of GDP in 2000.[4] In Ireland and Spain, grave private-sector imbalances were on the verge of wreaking havoc on budgetary finances. By 2008, the EMU framework's failure to bring about a convergence in competitiveness meant that the core Eurozone banking sector was interlocked with the fortunes of the periphery; the significant deviation in inflation averages – below-average inflation in the Eurozone core and higher-than average inflation in the periphery – fostered current account imbalances, which were financed to a very high degree by the core.[5] In an

---

1. European Commission, 'Economic crisis in Europe: causes, consequences, and responses', *European Economy 7*, 2009, p. 1.

2. *Ibid.*, p. 2.

3. A. Afonso, M. G. Attinasi, J. Catz, C. Checherita, C. Nickel, N. Leiner-Killinger, H. Maurer, Ph. Rother, M. Slavik, M. Trabandt, V. Valenta, A. van Riet, Th. Warmedinger, 'Euro area fiscal policies and the crisis', *ECB Occasional Paper Series No 109*, April 2010.

4. European Commission, 'The economic adjustment programme for Greece', *European Economy: Occasional Papers 61*, May 2010, p. 6.

5. R. Baldwin and D. Gros, 'Introduction: the euro in crisis – what to do?', in R. Baldwin, D. Gros and L. Laeven (eds), *Completing the Eurozone Rescue: What more needs to be done?* A Vox. EUorg Publication, Centre for Economic Policy Research, 2010.

extended period of unusually low interest rates and large global imbalances, poor regulatory frameworks meant that Eurozone banking systems, in both the core and the periphery, were excessively leveraged.

When movements in Greece's interest-rate spreads started to raise serious questions about its access to the markets, the Eurozone authorities assumed that this was a 'Greek crisis', to be contained within Greek borders. The limitations of the Eurozone's crisis-management strategy were soon exposed, including its purely reactive approach to market pressures – which further worsened the borrowing position of the weaker economies, as well as insufficient mechanisms of supervision and control.

This chapter analyses the conditions set for Greece's €110 billion stability package from the European Commission, the European Central Bank and the International Monetary Fund, unprecedented in financial history. The so-called 'economic adjustment programme of Greece', which Greece was called to implement in return, was certainly more than an 'external constraint'; it was a 'straitjacket', which raised the question of whether the country would be able to 'wear' it to the end.

A wake-up call

The global crisis was finally hitting home. Greek policy makers were certainly not the only ones trying to figure out how it would play out in the domestic economy. While international organisations and members of the Eurozone were constantly revising their macroeconomic projections downward, in September 2008, a very public warning by credit-rating agencies Standard & Poor's and Fitch was dismissed: Greece's credit rating was at stake, unless it succeeded in containing its public spending and reducing its public debt.[6] Domestic politics ruled, as a slim governmental majority kept interfering with government policy makers' room for maneuver: at the Ministry of Finance and the Prime Minister's office, the prevalent view was that 'to conduct economic policy, you must have left elections behind and must be able to tell the truth to the people'.[7]

While none of these two 'conditions' applied, the fiscal consolidation that had been theoretically achieved was far from sustainable. In the October 2008 EDP notification, subsequently validated by Eurostat,[8] the general government

6. B. Manessiotis, 'The root-causes of the Greek sovereign debt crisis', paper presented at the 2nd Bank of Greece workshop on the economies of Eastern European and Mediterranean Countries, Athens, May 2011, p. 20.

7. Interview 29.

8. Eurostat withdrew the reservation on the data reported by Greece in the April 2008 notification. *See* Eurostat News Release No 54/2008 of 18 April 2008 on the provision of data for the Excessive Deficit Procedure. Issues clarified since April 2008 concerned the recording of EU grants (in 2006 and 2007), statistical discrepancies (for 2007 data) and the coverage of source data for extra-budgetary funds, local government and social security funds. *See* European Commission, 'Eurostat news release, No 147', 22 October 2008.

deficit in 2006 was revised upwards to 2.6 per cent of GDP; it had reached 3.5 per cent in 2007, thus exceeding the 3 per cent reference value. The Commission adopted, on 18 February 2009, a report under Article 104(3), which initiated the EDP: the 2007 deficit and gross debt figures provided, at 3.5 per cent and 94.8 per cent respectively, *prima facie* evidence of the existence of an excessive deficit in Greece. Based on the 2005 amendments to the SGP, the Commission took into consideration the economic and budgetary background yet concluded that 'the excess over the reference value is neither exceptional nor temporary';[9] equally, high deficit levels, projected weak nominal GDP growth and positive and large stock-flow adjustments all suggested that the debt ratio could not be considered as 'sufficiently diminishing and approaching the reference value at a satisfactory pace'.[10] The Commission addressed its opinion to the Council that an excessive deficit existed in Greece on 24 March 2009, according to Article 104(5);[11] the Council would decide accordingly, in conformity with Article 104(6). The Commission also submitted a proposal for a 'Council recommendation' to be addressed to Greece, with a view to bringing the situation of an excessive deficit to an end according to Article 104(7). The Council concluded in April 27 that an excessive deficit existed in Greece.[12]

The extent to which Greece's fiscal deterioration could affect its standing in the markets was missed by the economic policy elite. This was understandable, given that 'market discipline' had been largely absent until the onset of the sub-prime crisis in the summer of 2007. During 2001–7, the prevalent mood of too-low risk premiums and too little differentiation meant that the spreads (yield differences between 10-year Greek and German government bonds) were on average 27 basis points (b.p.). In 2008, they increased from 40 b.p. in February to approximately 100 b.p. in October yet no one in the government thought of sounding the alarm.[13]

Policy makers' relaxed attitude began to raise a few eyebrows when Jean Claude Trichet, then President of the ECB, warned Greece, Italy and other Eurozone countries in March that widening spreads were a 'wake-up call' for policy makers, who had to 'be very cautious as regards fiscal policies'.[14] But if the continuous worsening of fiscal data in Greece was anything to go by, the call was not picked up. By the end of the year, revenue shortfall was in the 1.3

9. Commission of the European Communities, 'Report from the Commission, Greece: report prepared in accordance with Article 104(3) of the Treaty', SEC 197 final, Brussels, 18 February 2009, p. 5.

10. *Ibid.*, p. 7.

11. Commission of the European Communities, 'Commission Opinion on the existence of an excessive deficit in Greece', SEC (2009) 563 final, Brussels, 24 March 2009, p. 6.

12. 'Council Decision of 27 April 2009 on the existence of an excessive deficit in Greece' (2009/415/EC), *Official Journal of the European Union*, L 135, 30 May 2009, p. 22.

13. *See* N. Georgikopoulos and T. Efthimiadis, 'The development of the Greek-German government bond spreads', accessed 12 June 2011, http://www.europeanbusiness.gr/page.asp?pid=711.

14. G. Dinmore, J. Chung and R. Atkins, 'Trichet warning over bond spreads in Europe', *Financial Times*, March 6, 2008.

per cent of GDP range, while expenditure overruns had reached 1.2 per cent of GDP. In every Eurogroup meeting, the Greek Minister of Finance was bombarded with 'one question: what will you do with the markets?', to which the standard reply was, 'we will accept higher yields but we *will* borrow'.[15] To appease their partners, Greek policy makers would 'go out into the markets every month, the day before and the day of the Eurogroup meetings',[16] so that they could show up to the table with tangible evidence that Greece's market access remained intact. Worries temporarily subsided, as spreads did not follow an upward trend. In fact, from April 2009, the time of the excessive deficit decision, up to August 2009, when the crisis briefly eased, spreads were within the 110–160 b.p. range. It was the calm before the perfect storm.

It's the economy, stupid

In April, Greece was asked to 'strengthen the fiscal adjustment in 2009 through permanent measures, mainly on the expenditure side', a familiar request, if only previous Decisions had been read.[17] However, the implementation of the 2009 budget law, the deficit-reducing measures included in the January 2009 update of the stability programme and the additional set of measures to compensate for the higher-than-expected public deficit in 2008 (estimated at 5 per cent of GDP in the April 2009 EDP notification) that were announced in March fell well short of either the Council's public recommendations or the informal, behind-closed-doors, Eurogroup scolding. While ECB President Jean-Claude Trichet would walk into meetings with a paper showing labour cost trends and while Eurogroup partners suggested that Greece ought to follow the Irish example and proceed with wage reduction, 'the Greek side opted for a wage freeze, as a more politically palatable option'.[18]

The collective mentality of refusing to cut expenses and promoting watered-down measures till further notice, exemplified in the policy 'ostrichism' discussed in the previous chapter, was now deflecting both the country's commitments under the SGP and rising market pressures. Ministers 'could have been a lot stricter in taking measures' but, in the end, they simply were not.[19] The fact that European Parliament elections were scheduled in June did not help with policy resolve either. Once these were over, however, the Greek government announced, on 25 June 2009, an additional set of fiscal measures to be implemented in 2009, in order to 'safeguard' the budgetary implementation towards attaining the target of 3.7 per cent of GDP.[20]

---

15. Interview 29.

16. Interview 29.

17. Council of the European Union, 'Council Decision establishing whether effective action has been taken by Greece in response to the Council Recommendation of 27 April 2009', 15766/09, UEM 303, Brussels, 30 November 2009, p. 6.

18. Interview 29.

19. Interview 29 .

20. European Commission, 'SGP-implementation and follow-up to the Eurogroup in Prague (recent measures in Greece)', ECFIN/F3//ID (2009)/ARES/154115, Brussels, 2 July 2009, p. 2.

Any Minister of Finance would readily admit to his worst nightmare, being the debt bomb detonating on his watch.[21] All the signs were there: spreads rising, stern warnings from the Bank of Greece that the deficit would reach double digits and tougher language from the country's Eurozone partners: the Council had established a deadline of 27 October 2009 for Greece to take effective action to ensure progress along the fiscal-consolidation path. Fazed with the prospect of bearing the political cost associated with the required budgetary correction, Prime Minister Karamanlis decided that the government lacked the necessary legitimation to proceed. This required, in his calculations, a fresh political mandate; a snap general election was called for 4 October. With the year 2010 being a 'difficult and decisive one', the Greek people should 'choose a government that can lead the country out of this crisis'.[22]

Under the leadership of George Papandreou,[23] PASOK, the main opposition party took 43.9 per cent of the vote and won 160 seats in the 300-member parliament. Elected on the promise of a €3 billion stimulus to accelerate recovery – funds that would accrue from curbing tax evasion and increasing the tax burden on the rich – Papandreou pledged above-inflation increases in wages and benefits for public sector workers.[24] This was in line with his main campaign slogan, 'money exists'; after it was aired in the Thessaloniki International Fair, it became a catch-phrase, with a long-lasting, nationwide resonance.

Lies, damned lies, and statistics

Just weeks after his predecessor had announced that instead of the targeted 3.5 per cent the budget deficit would climb to approximately 6 per cent, new Finance Minister George Papakonstantinou revealed in Parliament, during the government's programmatic statements, that the deficit would actually be double the percentage projected. What would probably be the highest budget deficit in the Eurozone in 2009 did not constitute real news for the domestic policy elite: George Provopoulos, Governor of the Central Bank, had warned both contenders about the dire fiscal situation back in September. Right after the election, he visited the Ministry of Finance, where he publicly announced, hoping that he would set alarm bells ringing, that it would surpass 12 per cent.[25] Nothing much happened until two weeks later, when Papakonstantinou went to Brussels with the revised figure; once he announced that the budget deficit would hit 12.7 per cent of GDP, the news made international headlines and the true consequences of its size began to register.

---

21. Interview with the Minister of National Economy.
22. 'Greece PM confirms election date, 3 September 2009', *BBC News*, (accessed 12 August 2012) Online. Available: http://news.bbc.co.uk/2/hi/europe/8234843.stm.
23. *See* Appendix A. Bibliographical Data.
24. 'An emphatic win: George Papandreou's PASOK is victorious in Greece's election', *The Economist*, 5 October 2009.
25. Interview 33.

Initially, Eurozone members froze. Then they were overcome by 'a feeling of frustration': the revision was hyperbolic even by Greek standards; 'guilt also set in, as they had failed to monitor the unruly situation, in spite of clear signs over the summer that the previous government was off course'.[26] In spite of the bad news, Papakonstantinou proceeded to express his government's resolve to make a financial injection into the economy, which would be equivalent to 1 per cent of GDP. His partners' scepticism – how can you do that with this deficit? – was quieted when he promised, following a request by the Commission, that he would draw up a programme for the consolidation of the Greek economy. This would bring the budget deficit back to a single-digit number by 2010. In his first news conference following the meeting, he publicly stated that 'I told the Eurozone Finance Ministers' meeting that our measures to boost demand in order to stimulate economic recovery are non-negotiable'.[27]

Papakonstantinou's revision of the deficit figure, motivated by an intention not to whitewash the issue, proved particularly controversial. For one, it seemed like a poorly-thought-out repetition of the 2004 fiscal audit, even if the methodological issues under consideration were somewhat different. In fact, Eurostat went as far as to draw a public parallel between the 2004 and 2009 episodes: 'In both cases, in the aftermath of political elections, substantial revisions took place revealing a practice of widespread misreporting, in an environment in which checks and balances appear absent, information opaque and distorted, and institutions weak and poorly coordinated'.[28] Worse, it inflicted a nearly fatal blow to Greece's credibility, as a sense of 'here we go again' prevailed. If the 2004 fiscal audit had failed to teach a lesson or two and if, following five Eurostat reservations on the quality of data between 2005 and 2009, the same problem arose, how could the Greeks ever be trusted to report sound data? The revision irked Greece's partners, it irked Eurozone authorities and, more importantly, it attracted the attention of credit-rating agencies, with Fitch Ratings cutting the country's rating from A to A- two days later.

The damage to the Commission's standing was huge as well. It was severely criticised for not upholding its supervisory role under the EDP, accused of failing to do its job. The Commission retorted that it lacked the necessary tools, as Eurostat had no audit powers and had to accept national data as they were provided by the member states. In fact, when the Commission had asked for more powers[29] after

---

26. Interview 34.

27. 'Statement of George Papakonstantinou', cited in D. Yannopoulos, 'Mammoth deficit stuns EU', *Athens News*, 24 October 2009.

28. European Commission, 'Report on Greek government deficit and debt statistics', COM 1 final, January 2010, p. 20.

29. Following the 2004 inventory and the Council's request to strengthen the monitoring of the quality of the reported fiscal data, in 2005 the Commission proposed amendments to the legislation in force, i.e. Council Regulation (EC) No 3605/93, governing the quality of EDP data. The amendments in the Commission's proposal of 2005[3] sought to increase the transparency of the EDP-related statistics and, to that end, to strengthen the powers of Eurostat with respect to

the 'Greek case' in 2004, this request was flatly turned down by Germany and France. In addition, in July 2009, Joaquín Almunia, then the EU's monetary affairs commissioner, circulated a memorandum among European Finance Ministers, predicting that 'should these trends continue [budget implementation deviating significantly from the annual targets] over the year the central government deficit would exceed 10 per cent of GDP, which contrasts with the official annual target for the central government deficit of 5 per cent of GDP'.[30] Hence, Eurogroup members were well aware of Greek developments and were 'hardly innocent of the blood'.[31]

When the 27 October deadline was up, the Council concluded, as was widely expected, that Greece had not taken effective action in response to the Council Recommendation of 27 April 2009. Allowing for the adverse macroeconomic conditions, the significant deterioration in Greece's budgetary position in 2009 was mainly due to 'an insufficient response by the Greek authorities to the Council recommendation according to Article 104(7) of the Treaty of 27 April 2009'. The 2009 budget execution pointed, in fact, to sizeable expenditure overruns in 2009, of which more than half were channelled to higher-than-budgeted outlays for the compensation of employees and to increased capital spending. Most of the additional deficit-reducing measures announced in June 2009 had not been implemented. Worse, the large projected increase in the debt-to-GDP ratio resulted from insufficient efforts to control factors other than net borrowing, which contributed to the change in debt levels.[32] It was, effectively, yet another instance of 'the political system not standing up to vested interests'.[33]

Old habits are hard to break

Under increased pressure, in November, in its 2010 final budget draft, the Greek government pledged, to cut the deficit to 9.4 per cent of GDP in 2010. When the budget was debated in Parliament a few days later, Papakonstantinou spoke of a '*tour de force*': the government would stick to its pre-election pledge and,

---

data quality. However, the additional tools provided to the Commission by the Council Regulation (EC) No 2103/2005[4] were more limited than initially requested. In particular, there is no general obligation for member states to provide the Commission (Eurostat) with access to all the information requested for the purposes of the data-quality assessment and the scope of the methodological visits (only conducted in one member state since the adoption of the legislation) is confined to the purely statistical domain. *See* European Commission, 'Proposal for a Council Regulation (EU) No […]/[….] amending Regulation (EC) No 479/2009 as regards the quality of statistical data in the context of the excessive deficit procedure', COM(2010)53 final, 2010/0035 (NLE), Brussels, 15 February 2010.

30. European Commission, 'SGP-implementation and follow-up to the Eurogroup in Prague', p. 4.

31. Interview 34.

32. Commission of the European Communities, 'Recommendation for a Council Decision establishing whether effective action has been taken by Greece in response to the Council recommendation of 27 April 2009', SEC(2009) 1549 final, Brussels, 11 November 2009, p. 12.

33. Interview 35.

despite 'the unseen before fiscal derailment' of the previous ND government, provide €1 billion in the form of a contingent social-solidarity benefit.[34] There were also measures to raise pay and pensions above the rate of inflation, raise the unemployment benefit so that it would gradually reach 70 per cent of the basic salary, raise farmers' pensions by €30 from 1 October 2009 and an additional €20 from 1 July 2010, and hire 3,000 extra nurses in the National Health System.[35] Not persuaded, Fitch moved, on December 8, to cut Greece's credit-rating from A- to BBB+ with a negative outlook; this was the first time in ten years that Greece had fallen below the A investment grade. Almost a week later, on December 16, S&P cut Greece's rating to BBB+ from A-. Moody's followed suit, cutting Greek debt to A2 from A1 on December 22.

As the rain poured, the government had to become more ambitious. In the eagerly awaited Updated Stability and Growth Programme 2010–2013, presented on 15 January 2010, it promised to cut its budget by 4 percentage points to 8.7 per cent of GDP at the end of 2010.[36] In addition to addressing the double challenge of consolidating the country's fiscal position and securing the conditions for economic development, there was public mention of a third challenge: addressing the 'credibility deficit' that had been generated from large revisions in deficit figures and failed attempts at fiscal consolidation. Institutional reform would 'restore credibility in data, the budgeting process and the operation of the public sector more generally'.[37] A 'new growth paradigm', which would abandon 'the previous reliance on consumption as the driver of growth', was eerily reminiscent of another paradigm shift that had been announced in December 2005.[38]

The European Commission would have preferred to have seen greater resolve but the Greek government reassured it that 'this time, the cuts would have duration'.[39] Admitting that it was placed on a 'watch list', the government could still determine the country's political course, not bowing to threats of punishment.[40] Investor confidence plummeted, as the announced major overhaul of the tax system was referred to a process of social consultation, with a new law scheduled to come to Parliament in March. This seemed like a re-emergence of

34. Statement by G. Papakonstantinou in G. Bourdaras, 'G. Papakonstantinou: The 2010 budget is the toughest budget since the return to democracy due to fiscal derailment', *Kathimerini*, 8 December 2009 (accessed 5 August 2011) Online. Available: http://news.kathimerini.gr/4dcgi/_w_articles_economy_18_08/12/2009_382320 [in Greek].

35. Ministry of Finance, *Draft Budget 2010*, 5 November 2009.

36. Ministry of Finance, 'Update of the Hellenic Stability and Growth Programme including an Updated Reform Programme', Athens, January 2010, p. 21.

37. *Ibid.*, p. 4.

38. *See* discussion in Chapter Six.

39. Interview 34.

40. Interview with George Papakonstantinou, *Der Spiegel*, 14 December 2009 (accessed 12 August 2012) Online. Available: http://www.gpapak.gr/enimerosi/media/interviews/sinentefxi-g-papakonstantinou-sto-periodiko-per centE2per cent80per cent9Cder-spiegelper centE2per cent80per cent9D/.

the old practice of procrastinating as a way to avoid adopting politically costly reforms. Pushed for a more immediate and visible change of tune, the government announced, on February 9, a new policy package for the public sector. This included a wage freeze in the salaries of all government employees and a 10 per cent cut in allowances – from these cuts 'the performance incentive allowance', to which *all* public employees were, ironically, entitled, was exempted. Nevertheless, ADEDY, the civil servants' union, went on strike the next day.

There is no plan B

The more Greek policy makers talked about restoring the country's credibility, the more its lack of credibility raised the yield on 10-year government bonds. Papandreou asserted that the markets' 'vote of confidence' was evident in the January auction of Greek debt, which was five times over-subscribed, even if the spread between Greek bonds and German Bunds rose to a record of more than 300 basis points. Strongly denying newspaper reports that he was drawing up plans to bail out the Greek government, Papandreou publicly stated, on the fringes of the World Economic Forum in Davos: 'We need no bilateral loans. We haven't asked for any and don't need any'.[41] Not persuaded by the Greek government's endeavours, the Commission made an unprecedented move. It adopted an Opinion on the Greek Stability Programme for 2010–13, a Recommendation to give notice, under Article 126(9) of the Treaty, regarding the correction of the excessive deficit and a Recommendation under Article 121(4) of the Treaty on structural reforms. It also launched, following the significant revision of data in October 2008, an infringement procedure to ensure that Greek authorities complied with their duty to report reliable budgetary statistics. This would be 'the first time that the budgetary and economic surveillance instruments foreseen in the Treaty are used simultaneously and in an integrated way'.[42]

Public finger-pointing, however, may have had an unwelcome effect. A week later on 11 February, as spreads began to rise in the periphery, an *informal* meeting of heads of state gave out a very formal message: the 'Euro area member states will take determined and coordinated action, if needed, to safeguard financial stability in the euro area as a whole'. This was the first time that the notion of 'shared responsibility' came to the fore, with members expected to conduct 'sound national policies in line with the agreed rules'. Another novelty was mention of the IMF: 'The Commission will closely monitor the implementation of the recommendations [Commission Recommendation for a Council Opinion on the updated stability programme of Greece, 2010–2013] in liaison with the ECB and

41. C. Giles and R. Elgar, 'Greek PM denies reports of EU bail-out', *Financial Times*, 28 January 2010.

42. 'Commission assesses Stability Programme of Greece; makes recommendations to correct the excessive budget deficit, improve competitiveness through structural reforms and provide reliable statistics', IP/10/116, Brussels 3 February 2010, accessed 7 July 2011, http://europa.eu/rapid/press-release_IP-10–116_en.htm.

will propose needed additional measures, drawing on the expertise of the IMF'. The statement concluded with the declaration that 'the Greek government has not requested any financial support'.[43] For his part, Prime Minister Papandreou asserted that 'Greece never asked for help', adding that 'it will not be needing help in the future'.[44] Only a few days later, his Finance Minister said, 'we are basically trying to change the course of the Titanic'. He hastened to add, 'people think we are in a terrible mess. And we are.' Following the Minister's comments, the yield on Greece's two-year bond rose to 5.230 per cent, compared with 5.1547 per cent three days earlier.[45]

The issue of IMF involvement was, in fact, indicative of how Eurozone authorities approached the 'Greek problem'. Back in November, the Ministry of Finance had asked the Fund for technical assistance. There was no real system for budget control save for an arrangement of crude haggling, whereby line ministers regularly proceeded to authorise off-budget expenses that subsequently had to be paid for by the Finance Ministry.[46] As a rule, ministries would simply add items to their respective budgets, without ever examining the rationale or expected result of each expense; while items were never evaluated *ab initio*, Ministers expected that the requested funds would be granted automatically. The logic that prevailed was 'I want that much, where can I find it?' rather than 'this is how much I have got to spend, how I can spend it?'.[47] On top of this haphazard multi-polar power system, the budget lacked the requisite infrastructure to begin with: it incorporated 14,000 input line-items but made no use of output or performance information.[48] Following the 2009 deficit announcement, sorting out this mess required a colossal restructuring that the Greek public administration could not undertake on its own.

Prime Minister Papandreou was also in search of an ally. He could not persuade his European partners that a collective European response would calm the markets. They were in political denial: 'There is no bail out, there is no money, just do your job'.[49] In public, German Chancellor Angela Merkel declared: 'We have a treaty under which there is no possibility of paying to bail out states in difficulty'; 'Right now we can help Greece by stating clearly that it has to fulfil its duties'.[50] The Commission and the Eurogroup concurred; implementation of the

43. 'Statement by the Heads of State or Government of the European Union', Brussels 11 February 2010, accessed 12 February 2012, http://www.consilium.europa.eu/uedocs/cms_data/docs/pressdata/en/ec/112856.pdf.

44. St-M. Ishmael, 'Quote du jour, Greek machismo edition', *Financial Times*, 11 February, 2010.

45. S. Bodoni and E. Ross-Thomas, 'Europe economy chief calls for more steps by Greece (Update5)', *Bloomberg*, 15 February 2010. Papakonstantinou subsequently opined in a number of media outlets that his statement had no repercussions on the markets.

46. Interview 34; *see also* discussion in Chapter Six.

47. Interview 29.

48. I. Hawkesworth, D. Bergvall, R. Emery and J. Wehner, 'Budgeting in Greece', *OECD Journal on Budgeting*, 2008, vol. 8, no. 3, p. 13.

49. Interview 34.

50. 'Merkel in talks on crisis plan for Greece: reports', 3 March 2010 (accessed 5 August 2012).

measures would prove sufficient. Whenever the Greek side pressed the Eurogroup to come up with a plan B, 'the standard answer was 'there is no plan B".[51] A frustrated Papandreou thought, therefore, that he could use his ongoing dialogue with IMF officials as a 'counterweight', a strategy that was not risk-free. In some Greek political quarters, the IMF was considered 'the devil':[52] an enduring vein of anti-Americanism in Greek politics was a potentially disruptive force in building up a consensus around IMF aid. There were also serious doubts as to whether the IMF possessed the required rescue funds or, even if it did, whether they could be channelled to a Eurozone country; this would have probably required the formal consent of the Eurozone members sitting on its Board of Governors.

It should not have come as a surprise that the markets refused to buy Greece's Updated Stability Programme. In its formal opinion, the Council deemed that the risks in the implementation of the revised 2010 budgetary target of 8.7 per cent of GDP were large, 'especially when taking into account that the expected gains from the fight against tax evasion are optimistic'. In addition, budgetary consolidation for the years 2011 to 2013 was 'not fully backed with concrete measures'. The lack of a 'medium-term budgetary framework for a time-consistent fiscal planning' contributed to the 'poor record in terms of budgetary outcomes'. Deviation from targets – a major culprit in Greece's 'credibility deficit' – resulted from 'the scant centralisation of the budgetary process, a weak monitoring of public expenditure, and lack of accountability at the level of line ministries'. Upbeat revenue projections that were never realised in practice and structural and endemic problems related to the recording of Greek government accounts completed the picture.[53]

In a *déjà vu* move, which spoke volumes about the 'history' of EDP application, the Council decided to 'give notice' to Greece, according to Article 126(9) of the Treaty on the Functioning of the European Union (TFEU),[54] to take, within a specified time limit, measures for deficit reduction. This was the second time that the Council had made this decision; the first was on 17 February 2005, in accordance with then Article 104(9) of the Treaty Establishing the European Community. Greece was expected to submit a report by 16 March 2010, spelling out the measures that would achieve the 2010 budgetary targets, together with a calendar for implementation. It also had to submit, to the Council and the Commission, 'a report outlining the policy measures to comply with this Decision' by 15 May 2010 at the latest. Article 2 included a detailed description of the measures that Greece had to adopt.[55]

Online. Available: http://www.eubusiness.com/news-eu/greece-Eurozone.3fx.

51. Interview 34.

52. Interview 34.

53. Council of the European Union, 'Council Opinion on the Updated Stability Programme of Greece', 6560/10, UEM 49, Brussels, 16 February 2010.

54. *See* discussion in Chapter Six.

55. 'Council Decision of 16 February 2010 giving notice to Greece to take measures for the deficit reduction judged necessary in order to remedy the situation of excessive deficit' (2010/182/EU), *Official Journal of the European Union*, L 83, 16 February 2010.

Let's keep it in the family

The Greek government adopted a package of additional measures on 3 March; Papandreou finally faced up to the fact that he had to abandon the government's 'domestic' credibility and take back the promises to deliver wage increases, higher social spending and huge public investment in green development. 'External' credibility could no longer be ignored.[56] The measures that were put forward were unheard of – in terms of their 'permanent' character and their reach to the expenditure side of the budget – but were expected to contribute 2 per cent of GDP to the consolidation effort. Law 3833/2010, tabled in Parliament in accordance with the emergency procedure foreseen in the Greek Constitution,[57] was to be followed by a number of structural interventions, which would include a new law on the reform of the tax system, the implementation of tax-collection mechanisms and a fight against tax evasion.

On the day, the ECB Governing Council released a statement in which the additional fiscal measures were described as 'convincing'. Cutting public expenditure and adjusting public sector wages – a long-contested item in every interaction between Greece and Eurozone authorities – was 'a key signal both for the long-term fiscal sustainability and for substantially enhancing the price and cost competitiveness of the Greek economy'.[58] Market approval was also evident. Athens managed to sell €5 billion in 10-year bonds in an oversubscribed auction. Even if the coupon interest-rate on the bond was 6.25 per cent, about 2 percentage points more than Portugal's and double the rate paid by Germany, it supposedly 'settled the nerves of investors'.[59] Two days later, GSEE and ADEDY, the two largest unions, orchestrated a massive protest rally in Athens.

The Greek side rested assured that, with new measures announced, it was its partners' turn to bring something to the table. The Eurogroup's mood had certainly changed from 'there is no European solution' to 'we will see about a European solution';[60] financial assistance, however, was not just going to drop into the country's lap. Worse, bringing the IMF to Europe remained politically unpalatable. Every time that Papandreou raised the possibility, the collective response was a flat 'no'. Having realised that rising spreads and aggressive speculators would not simply go away, Papandreou indicated publicly that he preferred a 'European solution'; however, if that was not an option, he could always turn to the IMF as a 'measure of last resort'. Appearing at the European parliament's monetary and

---

56. Interview 36.

57. Law 3833/2010 'Protection of national economy, emergency measures to tackle the financial crisis', *Government Gazette*, No. 40A, 15 March 2010 [in Greek].

58. ECB, 'Statement by the ECB's Governing Council on the additional measures of the Greek government' (accessed 7 August 2012). Online. Available: http://www.ecb.int/press/pr/date/2010/html/pr100303.en.html

59. D. Oakley, K. Hope, and D. Kontogiannis, 'Strong demand for 10-year Greek bond', *Financial Times*, 4 March 2010.

60. Interview 34.

financial committee in Brussels, he reiterated his preference: 'We are part of the Eurozone and I want to show the world Europe can act together in a co-ordinated way'.[61]

'Europe', on the other hand, was not quite sure of how it wanted to act. It simply was 'forced' to act, as the possibility of a Eurozone member defaulting on its debt grew bigger day by day. The government managed to sell €5 billion in seven-year bonds in late March but did so at a high price; the average interest rate exceeded 6 per cent, which was no longer considered sustainable. Still, the Commission, the Council and the Eurogroup were 'extremely reluctant to agree on a financial mechanism to help Greece, as they considered it a bailout. The Germans, in particular, constantly brought up the constitutional hurdles they would face; they believed that, if created, this mechanism should be *ultima ratio*'.[62] The Eurogroup, the Commission and Greece, all realised that 'nothing could proceed until Germany said yes'.[63] Angela Merkel, the German Chancellor, did not want to make any moves until after 10 May, when she faced a key regional election in North Rhine-Westphalia; seen to be bowing to a fiscally irresponsible member state would hurt her politically. Greece, however, had to re-finance €8.5 billion in bonds that matured on May 19. If it failed to raise the funds in the markets, this *de facto* default would have probably blown the Chancellor's career and government away. Worse, default would have triggered, in the absence of a safety net, incalculable consequences for the Eurozone and for Germany's banks.

To present an agreement that would be considered credible by the markets, Greece, the Commission and the Eurogroup began with 19 May as the final deadline and counted the time backwards: 'how much earlier should an agreement have been reached? When should the Summit approve this plan? How should a disbursement take place? What sort of programme should be implemented and when should the starting date be? When should negotiations for such a programme start?'.[64] The 'agreement' reached at the Spring European Council (25–6 March) had all the same trappings of the compromise that had preceded it. For one, while the head of the IMF had declared that 'the Eurozone wants to deal with the problem itself, and I can understand that',[65] within two weeks' the IMF was actually brought in on the deal. Chancellor Merkel made a full U-turn, as she now made clear that the condition for aid *was* IMF involvement. In her interpretation, the Commission's handling of Greece was, in any case, useless; it had failed either to control or prevent the Greek crisis. At least, 'the IMF, had the respect of the markets, having conducted and implemented tens of bail-outs. The 'men in black'

61. K. Hope and D. Oakley, 'Papandreou prefers European solution over fund', *Financial Times*, March 19 2010.

62. Interview 35.

63. Interview 34.

64. Interview 34.

65. Statement by IMF Managing Director Dominique Strauss-Kahn in G. Wearden, 'Greece will come through crisis without bailout, IMF head says', *The Guardian*, March 8 2010.

should be brought in, as they outshone Eurozone authorities in credibility and expertise'.[66] The ECB, whose opposition to any IMF involvement had been the most vocal, quieted down.

Commissioner Barroso announced that 'we have solved this in the European family, in the euro area'. This was 'the European coordinated approach with the participation of the IMF'.[67] Given the 'exceptional problem' that had arisen, both the triggering of the mechanism and the implementation of conditionality were to be carried out by EU institutions. IMF expertise had come in useful, both in setting up the mechanism and in organising member contributions; IMF financial support would now 'come in full respect of euro area mechanisms'.[68] Careful to distinguish between 'substantial' IMF financing and 'a majority' of European financing, euro area member states appeared ready to contribute to co-ordinated bilateral loans; these were deemed compatible with the 'no-bail-out clause' – but their activation was not deemed pressing or immediate.

The 'European family', however, had a major political hurdle to overcome: Eurozone members had to sell the rescue package to their respective electorates and pass it through their parliaments. This was no easy task. Legally, the Treaty, which lacked a bail-out mechanism, featured a 'no-bail-out' clause (Article 125 TFEU). Politically, Eurozone members wanted to see proof that Greece would or could actually implement the adjustment measures that it had agreed to. They also wanted to be reassured that the Commission and the Greek government would finally settle the issue of Greek statistics; the government had already tabled a law for the institutional and operational independence of the National Statistical Service, thereafter named Hellenic Statistical Authority.

The Greeks were not going to be given a free ride. The agreed mechanism was considered '*ultima ratio*', to be used only if 'market financing was insufficient'. Disbursement would be decided 'by unanimity, subject to strong conditionality, and based on an assessment by the European Commission and the European Central Bank'. Euro member states were expected to participate on the basis of their respective ECB capital key. Financing would not be provided at average euro area interest rates; the aim was to set incentives 'to return to the markets as soon as possible by risk-adequate pricing'. Interest rates would be non-concessional, lacking any 'subsidy element'.[69] The text, agreed by an extraordinary meeting of the leaders of the 16 EU Eurozone member countries, came with no figures. If the 'punishment' undertones were left aside, this was definitely a first step towards a crisis-resolution mechanism. Would all the next steps resemble this one and how effective and credible could a mechanism built on such a 'reaction-reflex' principle be?

---

66. Interview 34.

67. José Manuel Durão Barroso, President of the European Commission, 'Statement at the press conference following the first day of the Spring European Council Brussels', SPEECH/10/132, Brussels, 25 March 2010.

68. *Ibid.*

69. 'Statement by the Heads of State and Government of the Euro Area', Brussels, 25 March 2010.

A cry for help

In a verbatim repetition of the 11 February statement, the 25 March Council Statement declared: 'The Greek government has not requested any financial support.' This triggered the opposite effect from the one that Eurozone authorities had hoped for, in that Fitch Ratings then downgraded Greece to BBB-, the lowest possible investment grade. The downgrade reflected 'the intensification of fiscal challenges in response to more adverse prospects for economic growth and increased interest costs', as well as 'the ongoing uncertainties about the government's financing strategy in the context of increased capital market volatility'.[70] The absence of a price tag on the promise of EU support evidently failed to reassure the markets. Directly questioning Eurozone authorities' resolve, Fitch asserted that 'the lack of clarity regarding the mechanism for timely external financial support may have hindered Greece's access to market finance at affordable cost and hence further undermined confidence in the capacity of the government to meet its fiscal targets'.[71] The US Treasury Secretary, who called his Greek counterpart three times a week, was astounded by the fact that 'Eurozone authorities could not draw the parallels between 'Lehman' and 'Greece'. Markets would not stop pushing and testing the country's and Eurozone's endurance; the only method that worked was the big bazooka, putting money on the table'.[72] On the day of the downgrade, the spread between 10-year Greek and German bonds widened by over 10 basis points, to 412.

Euro area members were left with few options and finally got the message. Seeking to safeguard 'financial stability in the Euro area as a whole',[73] they agreed, on 11 April, on the terms of the financial support and the 'method' that would be followed. Bilateral loans would be centrally pooled by the European Commission as part of a package that included International Monetary Fund financing; the latter stood ready to join in the effort, 'including through a multi-year stand-by arrangement, to the extent needed and requested by the Greek authorities'.[74] In the joint programme, covering a three-year period, the euro area member states would contribute, in the first year, up to €30 billion, with a further €10 billion coming from the IMF; support for the following years would be decided upon agreement with the programme's provisions. The choice of bilateral loans caused major

---

70. 'Fitch downgrades Greece to "BBB-"; outlook negative', 9 April 2010 (accessed 1 September 2012) . Online. Available: http://www.fitchratings.com/creditdesk/press_releases/detail.cfm?pr_id=565836&origin=home.

71. *Ibid.*

72. Interview 34.

73. 'Statement on the support to Greece by Euro area Member States', Brussels, 11 April 2010 (accessed 1 September 2011). Online. Available: http://www.Eurozone.europa.eu/media/596698/statement_on_support_to_greece_11_april_2010.pdf. The details of the agreement presented in this section are based on this statement.

74. 'Statement by IMF Managing Director Dominique Strauss-Kahn on Greece', press release No. 10/143, April 11 2010.

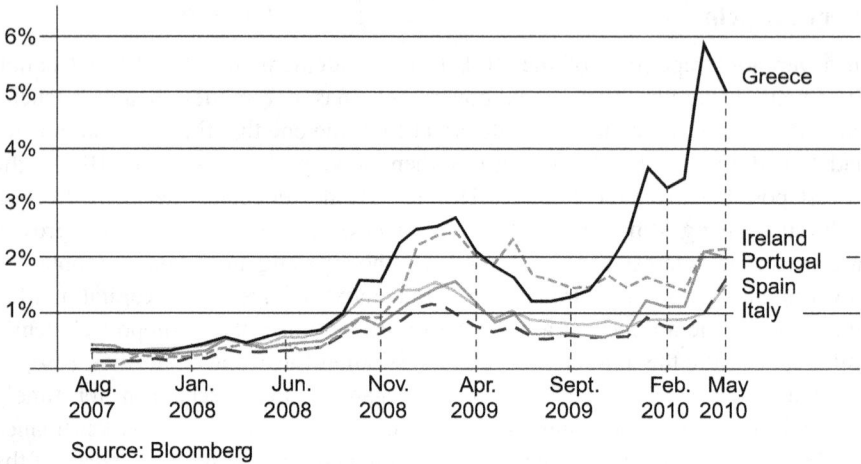

*Figure 7.1: Greece and PIIGS, 10-year sovereign bond spreads over German,
August 2007–May 2010*

friction between the Commission and the Eurogroup and was hardly welcomed by
Greece. The Commission was not in favour of an intergovernmental mechanism;
it preferred that its operation stuck to the 'Community method'. Weakened and
badly discredited by the Greek crisis, however, it had to bow to the complete and
unwavering opposition of the Germans, Dutch and Finns.[75]

The decision to activate support rested with the euro area members, while
disbursements would be decided by participating member states. Loans would be
granted on non-concessional interest rates as an incentive 'for Greece to return
to market financing'.[76] To set loan conditions, authorities agreed upon the IMF
pricing formula, albeit with some adjustments. Variable-rate loans would be
based on three-month Euribor[77], while fixed-rate loans would be based upon the
rates corresponding to Euribor swap rates for the relevant maturities. A charge of
300 basis points would be applied. A further 100 basis points would be charged
for amounts outstanding for more than three years. In conformity with IMF
charges, a one-off service fee of maximum 50 basis points would be charged to
cover operational costs. This last issue caused a battle of epic proportions during
negotiations. Greece and most of the other Eurozone members protested that this
charge should not be acceptable in the context of the 'European family'. Germany,
however, threatened that, without the charge, there would be no loan. Minister
of Finance Wolfgang Schäuble even asserted that he had already made the
announcement in the Bundestag; this charge was, in fact, one of the main reasons
for which the mechanism had been approved.[78]

---

75. Interview 34.

76. Eurogroup, 'Statement on the support to Greece by Euro area Member States'.

77. Euro Interbank Offered Rate, the rate at which euro interbank term deposits are being offered by
    one prime bank to another within the EMU zone.

78. Interview 34.

If the final agreement showed that 'responsibility and solidarity can go together',[79] it could certainly be argued that solidarity did not come cheap. A simple calculation raised the interest rate to around 5 per cent. The punishing conditions and tough language, however, were supposed to help Germany and, to a lesser extent, the Netherlands and Finland, sell the unprecedented financial support package to their Parliaments. Based on the Ecofin Council February recommendations, the Commission, in liaison with the ECB and the IMF would immediately start negotiations with the Greek authorities on a joint programme. The exact financing needs and the conditions attached to assistance were to be determined. Figure 7.1 shows the ten-year sovereign bond spreads of Greece (and those of the other PIIGS) over Germany. Within three years, Greece had gone from borrowing with rates comparable to those of Germany to losing access to the markets.

'Too little, too late'

While rescue talks were underway, the yield on 10-year Greek bonds rose to 8.28 per cent. The markets were, once more, questioning the novel process that was underway. George Provopoulos, Governor of the Bank of Greece, rushed to explain: 'Markets see the figures as bad [...] that borrowing costs will be again high in the coming years [...]. They estimate the debt will tend to increase instead of coming under control'.[80] When the April EDP notification figures were released, two days later, Greece's 2009 budget deficit rose to 13.6 per cent of GDP, the second highest after Ireland's. This was the final straw, subsequently described as a 'shock' by both the Minister of Finance and the head of the Public Debt Management Agency.[81] Greece's continued adherence to the Stability and Growth Programme would now be more aggressively contested, particularly as Eurostat left open the possibility of a further revision by 0.3 to 0.5 per cent of GDP.[82] While Moody's downgraded Greece's debt rating to A3,[83] placing it under review for a further downgrade, market movements were delivering a harsh verdict on Greek bond

79. 'Statement by the President of the European Commission on Greece', IP/10/415, Brussels, 11 April 2010.

80. K. Hope, 'Investors show concern as talks begin on Greek rescue package', *Financial Times*, 21 April 2010.

81. The head of the Public Debt Management Agency, Petros Christodoulou, admitted, in his testimony before a parliamentary committee investigating allegations that Greece's 2009 deficit had been deliberately inflated, that he was 'stunned' when, in a period when spreads had appeared to be settling down in April 2010, he found out there would be another upward revision of the 2009 deficit. *See* 'Debt management chief wants testimony released in full', *Athens News*, 14 March 2012 (accessed 15 May 2012). Online. Available: http://www.athensnews.gr/portal/1/54043.

82. Eurostat, 'Provision of deficit and debt data for 2009 – first notification', 55/2010, 22 April 2010 (accessed 12 February 2012) Online. Available: http://epp.eurostat.ec.europa.eu/cache-ITY_PUBLIC/2-22042010-BP/EN/2-22042010-BP-EN.PDF.

83. 'Rating action: Moody's downgrades Greece's sovereign ratings to A3; on review for further possible downgrade' (accessed 15 May 2012) Online. Available: http://www.moodys.com/research/Moodys-downgrades-Greeces-sovereign-ratings-to-A3-on-review-for--PR_198275.

prices, with the yield on a Greek 10-year bond rising to a record 8.92 per cent. With no options left, Papandreou informed his cabinet that he would seek to activate the mechanism: 'We must be honest, Greece is already under the surveillance of the EU and the IMF because of its high deficits and debt, which were created by the criminal policies of previous years'.[84] Formally asking for help was a critical turning point both for the Eurozone and for Greece. The strength of the currency bloc, presented on to the world stage as the most successful example of economic integration, would now come into question. The Greek economy, constituting only 2 per cent of the Eurozone's GDP,[85] was shaking the entire edifice to the core. Greece, on the other hand, was undergoing national humiliation, as it was the first Eurozone country to appeal for emergency Eurozone/IMF loans. The fact that the German Chancellor insisted on Athens presenting 'an absolutely credible savings programme'[86] was a not-so-subtle hint about the country's perceived rule-breaking and weak institutional capacity.[87]

Prime Minister Papandreou officially asked for the activation of the Greek Loan Facility (GLF) , which 'we have jointly created in the EU', in a speech broadcast live to the nation from the remote island of Kastelorizo; it was a matter of 'national and imperative need'. The newly released deficit figures were indicative 'of the inexplicable errors, omissions, criminal choices and the avalanche of problems bestowed by the previous government.'[88] Having inherited 'a ship that is about to sink', 'a country without prestige and credibility', Papandreou said that he hoped that the decision to create the mechanism would 'be enough to calm and bring markets to their senses, thus enabling us to continue to finance our country with lower interest rates'.[89] The markets did not respond, however, 'either because they did not believe in the EU's determination, or because some people decided to go on speculating'.[90] The decision to support Greece would give the country the time 'that the markets do not give us'. Aware that the prospect of external aid would bring with it images of European and IMF tutelage, together with a strict clampdown on policy options, he said that 'our final goal, our final destination is to liberate Greece from supervision, from trusteeship'.[91] Papandreou asked Finance Minister Papakonstantinou to make the formal application, which was a typical letter addressed to Dominic Strauss-Kahn, Jean-Claude Trichet, and Ollie Rhen.

---

84. K. Hope and A. Sakoui, 'Shaky start to Greek aid talks', *Financial Times*, April 23, 2010.

85. Baldwin and Gros, 'Introduction: the Euro in crisis – what to do?', p. 1.

86. T. Barber and K. Hope, 'Greece grasps for €30 bn rescue package', *Financial Times*, 23 April 2010.

87. K. Featherstone, 'The Greek sovereign debt crisis and EMU: a failing state in a skewed regime', *Journal of Common Market Studies* 2011, vol. 49, no. 2, p. 196.

88. 'Prime Minister's Statement', Prime Minister's Office, 23 April 2010 (accessed 1 September 2012). Online. Available: http://www.primeminister.gov.gr/english/2010/04/23/prime-ministers-statement/

89. *Ibid.*

90. *Ibid.*

91. *Ibid.*

Prior to the announcement, Papakonstantinou had made a round of phone calls, as he wanted to make sure that the countries were ready to commit financially – 'this is not working out, we are ready to apply, are you ready?'.[92]

In reality, Eurozone authorities and members had been bluffing. They had hoped that the *making* of the loan facility would be a sufficient incentive for the markets and that it would *not* need to be activated. Once the markets saw the 'loaded gun' on the table, they would be persuaded that the Eurozone authorities would protect their own. The risk of default would get smaller, the credit-rating agencies would temper their pessimistic assessments and the spreads would eventually fall. Now that the facility had to be activated, it required a Eurozone shift, both psychological – surrendering to the inevitable and accepting the markets' verdict – and political – explaining to the creditor countries' tax-payers why they should pick up the bill for rescuing Greece. Papandreou had completed his own political turnaround, 'credited' by the opposition with bringing the IMF to Greece. The bluff was called and the logic had failed; the gun came with 'too little' ammunition and was placed on the table 'too late'.

In a short joint statement, the European Commission, the European Central Bank and the Presidency of the Eurogroup asserted that support would be based on the programme that was being prepared by the Commission, the ECB and the IMF, together with Greek authorities.[93] A few days later, Standard & Poor's downgraded Greece from BBB+ to BB+, effectively questioning the ability of everyone that touched upon the 'Greek problem' to map out a credible path to Eurozone stability. Portugal was downgraded to A-, while, confirming fears of a contagion effect, Spain and Ireland came under severe pressure. With market speculation factoring in a potential restructuring of the Greek debt, the President of the Commission had to declare publicly that 'debt restructuring in an euro area Member State is not an option and is not going to be part of the joint programme'. Moreover, the Commission would 'watch closely the behaviour of financial markets',[94] considering a regulatory framework for credit-rating agencies. In reality, debt-restructuring had indeed been considered in March, when the IMF had completed its first evaluation of the Greek economy; as a policy option, however, it met with the stiff resistance from Eurozone authorities and, in particular, the ECB, which was concerned about its effects on the financial stability of the Eurozone. 'Core' banks also lobbied against it, as their exposure to Greek bonds was calculated then at approximately €76 billion.[95]

---

92. Interview 34.

93. 'Joint statement by European Commission, European Central Bank and Presidency of the Euro-group on Greece', IP/10/446, Brussels 23 April 2010.

94. 'Statement by President Barroso on Greece', MEMO 10/157, Brussels 28 April 2010.

95. Interview 36.

The negotiations

When high-level officials from the Commission, the ECB and the IMF, the troika of creditors, made the rounds of Greek ministries, they worked 'day and night' to formulate a 'multi-annual programme' that would 'reverse the debt spiral of Greece and restore its overall economic competitiveness'.[96] Were there any 'real' negotiations with the Greek authorities however? Greece had its back to the wall. The real problem was 'that for thirty years you were only handing out benefits and privileges; and, all of a sudden, you had to bring the whole edifice down. How could you persuade the troika that you could do that and how could you persuade the Greek people that you would do that? The basic problem was persuasion'.[97]

In the event, the prospect of a Greek default cast an ugly shadow and time was pressing – the government had to tackle sizeable fiscal financing needs by 19 May. To calm the markets, all sides agreed that the fiscal measures should be front-loaded. This was the easy part. Major tensions erupted when it came to determining the time frame. The IMF was more flexible regarding the implementation schedule; the Eurogroup concurred with this view but had no power to persuade the Commission and the ECB, the formal and authoritative parties to the negotiations, that piled on the pressure for shorter deadlines; they were concerned that 'the Germans would otherwise not approve the programme'.[98] No one cracked but there was strain; this was the first time that all the organisations worked together.

The troika and the Greek side worked on the 'standard IMF template: any memorandum would include a section on fiscal policies, one on financial sector policies, and one on structural policies. There was nothing original about the structure of the Memorandum text – you only had to look at the Portuguese that followed – it was merely adjusted to the realities of the country in need of assistance'.[99] Every line was up for discussion, even if the major macroeconomic adjustment that had to be undertaken, especially in the public sector, was not negotiable: the fiscal balance would be reduced from almost 14 per cent of GDP in 2009 to below 3 per cent of GDP in 2014, while the debt ratio would start declining in 2014; the current account balance would fall to around 5.5 per cent of GDP in 2013, while net external debt would start declining in 2013 after peaking at just below 120 per cent of GDP.

Every discussion would begin with 'in the first year you have to reduce the deficit by this much'[100] and continue with an exacting analysis of the Greek side's proposals. Greek authorities, who had never engaged in an exercise of quantifying targets before, had difficulty in persuading the troika that the measures for curbing tax evasion would work or that cutting back on operational costs and closing down public organisations would produce the required deficit reduction. IMF

---

96. 'Statement by Commissioner Rehn on Greece', 29 April 2010, (accessed 5 May 2012). On-line. Available: http://ec.europa.eu/economy_finance/articles/eu_economic_situation/2010–04–29-statement-commissioner-rehn-on-greece_en.htm.

97. Interview 35.

98. Interview 34.

99. Interview 34.

100. Interview 34.

experience from implementation failures in other countries weighed heavily on the troika's responses; measures which took two to four years to produce results were not deemed 'acceptable'. Given the size of the consolidation required, the IMF was in favour of measures that produced a direct impact on the deficit, such as terminating the thirteenth and fourteenth salaries (Christmas, Easter, and holiday bonuses) in the public sector. The ECB and the Commission concurred, even if national sensibilities were ruffled. 'The measures were just too hard for the system to digest, they ran counter to the credo of the Greek system and the Greek society – by accepting them, the PASOK government was self-destructing'.[101]

The most difficult part of the process, which became even more difficult as time progressed, was spelling out, to the country's EU partners and the IMF, a specific amount of aid – the sheer scale and their having to justify it made Greek authorities extremely apprehensive. Another thorny issue was restoring competitiveness; for the troika, this was essentially a labour cost issue whereas for the government it was a structural adjustment issue. The government resisted the reduction of private-sector salaries, suggesting that these would effectively be restrained as a reflection of developments in the public sector as well as by changes in the system of collective bargaining.

Ministers would subsequently admit that they had very little time, only a few hours, to read, understand, evaluate and approve the part of the agreement which concerned their Ministry's commitments for the next three years. Aleka Katseli, then Minister for the Economy, Competitiveness and Shipping, publicly acknowledged that she read it in 'three hours, on a Saturday', while Michalis Chrysohoidis, Citizens' Protection Minister, said that 'it was not his job (to read it)'.[102] On 2 May, the programme was formally completed, with the Eurogroup unanimously agreeing to activate stability support. The Greek side had one 'basic choice' to make: it had to choose between 'collapse and salvation'.[103]

Aware that this was the most painful fiscal adjustment programme ever to be implemented, the Greek government's goal was 'not to absorb the entire aid package but return to the markets as soon as possible, without having to pay predatory interest rates'. The Finance Minister turned against 'the international markets which do not give us the opportunity to make the adjustments that we consider necessary'. At least, now it was up to Greece to decide when to return to the markets.[104]

Unprecedented 'in the scope of the national effort required, as well as in the scale of the financial support, €110 billion',[105] the programme gave Greece the

101. Interview 36.

102. 'Chysochoidis-Katseli insist that they did not read the debt agreement', 24 January 2012, (accessed 2 March 2012). Online. Available: http://www.capital.gr/news.asp?id=1388352 [in Greek].

103. Ministry of Finance, 'Press conference regarding the Program of Economic Policy for the Support Mechanism from the Eurozone and the International Monetary Fund', Sunday 2 May 2010.

104. *Ibid.*

105. 'Commissioner Olli Rehn and IMF Managing Director Dominique Strauss-Kahn, Joint Statement 2 May 2010'. All quotes in this paragraph have been taken from the joint statement.

significant breathing space that it needed. The 'great sacrifice' that was demanded from the Greek people would eventually pay off when Greece's debt was brought down and its competitiveness restored. The programme was still designed with 'fairness in mind', so as 'to protect the poorest and most vulnerable, and ask for a fair sharing of the burden across Greek society'. With an air of optimism, Commissioner Olli Rehn and IMF Managing Director Dominique Strauss-Kahn held: 'if implemented effectively – and we believe it will be – the program will lead to a more dynamic economy that will deliver the growth, jobs, and prosperity that Greece needs in the future'. Critical to implementation was, of course, a 'national commitment that went beyond political party lines'.[106]

A twenty-four-hour, nation-wide strike, during which three Athens bank employees died in a blaze started by a petrol bomb, signalled the extent of public opposition to the agreement's measures. The next day, 6 May, the Greek parliament voted on the activation of the Memorandum. Law 3845/2010 establishing 'measures to implement the mechanism to support the Greek economy by the Member States of the euro area and the International Monetary Fund'[107] passed by 172 votes to 121 in the 300-member chamber. With political commitment to the programme having acquired parliamentary approval, the Governing Council of the ECB made an 'exceptional' and 'temporary' suspension: the marketable debt instruments issued by the Greek Government or guaranteed by the Greek Government would retain a quality standard sufficient for their continued eligibility as collateral for eurosystem monetary policy operations, irrespective of any external credit assessment.[108] This was put in place 'with a view to contributing to the soundness of financial institutions, thereby strengthening the stability of the financial system as a whole and protecting the customers of those institutions';[109] it would be upheld until the stability of the financial system allowed the normal application of the Eurosystem framework for monetary-policy operations.

The markets were still not persuaded, however. The gun on the table was hardly a big bazooka. The markets were now out to test – given the novelty of the GLF and the fractious support which underlay it – whether the gun could or would be fired. To Eurozone authorities' dismay, Greece's ten-year bond spreads reached 1287 points on 7 May. Acknowledging the risk of contagion – Spain and Portugal were expected to take significant consolidation measures in 2010 and 2011 in order to calm the markets – an extraordinary Ecofin meeting on 9 May decided 'on a comprehensive package of measures to preserve financial stability in Europe'. The threat was considered systemic, after Jean-Claude Trichet,

---

106. *Ibid.*

107. Law 3845/2010 'Measures for the implementation of the support mechanism of the Greek economy by the Member States of the euro area and the International Monetary Fund', *Government Gazette*, No 65A, 6 May 2010 [in Greek].

108. 'Decision of the European Central Bank of 6 May 2010 on temporary measures relating to the eligibility of marketable debt instruments issued or guaranteed by the Greek Government' (ECB/2010/3) (2010/268/EU), *Official Journal of the European Union*, L 117/102, 11 May 2010.

109. *Ibid.*

Governor of the ECB, warned that the situation in world markets resembled 'the demise of Lehman Brothers in 2008'. Pressure came from overseas as well. US President Obama impressed upon Eurozone leaders 'the urgency of resolution'.[110] The final agreement created the European Financial Stabilisation Mechanism (EFSM), an EU27 instrument based on Article 122.2, and the European Financial Stability Facility (EFSF), a special-purpose vehicle for the euro area, with a total firing power of €500 billion. The IMF would participate in these financing arrangements with an additional contribution of at least €250 billion, bringing the total amount to €750 billion. The Greek Loan Facility, the establishment of the European stabilisation mechanism and a strong commitment to accelerated fiscal consolidation were expected to restore stability in the Eurozone. The Council also announced its intention to strengthen the governance of the euro area through enhanced economic surveillance and co-ordination, reinforced rules for surveillance of euro countries and a robust framework for crisis management; and to make rapid progress on financial-market regulation and supervision.[111] On the same day, the Council moved to adopt the Commission's recommendation, according to Articles 126 (9) and 136 of the Treaty, that Greece would 'put an end to the present excessive deficit situation as rapidly as possible and, at the latest, by the deadline of 2014'. The adjustment path included a detailed account of the measures that had to be implemented between June 2010 up to September 2011 (Article 2).[112]

Conclusion: responsibility and solidarity in short supply

It is no accident that some policy makers would suggest: 'if the Memorandum did not exist, we would have to invent it'.[113] The Greek sovereign-debt crisis demonstrated that Greek policy makers had failed to exercise the political will or develop the necessary institutions that would have put an end to the fiscal derailment and the lack of structural adjustment that had finally brought the country to the brink of insolvency. As a result, they had, yet again, to resort to some 'external constraint': 'Without the Memorandum there was no way that any government would ever be able to take half the measures that were taken'.[114] This was, at best, an unfortunate repetition of the pre-EMU adjustment approach. The idea that 'if EMU did not exist, we would have to invent it' had become a

---

110. B. Hall, Q. Peel, and R. Atkins, 'Twelve hours that tested the limits of the Union', *Financial Times*, 11 May 2010.

111. Council of the European Union, 'Council conclusions: Economic and Financial Affairs Council Extraordinary meeting', Brussels, 9/10 May 2010.

112. 'Council Decision of 10 May 2010 addressed to Greece with a view to reinforcing and deepening fiscal surveillance and giving notice to Greece to take measures for the deficit reduction judged necessary to remedy the situation of excessive deficit' (2010/320/EU), *Official Journal of the European Communities*, L 145, 11 June 2010.

113. Interview 36.

114. Interview 34.

mantra for the Ministers of Finance who were trying to pass the 'tough' nominal convergence measures during 1994–9.[115]

Why was it that Greek policy makers consistently failed to put their house in order? A good starting point for conceptualising Greek economic performance under EMU is provided by the concept of 'complementarity', whereby actors adjust institutions to enhance the productivity of other institutions, in the service of economic performance and efficiency.

Streeck however suggests that:

> most economic systems command a great deal of slack; that the time lag between decisions on institutional structures and their economic effects is long; and that an unpredictably changing environment permanently resets the conditions of economic performance, rendering it futile to follow current performance requirements narrowly.[116]

For an entire decade, Greek society and its governing elite were in mutually reinforcing denial, sheltered by, in turns, EU funds and debt-led growth and conditioned by a continuous and often meritless expansion of wages and benefits. The ostrich approach worked superbly, allowing Greek policy makers to stick to the domestic policy path while ignoring national-level responsibilities attached to Eurozone membership. Following Streeck, this could constitute proof that, given 'slack', the 'time lag' and the 'unpredictably changing environment' policy actors 'rationally neglect economic complementarity and pursue other targets such as social stability'.[117] It is a matter of interpretation whether, in the Greek case, *buying* social stability – public debt to GDP ballooned from 48.3 per cent in the 1974–85 period to 142.8 per cent in 2010 – had come about as a result of some master plan. Here was a long-drawn process of *failing* to develop institutional complementarities, one which had started, in fact, in 1974 and had spanned three decades; this resulted, quite ironically, from the short-term horizons of policy makers, who prepared 'adjustment' plans, all the time with an eye on winning the next election.

Greece was also a typical South-European economy, which 'lacked the institutional capacity to ensure economic efficiency';[118] even in the areas of shipping and tourism, it never succeeded in developing a 'comparative institutional advantage'. In their 'revised typology of capitalist varieties', Hancké, Rhodes and Thatcher bring the state back in, as 'past forms of coordination between labour, the state, and firms, based on pre-existing coalitions and institutionally shaped

115. *See* discussion in Chapter Three.

116. W. Streeck, 'Requirements for a useful concept of complementarity', in C. Crouch, W. Streeck, R. Boyer, B. Amable, P. A. Hall and G. Jackson, 'Dialogue on institutional complementarity', *Socio-Economic Review* 2005, vol. 3, no. 2, pp. 359–82.

117. *Ibid.*

118. S. Zambarloukou, 'Collective bargaining and social pacts: Greece in comparative perspective', *European Journal of Industrial Relations* 2006, vol. 12, no. 2, pp. 211–29, p. 215.

interests, will condition national responses to exogenous shocks';[119] they even posit that economic governance is built in large part on elite networks that seek 'to control the strategic levers of the economy and state at politically opportune moments';[120] they are, however, wrong to leave government policy actors out and not to delve deeper and further. In the Greek case, actors not only acted as policy monopolists across a range of areas but also created the breeding ground for rent-seeking networks to emerge and prosper.

In fact, if institutional complementarities – developing complementary practices and transposing them from one sphere of the economy to the other – could explain positive outcomes, here was a textbook case of how institutional *non*-complementarities, or perhaps negative complementarities, abounded at the expense of national economic performance: the administrative burden was exceptionally high; regulation of markets was excessive; government intervention limited competition as well as resource allocation and pricing decisions in crucial network industries; professional services regarding entry and price-setting were heavily controlled; while the business environment was, on the whole, unattractive.[121]

Allowing for the Eurozone's 'systemic failure', which 'exacerbated a boom in capital flows and credit and complicated its aftermath after the boom turned to bust',[122] the problem with Greece's capitalist variety was that policy makers made no effort to shake off the country's weak institutional capacity or calculate how its concomitant credibility deficit could prove as harmful as its fiscal deficits. The unfortunate reporting of official Greek statistics offered a major example. Following the 2004 fiscal audit, five Eurostat reservations on the quality of data between 2005 and 2009 failed to remove political control from the the National Statistical Service's management. In one of the more detrimental episodes, the 2009 budget deficit was revised five times: the 2009 budget projected a budget deficit of below 3 per cent; this doubled to 6 per cent in October 2009, at the time that it was reported to the Commission. The new government shortly after revised the figure to 12.7 per cent of GDP, only for Eurostat to revise it again to 13.6 in the April EDP notification. The final figure, as it was reported in the November EDP notification, was 15.6 per cent.

Policy makers admitting that 'successive governments have promised things that haven't happened'[123] was not good enough. The 2010 January Update of the Stability and Growth Programme, much anticipated by the Commission, the

---

119. B. Hancké, M. Rhodes and M. Thatcher, 'Beyond varieties of capitalism' in B. Hancké, (ed.), *Debating Varieties of Capitalism: A reader*, Oxford, Oxford University Press, 2009, p. 294.

120. *Ibid.*, p. 285.

121. T. Pelagidis, *The Greek Paradox of Falling Competitiveness and Weak Institutions in a High GDP Growth Rate Context (1995–2008)*, *GreeSE Paper No 38*, Hellenic Observatory Papers on Greece and Southeast Europe, London, 2010, p. 13.

122. INET Council on the Eurozone Crisis, 'Breaking the deadlock: a path out of the crisis', *Institute for New Economic Thinking*, 23 July 2012.

123. Statement of George Papakonstantinou in J. Hughes and C. Giles, 'Greek "credibility deficit" its key issue', *Financial Times*, 16 December 2009.

Council and the markets, announced the strategy of 'changing the process of budgeting, monitoring and evaluating its implementation, and moving towards a programme-based budget', in the context of improving fiscal management.[124] A closer look of the 2009 January Update would reveal that 'a new system of programme budgeting' had also been announced in the previous year.[125] This stable pattern – of announcing measures and postponing their implementation to a future date, in the hope that the political cost or their actual setting up and application would fall on to the next government – caused grave damage to the country's ability to make credible commitments. The fact that it reappeared in a year when Greece was facing increased scrutiny, explained why neither the sizeable fiscal-consolidation decisions that were included in the 2010 budget, nor the additional measures that were taken in January, February and March 2010 were enough to persuade the markets to change their verdict.

In like manner, policy makers constantly defied pledges to curtail the public sector, a major target set in every stability and growth programme; during the 2000–8 period, when Greece's strong growth performance was reflected in a domestic demand boom, the wage bill of the general government increased by almost 100 per cent, to €27,480 million (11.4 per cent of GDP), at a time when nominal GDP increased by only 74 per cent. In 2009, the year that policy makers were theoretically trying to persuade the markets of their commitment to reform, they increased the public wage bill further, by 7.5 per cent in 2009, to €29,460 million (12.4 per cent of GDP).[126] In fact, the wage and pension bill amounted, in 2009, to three-quarters of total primary expenditure. Locked in the imperatives that maintained the operation of the clientelistic state, policy makers had obviously disconnected their decisions from the EDP obligations with which they were simultaneously trying to comply. When Greece was called out by the Commission in 2008 for its lack of fiscal discipline – and the potential effect of that on debt sustainability – 'it promised "full co-operation"; this usually worked as a strategy for avoiding sanctions'. [127] Not that any country had been subjected to sanctions in the first place.

The Eurozone, its institutions and its leading authorities suffered from their own credibility deficit. The Stability and Growth Pact had failed, as Tables 7.1 and 7.2 suggest, in instilling fiscal discipline across the board. In 2009, 12 out of the 17 Eurozone countries – including model students Spain and Ireland, which had never breached the rules – were in the EDP, while two more were added in 2010. When markets, which had operated for a decade under the naïve assumption that no euro area member could default, began to price in sovereign risk, they exposed the ostrich-like strategy of the Eurozone authorities. With the possible exception of the ECB, Eurozone authorities, Eurozone members and

---

124. Ministry of Finance, 'Update of the Hellenic Stability and Growth Programme, including an Updated Reform Programme', Athens, January 2010, p. 14.

125. *See* discussion in Chapter Six.

126. European Commission, 'The economic adjustment programme for Greece', p. 16.

127. Interview 29.

Greece failed to understand how markets saw, analysed and assessed a country's economic situation. Painful realisations began to sink in after the event: 'The way the markets see your economy, is a reality that you cannot ignore. No matter what political 'wrapper' you choose to put on it, if they think it is in bad shape they will not buy'.[128]

The markets were, in fact, not appeased but continued relentlessly to test the political resolve to 'ensure the stability of the Eurozone'. This was the question of the big bazooka, of throwing enough money at the problem to prove the project's 'irreversibility' by deeds rather than words. The fact that the funds provided were considered 'too little, too late' betrayed the genuine ignorance of Eurozone members, who appeared unable to think outside the Maastricht box. Reluctant to acknowledge that the Eurozone's systemic failures were creating a chasm between the core and the periphery, Eurozone authorities continued to work on the assumption that a greater emphasis on rules and conditions would bring about the desired compliance; but all the while, the national political systems were pulling in the opposite direction. The inevitable result was that market confidence remained low, constantly raising the spectre of 'contagion': what if systemic risk materialised and propagated throughout the Eurozone?

128. Interview 34.

Table 7.1: How the Stability and Growth Pact failed I, deficit as a percentage of GDP

Country	2000	2001	2002	2003	2004	2005	2006	2007	2008	2009	2010
Austria	-1,70	0,00	-0,70	-1,50	-4,40	-1,70	-1,50	-0,90	-0,90	-4,10	-4,40
Belgium	0,00	0,40	-0,10	-0,10	-0,30	-2,70	0,10	-0,30	-1,30	-5,80	-4,10
Cyprus	-2,30	-2,20	-4,40	-6,60	-4,10	-2,40	-1,20	3,50	0,90	-6,10	-5,30
Estonia	-0,20	-0,10	0,30	1,70	1,6	1,6	2,50	2,40	-2,90	-2,00	0,20
Finland	6,90	5,10	4,10	2,60	2,50	2,80	4,10	5,30	4,3	-2,50	-2,50
France	-1,50	-1,50	-3,10	-4,10	-3,60	-2,90	-2,30	-2,70	-3,30	-7,50	-7,10
Germany	1,10	-3,10	-3,80	-4,20	-3,80	-3,30	1,60	0,20	-0,10	-3,20	-4,30
Greece	-3,70	-4,50	-4,8	-5,60	-7,50	-5,20	-5,70	-6,50	-9,80	-15,80	-10,60
Ireland	4,70	0,90	-0,40	0,40	1,40	1,70	2,90	0,10	-7,30	-14,20	-31,30
Italy	-0,80	-3,10	-3,10	-3,60	-3,50	-4,40	-3,40	-1,60	-2,70	-5,40	-4,60
Luxembourg	6,00	6,10	2,10	0,50	-1,10	0,00	1,40	3,70	3,00	-0,90	-1,10
Malta	-5,80	-6,40	-5,80	-9,20	-4,70	-2,90	-2,80	-2,40	-4,60	-3,70	-3,60
Netherlands	2,00	-0,20	-2,10	-3,10	-1,70	-0,30	0,00	0,20	0,50	-5,60	-5,10
Portugal	-2,90	-4,30	-2,90	-3,00	-3,40	-5,90	-4,10	-3,10	-3,60	-10,10	-9,80
Slovakia	-12,30	-6,50	-8,20	-2,80	-2,40	-2,8	-3,20	-1,80	-2,10	-8,00	-7,70
Slovenia	-3,70	-4,00	-2,40	-2,70	-2,30	-1,05	-1,40	0,00	-1,90	-6,10	-5,80
Spain	-0,90	0,50	-0,20	-0,30	-0,10	1,30	2,40	1,90	-4,50	-11,20	-9,30

Exceeds the limit set by the Stability and Growth Pact (-3% of GDP)

Source: Eurostat

Table 7.2: How the Stability and Growth Pact failed II, debt as a percentage of GDP

Country	2000	2001	2002	2003	2004	2005	2006	2007	2008	2009	2010
Austria	66,20	66,80	66,20	65,30	64,70	64,20	62,30	60,20	63,80	69,50	71,80
Belgium	107,80	106,50	103,40	98,40	94,00	92,00	88,00	84,10	89,30	95,90	96,20
Cyprus	59,60	61,20	65,10	69,70	70,90	69,40	64,70	58,80	48,90	58,50	61,50
Estonia	5,10	4,80	5,70	5,60	5,00	4,60	4,40	3,70	4,50	7,20	6,70
Finland	43,80	42,50	41,50	44,50	44,40	41,70	39,60	3,520	33,90	43,30	48,30
France	57,30	56,90	58,80	62,90	64,90	66,40	63,70	64,20	68,20	79,00	82,30
Germany	60,20	59,10	60,70	64,40	66,30	68,60	68,10	65,20	66,70	74,40	83,20
Greece	103,40	103,70	101,70	97,40	98,60	100,00	106,10	107,40	113,00	129,30	144,90
Ireland	37,50	35,20	31,90	30,70	29,40	27,20	24,70	24,80	44,20	65,20	92,50
Italy	108,50	108,20	105,10	103,90	103,40	105,40	106,10	103,10	105,80	115,50	118,40
Luxembourg	6,20	6,30	6,30	6,1	6,30	6,10	6,70	6,70	13,70	14,80	19,10
Malta	54,90	60,90	59,10	67,60	71,70	69,70	64,10	62,10	62,20	67,80	69,00
Netherlands	53,80	50,70	50,50	52,00	52,40	51,80	47,40	45,30	58,50	60,80	62,90
Portugal	48,50	51,20	53,80	55,90	57,60	62,80	63,90	68,30	71,60	83,00	93,30
Slovakia	50,30	48,90	43,40	42,40	41,50	34,20	30,50	29,60	27,80	35,50	41,00
Slovenia	26,30	26,50	27,80	27,20	27,30	26,70	26,40	23,10	21,90	35,30	38,80
Spain	59,40	55,60	52,60	48,80	46,30	43,10	39,60	36,20	40,10	53,80	61,00

  Exceeds the limit set by the Stability and Growth Pact (60% of GDP)

Source: Eurostat

chapter eight | conclusion: owning and sharing responsibility

If numbers tell the truth, then the Greek sovereign debt crisis has indeed reached epic proportions. The economy has entered its sixth year of recession, public debt has climbed to 156.9 per cent of GDP, and unemployment has soared, exceeding 60 per cent among young people; worse, the adjustment process is now expected to continue well beyond the end of the forecast horizon in 2014[1]. The Athens Stock Exchange has lost almost 90 per cent of its value, major companies have relocated their headquarters and switched their primary stock listings and the number of small and medium-sized enterprises (SMEs), the 'backbone' of the Greek economy, has been reduced by 90,000 between 2008 and 2011. Amidst the turmoil, Greece is also facing a serious crisis of identity, no longer able to sustain the Europeanisation and modernisation façade of the good EMU years. The city centre has repeatedly played host to street rallies and demonstrations, during which there has been, at times, extensive vandalism: of hotels, monuments and even the parliament's grounds; public sector strikes have disrupted services; and petty crime is on the rise. Having seemingly resigned to its debtor status, Greek society is reaching breaking point – in the last two years, the suicide rate, typically one of the lowest in Europe, has jumped up, the number of homeless has increased by about 20–25 per cent and bank loans have hit a 25 per cent default rate.

Greece banked on EMU yet came close to insolvency. How did it happen that great expectations turned to dust so quickly? Following a long-drawn process of maladjustment, Greek policy makers stuck to what they knew best: they borrowed in order to finance unsustainable development; they allowed expenditure on the public sector to balloon, with meritless wage increases, benefits, and pensions; and, in the end, they generated comfortable lifestyles that were parasitic on the state – all this, at the expense of real growth and the modernisation of the economy. A profoundly distorted conception of the social contract was at work, but one that all parties appeared to be content with. Special interests of all kinds continually popped up, helping themselves to a slice of an ever-expanding pie. This catastrophic entanglement began to lose its appeal, when it became obvious that Greece would have to struggle to avoid default. The crisis could 'force' or bring about a new form of social contract. Difficult reforms agreed with the country's creditors, however, would have to break thirty year old practices of corruption, cronyism, and clientelism.

Is Greece a case of economic delinquency or a victim of systemic failure? The question and its answer have wider resonance: the Euro project – a currency

---

1.   European Commission, 'European Economic Forecast Autumn 2012', *European Economy 7*, 2012, p. 4.

without a state – was always going to be about owning and sharing responsibility in a less-than-optimal monetary union in a more-than-troubled world. Delinquency in economic and fiscal management was rampant, well before Greece joined the EMU, and well after, as this book has thoroughly documented. However, that the country's refinancing difficulties 'triggered a systemic crisis for the euro that brought global financial markets to the brink'[2] suggests that the European monetary system itself was deeply flawed.

Weak institutional capacity and the road not taken

This book has offered an analytical narrative of how distinctive patterns of national economic-policy formation have tended to persist in the face of significant pressures to change, including entry to the EEC, EMU membership, a severe sovereign-debt crisis, and the securing of bailout loans on the basis of conditionality. Throughout each episode, the domestic institutional framework has provided for weak capacity and strong incentives regarding the creative interpretation of rules and non-compliance. In an interesting twist, deterioration in the quality of institutions has resulted from policy actors creating laws and practices that enabled and legitimated unaccountable and non-transparent behaviour. Economic policy-making was typically 'structured around the Minister and his entourage; his personality, education, and the people surrounding him were crucial to the kinds of choices he made'.[3] With 'a premium placed on personalities – Greece is not Germany, Switzerland or Britain',[4] and the absence of a strong and independent civil service, questions of accountability and responsibility did not rank highly in importance, particularly whenever a Minister enjoyed the Prime Minister's trust or friendship. As a result, setting ministry objectives and performance criteria became irrelevant over time, the performance of Ministers, most of whom were economists educated in top universities in the UK and the US, wildly variable.

Weak institutional capacity also showed in a Greek civil service which was 'not fit for purpose' – a fact that would disrupt any attempt at rational planning and strategic decision-making. Even though there were organisation charts that meticulously mapped positions and hierarchies, 'the problem was in actual operation, in achieving proper execution and in having under one's supervision people willing to work'.[5] Bureaucratic clientelism, the 'systematic infiltration of the state machine by party devotees and the allocations of favours through it'[6], formally replaced more orthodox forms of recruitment, appointment and

---

2. R. Baldwin and D. Gros, 'Introduction: the euro in crisis – what to do?' in R. Baldwin, D. Gros and L. Laeven , (eds), *Completing the Eurozone Rescue: What more needs to be done?* A Vox. EUorg publication, Centre for Economic Policy Research, June 2010, p. 1.

3. Interview 10.

4. Interview 17.

5. Interview 10.

6. C. Lyrintzis, 'Political parties in post-Junta Greece: a case of "bureaucratic clientelism?"' in G. Pridham, (ed.), *The New Mediterranean Democracies,* London, Frank Cass, 1984, p. 103.

promotion, both at the top – following each government turnover, a large and often fluctuating number of top administrative posts were filled by appointees of the governing elite – and at the bottom, since recruitment of employees at the lower levels and in-service transfers were typically based on particularistic criteria, such as political-party affiliation.[7] The two tended to feed off each other, with ministers routinely complaining of 'the inefficiency and lack of high calibre personnel which leads us to bring in outside people in order to assist the government with its work'.[8]

Dispensing with the grave responsibility that came with using the public sector as an employment tool did not really make sense – this was a practice that eager politicians operating in an antagonistic party system had sworn by; state employment, in fact, ballooned with every election,[9] while, following EMU accession, the bulk of government borrowing went to pay the wage bill in the public sector and on pension outlays.[10] In this 'system', rocketing costs simply served to intensify the effects of fragmentation of power, lack of co-ordination and random dispersion of (any) expertise and technical knowledge.

A 2011 OECD report recorded precisely the shortcomings of public governance in Greece, emphasising 'legal formalism' and limited attempts to introduce performance-based management of human resources. The culture and framework that has emerged paralyses civil servants, as it does not provide incentives for policy initiative; expects proposed actions to be accompanied by a legal text; privileges the observance and development of administrative processes at the expense of developing policy substance; and slows down the work of the administration.[11] As a result, 'inadequate data collection schemes and the absence of precise data' negatively affected reform strategies because they 'lack a strong evidence base which would justify, support – and quantify – effective and efficient policy decisions'.[12] The high ministerial turnover, discussed in Chapter Six, has further disrupted policy implementation, particularly as co-operation and co-ordination between and within ministries has not been dependent on formal

7. D. Sotiropoulos, 'Democratization, administrative reform and the state in Greece, Italy, Portugal and Spain: is there a "model" of South European bureaucracy?', *Discussion Paper No. 17*, The Hellenic Observatory /The European Institute, April 2004, pp. 33–4.

8. Interview 39.

9. C. Spanou, 'Elections and public administration: the electoral mobilisation of intra-administrative patronage mechanisms' in C. Lyrintzis and E. Nicolacopoulos, (eds), *Elections and Political Parties in the 1980s: Developments and prospects of the political system* (Athens: Themelio, 1990), pp. 165–99 [in Greek].

10. V. Rapanos, 'Size and range of activities of the public sector', *Working Paper*, Foundation for Economic and Industrial Research (IOBE), November 2009, p. 42 [in Greek].

11. OECD, *Greece: Review of the Central Administration*, OECD Public Governance Reviews, OECD Publishing, 2011 (accessed 2 October 2012). Online. Available: *http://dx.doi.org/10.1787/9789264102880-en*, p. 27.

12. *Ibid.* p. 9.

channels but took place on an *ad hoc* basis.[13] Under these framework conditions, there have arisen, the report continues, 'ample opportunities for rent seeking', particularly with the emergence of 'special secretariats' that muddled the political/ administrative interface, 'providing a screen for individual behaviours that undermine the common good'.[14]

Greece's particular version of crony capitalism – certainly a distorted version of the textbook model of 'Mediterranean capitalism' – negatively affected dynamism and opportunity in the economy, while bowing to ever-increasing demands for state largesse. The country exhibited 'one of the most restrictive systems of product market regulations' by OECD standards, with various barriers to entry and restrictions on fees and prices in key sectors, leading to 'high rents, low innovation and job creation and reduction in competitiveness'.[15] Political connections proved, time and again, more important than business plans, as government contracts were secured under less-than-transparent procedures. Successive governments, with the power to issue or withhold licenses, subsidies and other discriminatory privileges, favoured particular conglomerates – in sectors ranging from health-care to energy, telecommunications and public works – in exchange for serious 'kickbacks' and 'sweeteners' (often calculated and given out as a percentage of the final contract); even foreign multinationals learned to play the game as they routinely bribed government officials in order to promote lucrative deals;[16] this give-and-take became so pervasive – as already high levels of deficits and debt continued to rise – that privileges and subsidies trickled down to smaller firms, further augmenting the demand for entitlements for those even further down the line. In the absence of independent agencies to monitor rampant billing fraud, special interests skewed important policy decisions and harmed the public interest.

Policy actors' practical impunity from such practices[17] served to weaken the rule of law,[18] reinforcing an idiosyncratic culture of anomie that has pervaded Greek society. Along with grand corruption that has gone largely unchecked, petty corruption has thrived. In the 2011 'national survey on corruption', published by Transparency International Greece, the estimated cost of petty corruption was €554 million in 2011, down from €632 million in 2010; due to the crisis, the size of bribes was reduced, with the survey calculating that the average bribe requested

---

13. Interview 6; interview 9; interview 11; interview 12.

14. OECD, *Greece: Review of the Central Administration*, p. 31.

15. OECD, *Economic Surveys Greece*, Paris, OECD, August 2011, p. 15.

16. The cases of DePuy International Ltd and Siemens AG have been highly publicised. For a recent reference, see M. Walker, 'Tragic flaw: graft feeds Greek crisis', *Wall Street Journal*, April 15, 2012.

17. In April 2012, a former Greek Defence Minister was remanded in custody, pending trial over suspicion of money-laundering and corruption. He is one of only a handful of Greek officials ever held accountable for such activities.

18. For an analysis of the substantial costs associated with the inefficiency of the judiciary, *see* M. Mitsopoulos and T. Pelagidis, *Understanding the Crisis in Greece: From boom to bust*, London: Palgrave Macmillan, 2012, pp. 55–106.

in the public sector was €1,399 and €1,406 in the private sector.[19] These costs were still calculable – in contrast to the incalculable cost of the corrupt practices that created the incentives for even more corrupt practices.

Greek citizens appeared to live in a state of 'corrupt legality', typified by 'broad scale acceptance of and participation in corruption', in spite of the fact that they condemned it:[20] according to a specially commissioned Eurobarometer poll on corruption, the majority (74 per cent) of Europeans believed that corruption is a major problem in their country; respondents in Greece, however, were the most likely (98 per cent) to think that it was a major problem that exists at all institutional levels, national, local, and regional (95 per cent). They were also the most likely of all Europeans to think that corruption is more widespread in their country than elsewhere and that corruption is part of their business culture (88 per cent).[21] This national-level evaluation was 'corroborated' by Greece's international ranking in the Corruption Perception Index (CPI), which keeps scores of more than 180 countries according to their perceived level of corruption. Greece ranked 80th for 2011, well behind the other PIIGS countries (Ireland ranks 19th, Spain 31st, Portugal 32nd, and Italy 69th).[22]

As corruption became systemic and was accepted as being so,[23] policy actors had few incentives (and even fewer resources) to simplify the complex and opaque frameworks governing public sector–citizen interactions or create effective systems for detecting and punishing offenders. Nowhere has this been more evident than in the repeated failures to reform tax-collection and curb tax-evasion. The fact that, between 1974 and 2011, 37 tax laws (including presidential and legislative decrees) have been instituted – a 'practice' which amounts to a phenomenal average of one law per year – effectively suggests the lightness, amateurishness and casualness with which rule-making was undertaken. The results have been, predictably, meagre; while Greek government expenditure has been broadly comparable with the EU average, government revenue has systematically trailed behind, pointing to a direct link between tax-evasion and Greece's deficits and, more importantly, to successive governments' inability to collect direct taxes.[24] This trend, which as discussed in Chapter Three, first emerged in the 1980s, has continued unabated: personal-income-tax revenues were more than 5 per cent of GDP below the euro area average in 2010, although statutory rates were not especially low. In fact, according to OECD calculations, 'If Greece collected its

19. 'National Survey on Corruption in Greece', *Transparency International Greece*, 2011.

20. 'Executive summary', *National Integrity Assessment System: Greece*, Transparency International Greece, 2012.

21. 'Corruption Report', *Special Eurobarometer 374*, February 2012.

22. Transparency International, *Corruption Perceptions Index 2011*, 2011.

23. 'Our basic problem is systemic corruption': statement of George Papandreou (former Prime Minister) after he took office, cited in M. Walker, 'Tragic flaw: graft feeds Greek crisis'.

24. C. Meghir, D. Vayanos, N. Vettas, 'The economic crisis in Greece: a time of reform and opportunity', 5 August 2010 (accessed 10 October 2012). Online. Available: http://greekeconomistsforreform. com/wp-content/uploads/Reform.pdf.

VAT, social security contributions and corporate income tax with the average efficiency of OECD countries, tax revenues could rise by nearly 5% of GDP'.[25]

In a revealing data-processing exercise by the Ministry of Finance, the picture that emerged was bleak: six out of ten professionals, traders and owners of small industries declared, in 2011, income under the tax-free boundary of €12,000; 457,377 (out of a total of 779,319) professionals and traders declared an average personal income of €7,500 (the poverty line is set at €7,400).[26] The extent to which vested interests have managed to protect their rents, in spite of grandiloquent public statements, speaks volumes: a survey on tax evasion has uncovered that banks in Greece have adapted their lending policy on the basis of semi-formal rather than declared income (the average self-employed Greek appeared to spend 82 per cent of monthly reported income on servicing debt, with some professions spending more than 100 per cent, while the incoming/lending ratio does not typically exceed 30 per cent across European banks). Targeting self-employment and using individual-level household lending data across four credit products, the amount of income that went untaxed in Greece for 2009 was estimated to have reached €28 billion, 'accounting for 31 per cent of the deficit for 2009 or 48 per cent for 2008'.[27] Professionals in medicine, engineering, education, accounting, financial services and law have been the worst offenders – parliamentarians, however, keen to protect 'their own', have systematically avoided targeting these occupations, promoting the mildest of reforms.[28]

This enduring policy behaviour explains why the designers of the first adjustment programme did not explicitly 'envisage gains from the fight against tax evasion';[29] following five reviews, the evaluation presented in the second adjustment programme suggested that 'tax and social security evasion may have actually increased in 2011, against the backdrop of negative economic growth and increased liquidity constraints of taxpayers'.[30] Creating a regime of tax discipline and improving compliance has been difficult, particularly because the enactment of laws has been negated by policy makers' dangerous negligence or plain inaction. Characteristically, in the autumn of 2010, Christine Lagarde, then French Finance Minister, in a bid to help the Greek Ministry of Finance clamp down on potential tax evasion, handed a list of bank accounts with information on Greek customers at the HSBC Bank in Switzerland. While France collected

---

25. OECD, *Economic Surveys Greece*, p. 10.

26. N. Siomopoulos, '457.377 professionals have declared an income of €7.500', *To Vima*, 9 September 201 (accessed 25 September 2012) . Online. Available: http://www.tovima.gr/finance/article/?aid=473905 [in Greek].

27. N. Artavanis, A. Morse and M. Tsoutsoura, 'Tax evasion across industries: soft credit evidence from Greece', *Chicago Booth Paper No. 12–25*, Chicago Booth: Farma-Miller Center for Research in Finance, 25 June 2012, p. 29.

28. *Ibid.*

29. European Commission, 'The Economic Adjustment Programme for Greece', *European Economy: Occasional Papers 61*, May 2010, p. 28.

30. European Commission, 'The Second Economic Adjustment Programme for Greece', *European Economy: Occasional Papers 94*, March 2012, p. 34.

half a billion euro from its own tax offenders, Giorgos Papakonstantinou and his successor Evangelos Venizelos were hard pressed, two years later, to explain why, in a period of severe austerity, with standards of living constantly eroding due to wage and pension cuts, and formal recognition that 'the reduction in tax evasion will lead to a fairer sharing of the adjustment burden'[31], they had taken no action on the list. Two more headline-making lists have been circulating, theoretically awaiting for further investigation: one involves 400 purchases of high-end London properties by Greek nationals; the other, the names of 54,000 individuals said to have deposited, during 2009–12, a total amount of €22 billion in foreign banks abroad.[32]

At the core of Greece's weak institutional capacity lay an almost complete disregard for monitoring and evaluation mechanisms. Starting with the state budget, whose 'function' was thoroughly analysed in Chapters Six and Seven, it emerged that successive governments failed to develop even basic tools for controlling public finances: annual spending caps, borrowing limits, procedures for controlling expenditure, the obligation to regularly publish data on budget execution and the introduction of a realistic medium-term budget were continuously announced but, in one way or another, did not materialise. At the same time, informal norms – ministers' tendency to shift responsibility for cutting expenses to others, in order to 'keep their mini-dominion and satisfy their clientele'[33] – repeatedly prevailed over formal arrangements.

Excesses and distortions were bound to multiply; until 2010, when a census was launched at the behest of the country's creditors, there was no registry and hence no official number of public sector employees. As of July 2010, it had emerged that 768,009 employees were employed in decentralised administrations, independent authorities, ministries and public bodies, and municipalities, with the disclaimer that 'not all personnel information has been verified by their respective Personnel Divisions yet'.[34] This kind of non-transparency, allowing for the creation of pay scales, benefits, and pensions typically unrelated to effort and merit has been, in fact, endemic, multiplied by the universal lack of instruments for overseeing and effectively supervising an over-stretched public sector.

Steadily contributing to the rise of public debt, public sector enterprises in Greece have operated under a regime of mismanagement, soft budget constraints and weak accountability: 'an inadequate programme for controlling expenditure would typically lead to the creation of an auditing committee, which would develop another auditing system; its development, however, would remain on paper, with managers, high-ranking and middle-ranking officials operating in their

31. European Commission, 'The Second Economic Adjustment Programme', p. 34.

32. K. Hope, 'Greece: held to account', *Financial Times*, 2 November 2012.

33. Interview 29.

34. Ministry of Administrative Reform and E-Government and Ministry of Finance, 'Registry of public sector employees', October 9 2012 (accessed 2 October 2012) . Online. Available: http://apografi.yap.gov.gr/apografi/english.html.

usual, scot-free ways'.[35] In fact, combined public sector enterprise losses in 2009 amounted to ¾ per cent of GDP; they also accounted, according to the OECD, for the last upward revision of the 2009 general government debt by 11 per cent of GDP in November 2010, when they were finally included in general government sector expenditure.

As waste went unchecked and unpunished over a long time, it was perversely legitimated. Policy-actors were instrumental in this respect: they appointed the management in public sector enterprises, as a matter of course, because 'you cannot pretend that you are not the main shareholder';[36] they provided disguised subsidies, hindering competition in key sectors, a practice that dated back to the 1990s; they opted for stock-market flotations during the supposed privatisation phase of 1998–2008 period, to protect their clienteles – 'public sector employees accepted this change of ownership only because their status and privileges remained unchanged';[37] and, finally, they repeatedly encroached upon the same laws on transparency in operation that they had previously voted for. Successive ministers reinforced their predecessors' lax supervision, 'turning a blind eye to the fact that the adoption of international accounting standards in public enterprises' financial statements remained on paper'.[38] The financial accounts of the nine most loss-making public enterprises supervised by the Special Secretariat of Public Enterprises were finally published for the first time in October 2010. In November, the Ministry of Finance proceeded to publish the financial accounts (for the first semester 2010) of 30 out of the 52 public enterprises as well as the payroll of all of 52 enterprises. By the end of 2010, the financial statements for the period January to September 2010 were published for 48 public enterprises (supervised by the Special Secretariat) as well as data on employment and the payroll of all 52 enterprises.[39]

Irresponsible and unaccounted-for spending also pervaded the Greek pension system, posing a significant risk for the long-term sustainability of public finances; attempts to rationalise Greek public-pension entitlements, which were 'among the most generous in the OECD', repeatedly failed, as suggested in Chapter Six. The political cost of reform outweighed the system's obviously irrational bloating, all the while Commission warnings about the budgetary impact of ageing went unheeded. Public-pension reform did take off in July 2010, however, 'externally' instigated by the country's Memorandum with the troika. The reform finally introduced 'homogeneous rules on entitlements, contributions, accumulation rules and indexation of pension rights that limit pension expenditure increase to 2.5% of GDP, or, in other words, pensions expenditure of 14.9% of GDP in 2060'.[40] Two

---

35. Interview 41.

36. Interview 37.

37. Interview 20.

38. Interview 38.

39. Ministry of Finance, *Hellenic National Reform Programme 2011–2014*, Athens, April 2011, p. 19.

40. *Ibid.*, p. 14.

years later, the combination of poor electronic data-processing and incapacity to promote the electronic interconnection between registries, insurance funds and the General Secretariat of Information Systems (the organisation responsible for developing and operating large-scale integrated IT systems, including TAXIS for taxation and TAXISnet for web-based tax services to citizens and corporations) forced policy makers to admit that the system was 'blind'. According to Ministry of Labour, Social Security and Welfare calculations, the collection of pensions by fake beneficiaries – after two audits, their number was approximately 42,000, including 3,700 people collecting pensions for their dead relatives – cost the funds €400 million annually.[41]

Return to the research hypotheses

Bringing together this analysis and the three hypotheses offers a few interesting conclusions.

> H1 National and EMU frameworks competed for influence over the goals and direction of economic policy, the outcome depending on the compliance mechanisms and the incentives available to policy makers for dodging rules or free-riding.

The notion of 'competition' proved here over-rated. With the exception of monetary policy, conducted at the supranational level, soft EMU compliance mechanisms and sanctions on the fiscal front rendered economic policy-making 'national' and therefore susceptible to the usual political calculations. The stop-go policies of the 1980s, whereby stabilisation programmes attached to EC loans were followed by profligate spending, simply mutated, once Greece joined the euro; cheap credit ensured that debt-funded overspending could continue, seemingly *ad infinitum*, without the need for stabilisation (instead, feeble gradual-adjustment schemes with muddled targets and objectives were proposed). Cushioned from real adjustment, the politicisation of the economy, expressed in electoral cycles, continued unabated: each election cost, according to a 2012 study, a loss of revenue equal to 0.18 per cent of GDP, making the total for the thirteen elections that have taken place between 1974 and 2009 more than €5 billion in 2010 prices.[42]

> H2 It is the capture of reform by powerful political and economic actors rather than its design that deals the fatal blow to policy change.

Apart from the nominal convergence endeavour, there was no real drive for policy change, as the external-constraint strategy never developed into a proper

---

41. Ministry of Labour, Social Security, and Welfare, *Ariadne Plan*, Athens, October 2012 [in Greek].

42. N. Christodoulakis, 'Greek crisis in perspective: origins, effects and ways-out' in S. N. Durlauf and L. E. Blume (eds), *The New Palgrave Dictionary of Economics*, Palgrave Macmillan, 2012, Online Edition (accessed 30 April 2012). Online. Available: http://www.dictionaryofeconomics. com/article?id=pde2012_G000221, p. 13.

adjustment strategy. The entanglement between political and economic actors became stronger, as there were, over time, more 'rents' to be extracted – generous EU transfers from the 1980s and 1990s, gave way, following financial-sector liberalisation and low interest rates, to the massive boom in residential investment during the good EMU years. In a framework of endemic corruption and political patronage, capturing reform became semi-institutionalised, with smaller and bigger special interests expertly organised for upholding the *status quo*.

Weak institutional capacity predictably translated into poor reform design: there was window-dressing and a semblance of 'reform' strategies but they were typically exhausted in instituting laws, agencies, and bodies that failed to take root or were negated in practice while, following EMU accession, 'strong growth' kept everyone afloat. The system worked smoothly, activating the ostrich-like behaviour of both national policy leaders and Eurozone authorities. For better or worse, EMU economic governance left a lot of loopholes: economic co-ordination was low; fiscal oversight was patchy; the extent of EU economies' interdependence underestimated; and tools to tackle macroeconomic imbalances were lacking. In this way, it perversely (re)created the rather 'familiar' domestic environment of laxity, slackness and impunity. From this follows the third hypothesis.

> H3 Policy makers' subsequent ability to impose a new policy direction becomes more asymmetric and certainly more costly, while the propensity of domestic institutions to breed policy stasis becomes stronger.

The Greek sovereign-debt crisis exposed the failings of a long period of maladjustment, bringing markets to a halt and the Eurozone to the brink. Reversing the debt build-up and promoting sustainable growth – based on investment and exports rather than consumption – required nothing less than a major policy shift. Greek policy makers, however, have only been able to promote fiscal adjustment and pension reform primarily with horizontal cuts. Asymmetry has been evident in the imbalance in the reform mix – despite taking steps in structural adjustment, policy makers repeatedly backtracked on measures related to wage agreements at the level of individual firms, while the full opening-up of the regulated professions remained broadly on paper. The ambitious privatisation programme, which was supposed to encourage foreign direct investment (FDI) and other private investment, while reducing public debt, was seriously watered down. In its initial estimates, the government anticipated €50 billion in proceeds over the lifetime of the programme; this figure was then revised to €19 billion through 2015. In April 2012, when the last credible figures were published, it emerged that the Hellenic Republic Asset Development Fund (HRADF), an organisation set up to oversee the privatisation revenue goal, had completed 'a number of important projects with a total yield of €1.8 billion in accruals';[43] these modest results have been

---

43. Ministry of Finance, *Hellenic National Reform Programme 2012–2015: Report on the progress towards 'Europe 2020' and the implementation of the Euro plus Pact commitments*, Athens, April 2012, p. 13.

linked to fierce opposition from trade unions, law-makers and civil servants – adept at presenting dozens of regulatory and administrative obstacles, on top of foreign investors' concern over the unfavourable business environment.

Following the derailment of the second adjustment programme agreed in March 2012, Greece has struggled to secure a two-year extension to meet its budget targets; the adoption, in November, of 'a substantial set of reforms' as well as 'a convincing budget for 2013' theoretically show 'the resolve of the Greek authorities to bring the programme back on track';[44] a strong tendency towards policy stasis has been evident, with 'legitimate doubts' about government ownership of reforms openly and repeatedly raised.[45] 'The real problem is that even whenever progress is made, this is in order to get the next instalment, not because there is genuine belief that these reforms are good for the economy and the society.'[46] The troika's doubts have been complemented by the OECD's evaluation that, in the planning of key reforms, including in the areas of privatisation, fiscal consolidation, debt reduction, tax-collection and enhanced competitiveness, the civil administration could not perform its role: there was 'no obvious ownership of the reform agenda either with specific entities at the Centre of Government, or shared by these entities'.[47]

Due to serious past policy inertia and creditors' failure to radically rethink the reform programme, in the face of repeatedly missed projections and continued recession, Greece verges, once more, on a politically and economically untenable situation. The debt-sustainability analysis, which envisaged a debt-to-GDP ratio of 120 per cent in 2020, has been practically negated, causing a serious rift among troika members. At the same time, the new austerity package and the 2013 budget, passed by the parliament in a bid to restore the country's credibility and persuade the troika to disburse the much awaited €31.5 billion instalment, envisages new cuts in public spending – while the economy is shrinking for a sixth consecutive year. Unemployment has risen to an unprecedented 27 per cent (with youth unemployment pushed far above 60 per cent),[48] tearing the social fabric apart. According to the 2011 Survey of Income and Living Conditions of Households, income inequality has deepened; 'the share of the income of the wealthiest 20 per cent of the population is 6.0 times higher than the income of the poorest 20 per cent of the population': only Latvia and Romania have fared worse than Greece.[49]

44. 'Eurogroup statement on Greece', 12 November 2012 (accessed 13 November 2012). Online. Available: http://www.consilium.europa.eu/uedocs/cms_data/docs/pressdata/en/ecofin/133445.pdf.

45. European Commission, 'The Second Economic Adjustment Programme', p. 1.

46. Interview 35.

47. OECD, *Greece: Review of the Central Administration*, p. 46.

48. Eurostat, 'Unemployment Statistics' (accessed 15 May 2013).Online. Available: http://epp.eurostat.ec.europa.eu/statistics_explained/index.php/Unemployment_statistics

49. Hellenic Statistical Authority, 'Press release: statistics on income and living conditions 2011, income inequality', Piraeus 2 November 2012 (accessed 5 November 2012). Online. Available: http://www.statistics.gr/portal/page/portal/ESYE/BUCKET/A0802/PressReleases/A0802_

In the same survey, material deprivation appears to have made inroads into the 'non-poor population': children under 18 years old have been affected by 16.4 per cent, the population aged 65 and over by 13.1 per cent, and the population aged 18–64 years old by 15.4 per cent.[50]

Between policy change and institutional stasis

It was stated from the outset that the approach adopted here would be one of, following Hodson, theory-testing[51] – bringing together specific hypotheses about policy-actors' preferences and institutional contexts and determining their 'fit' with fresh empirical evidence. This was an optimal strategy from the point of view of writing the book: it enabled me to engage with a series of highly interesting theories that were sufficiently 'open' both to accommodate a chronologically long process of adjustment and to engage in creative 'dialogue' with one another. Economic delinquency or systemic failure was always going to be analysed through the role of political leadership and democratic institutions, including 'institutionalised' norms – after all, institutions have been known to fall prey to the abuse of political power or become repositories for economic inefficiency.[52] With institutional arrangements at Eurozone level creating another layer of rules and instruments – potentially multiplying the mixture of incentives (including incentives for non-compliance) as well as the opportunities for economic policy success or failure – it would have been unwise to employ a single conceptual framework.

Chapter Three presented the historical dimensions of Greece's political economy. Confirming historical institutionalist analysis, the choice of institutional framework did have profound consequences for the growth prospects and efficiency of the economy. Its politicisation, resulting from the intense politicisation of *national* politics – the antagonistic party system, the electoral system(s) which delivered strong majority governments, the centralisation of the executive, the patron–client relationships in the public sector – was imprinted upon the stop-go cyclical pattern of debt-led growth followed by stabilisation programmes. The 'lock-in' that ensued, which cruelly exposed the absence of a Greek development

SFA10_DT_AN_00_2011_06_F_EN.pdf.

50. Material deprivation items include enforced incapacity to face unexpected financial expenses; inability to afford one week's annual holiday away from home, a meal with meat, chicken, fish or vegetarian equivalent every second day, the adequate heating of a dwelling, or durable goods like a washing machine, colour TV, telephone, mobile telephone or car; or being confronted with payment arrears, such as mortgage or rent, utility bills, hire-purchase instalments or other loan payment. Hellenic Statistical Authority, 'Press release: statistics on income and living conditions 2011, living conditions indicators', Piraeus, 2 November 2012 (accessed 5 November 2012). Online. Available: http://www.statistics.gr/portal/page/portal/ESYE/BUCKET/A0802/PressReleases/A0802_SFA10_DT_AN_00_2011_08_F_EN.pdf.

51. D. Hodson, *Governing the Euro Area in Good Times & Bad*, Oxford, Oxford University Press, 2011, p. 15.

52. M. Rutherford, *Institutions in Economics: The old and the new institutionalism*, Cambridge, Cambridge University Press, 1994, p. 180.

strategy, generated a sub-optimal path for adjustment; the chapter showed, in fact, that EEC accession neither acted as a critical juncture nor created the conditions for a different, non-path-dependent pattern of change. The 'social restitution' and 'compensatory justice' legacy of the restoration of democracy in 1974 proved stronger. As a result, the opening-up of the economy to the world market, a corollary of EEC membership, coincided with a period of increasing import penetration, sharply deteriorating export performance and a further widening of Greece's trade gap with its partners, whether appraised in terms of structural differences or *per capita* growth rate.[53]

In terms of exercising agency, policy-actors wasted substantial EEC transfers that accrued to Greece over this period, primarily on domestic consumption, while they also failed to abide by the conditions set by the balance of payments loans. Their patent inability to follow formal rules and persistent postponing of necessary fiscal and wage adjustments showed, *pace* rational choice explanations of economic decision-making, that, here was a case of a perverse equilibrium, associated with the deepening of political control over the economy. This sort of 'equilibrium' was maintained through the distribution of privileges and subsidies; the more these were handed out, the bigger the demand for them became, ballooning the budget deficit and the public debt in the process. As inefficient productive structures survived with the selective provision of funds from state-controlled banks, generous insurance and pension coverage was given to large groups of the population without matching contributions to the social security system, and public sector employment satisfied clientelistic goals, informal norms, including rent-seeking, corruption and cronyism, gradually became institutionalised. This suggests that institutionalists of both kinds ought perhaps to investigate more the relationship between the inability (and unwillingness) of policy makers to change formal rules and the eventual institutionalisation of informal norms.

Chapter Four explored the creation of EMU as an 'external-constraint' strategy and policy makers' subsequent efforts to import its discipline to the Greek political system. An important finding of this chapter was that the personalisation of leadership trumped government and bureaucratic structures in a domestic setting, where formal rules allowed for this kind of tampering. In a supranational setting, however, where power was re-shuffled, personalisation *diminished* Greek policy entrepreneurship, because the weakness of domestic infrastructure institutions affected the formulation of the national position and therefore undermined political performance. The chapter also revisited the idea of a Maastricht lock-in; the formal institutions that were established were not 'moral-hazard'-proof nor immune to political risks; as a result, they could not be construed as 'stable', either as forums for strategic interaction or as predictable structures of co-ordination and discipline. While institutional designers were well aware of unco-operative patterns of behaviour, theorists were rather vague about how these would unfold.

---

53. T. Fotopoulos, 'Economic restructuring and the debt problem: the Greek case', *International Review of Applied Economics*, 1992, vol. 6, no. 1, pp. 38–64.

But one only had to look at the domestic setting, the compliance 'history' of national executives with rules set, to have determined the extent to which credible commitments at EMU level would stick.

Chapter Five took up the question of preference-formation. Nominal convergence achieved, the real question raised was whether domestic policy makers could break the path(s) generated by the politicised economy – *if* they even wanted to – and proceed with the reforms necessary to strengthen the economy's competitiveness and improve the conditions for sustainable growth and employment-creation. With historical- and rational-choice analysis converging on the importance of institutional setting, where power and problem-solving meet,[54] the chapter drew attention to the notion of *relevant* setting. It was argued that, in the absence of fiscal institutional arrangements of an ECB type, which lengthened actors' time horizons, removed certain policy options from the agenda and isolated electoral calculations, the government's preferences could remain, following EMU accession, politically sensitive to the electorate and election returns. Another issue taken up was that of the economy's 'institutional complementarities', as elaborated by Hall and Soskice.[55] Critical to Greece's economic performance, their absence yet appeared to go unnoticed at Eurozone level. The country's 'Mediterranean capitalism' was a poor match, if the state of the labour and product markets was to be seriously taken into account; in reality, the discretionary framework of regulations which led to a large shadow economy, the taxes and fees imposed on economic activities and the high incidence of corruption exhibited 'pronounced signs of a transition country'.[56] The fact that institutional divergence could endure, *pace* the optimism of Hall and Soskice that national political economies (adjusting to contemporary challenges) change,[57] and the implications of this endurance in a less-than-optimal monetary union were missed.

Chapter Six revisited theories of fiscal governance in the light of Greece's systematic non-compliance with the Stability and Growth Pact. Hallerberg, Strauch, and von Hagen[58] and Hallerberg and Bridwell[59] begin with national

---

54. I. Katznelson, and B. R. Weingast, 'Intersections between historical and rational choice insti-tutionalism', in I. Katznelson and B. R. Weingast, (eds), *Preferences and Situations: Points of intersection between historical and rational choice institutionalism*, New York, Russell Sage Foundation, 2005, p. 16.

55. P. A. Hall and D. Soskice, 'An introduction to varieties of capitalism', in P. A. Hall and D. Soskice, (eds), *Varieties of Capitalism: The institutional foundations of comparative advantage*, Oxford, Oxford University Press, 2001, p. 18.

56. N. Karagiannis, and A. Kondeas, 'The Greek financial crisis and a developmental path to recov-ery: lessons and options', *Real-World Economics Review*, 2012, No. 60, p. 56.

57. Hall and Soskice, 'An introduction to varieties of capitalism', p. 65.

58. M. Hallerberg, R. Strauch and J. von Hagen, *Fiscal Governance: Evidence from Europe*, Cambridge, Cambridge University Press, 2009.

59. M. Hallerberg, and J. Bridwell, 'Fiscal policy context: co-ordination and discipline, the Stability and Growth Pact, and domestic fiscal regimes', in K. Dyson (ed.), *The Euro at Ten: Europeanization, power, and convergence*, Oxford, Oxford University Press, 2008.

budgetary institutions, assuming that delegation states, where strong ministers of finance assume control of the budget process, are more likely to run excessive deficits. In contrast to the track record of Spain and Ireland, two delegation states whose model fiscal behaviour was repeatedly praised until 2008, Greece seemed, on the surface, to offer a perfect fit with this model. When considering the 'strength' of Greek ministers, however, it emerged not only that the power to control the process varied widely but, more importantly, the resolve to develop the institutions to make delegation work was wanting. Repeatedly cautioned that, at the heart of Greece's fiscal vulnerabilities, lay the domestic budgetary framework, both in the preparation of the budget and in its execution,[60] Greek policy makers chose either not to create the necessary institutional conditions, or, once they had created them, to undermine them. This is an important finding, raising the question of how, in the context of EMU-level economic-policy co-ordination, institutions can be designed so as to reduce political risk-taking by policy makers.

The chapter also proposed the concept of 'ostrichism', to explain why, in the face of Greece's serious fiscal imbalances and protracted losses of competitiveness, Greek policy makers succeeded in burying their heads in the sand, almost uninterrupted, until well into 2009. Routine deviation from targets, over-optimistic assessment of planned procedures and missed structural-reform timetables quickly came to define the Greek approach to its EMU obligations. For better or worse, Eurozone authorities who failed to follow *their own* rules or, at least, to provide deterrents to make it harder for Eurozone members not to follow them, subscribed to their own version of ostrichism. How did this change in the system's operation come about? Bringing in Mahoney and Thelen's theory of gradual institutional change,[61] provided an important tool for understanding how, over time, rule-breaking practices can themselves become 'rules'.[62] In the Greek case, however, veto-capabilities and discretion levels in interpretation/enforcement proved secondary in importance to the centrality of a weak institutional environment and actors' near-institutionalised belief that the rules, even the formal ones, would not be followed. The political relationships that lay beneath the support and creation for EMU kept only the semblance of monitoring, supervision, and co-ordination going. Politics usurped the domestic level, as well: actors' systematic non-enforcement of EMU's fiscal framework became, *pace* Mahoney and Thelen, an important source of institutional stability.

Chapter Seven traced the notion of institutional complementarities back to Greece's economic performance in the Eurozone. Greek policy makers successfully managed to both avoid improving fiscal governance, and put off

---

60. Commission of the European Communities, 'Report from the Commission, Greece: Report prepared in accordance with Article 104(3) of the Treaty', Brussels, 18 February 2009, p. 8.

61. J. Mahoney and K. Thelen, 'A theory of gradual institutional change' in J. Mahoney and K. Thelen (eds), *Explaining Institutional Change: Ambiguity, agency, and power*, Cambridge, Cambridge University Press, 2010, p. 31.

62. A. Scheingate, 'Rethinking rules: creativity and constraint in the U.S. House of Representatives', in Mahoney and Thelen, *Explaining Institutional Change*, p. 183.

labour and product market reform. At the same time, EMU remained – even before the onset of the credit crisis in 2007 – 'unfinished business'.[63] Fiscal discipline was not a policy priority, while euro area economies lagged behind other advanced economies in the pursuit of structural reform – by adjusting their 'compliance' strategies, Greek policy-actors simply followed this 'rule'. In an interesting way, Greek policy makers who operated in the reform-proof, path-dependent domestic institutional environment found that the fit of institutions at EMU level was also far from perfect – a 'lesson' that must have been useful, when they calculated the 'costs' associated with non-adjustment. Hence, an important finding of this chapter, in terms of the wider discussion on designing institutions that foster compliance, is that formal structures prove partially and transitorily effective, particularly when, with their behaviour, policy actors nullify the intrinsic notion of credible commitment; it follows that policy actors can make formal structures work only if they understand, accept and agree with the political constraints that are attached to their operation.

The euro crisis: re-balancing national independence and supranational interdependence?

In seeking to answer whether Greece is a case of economic delinquency or has fallen victim to systemic failure, this book speaks directly to three debates about the way EMU has redefined the balance between national independence and supranational interdependence. First, whether a more centralised approach to economic policy in the Eurozone will work, where the previous governance method failed to provide a co-ordinated fiscal and monetary response? Second, how has the IMF/EU experiment in problem-solving fared, given the perceived and growing chasm between core and periphery? Third, who makes economic policy in the Eurozone and for whom, when the democratic deficit appears to be widening?

After more than twenty meetings, including meetings of the Eurogroup, Ecofin, and European Council, and a good number of Emergency, EU leaders', and EU summits, members of the euro have been told – in two 'European Council Conclusions' and in the report prepared by the President of the European Council Herman Van Rompuy – that they are moving towards a 'Genuine Economic and Monetary Union'.[64] While the report envisages a decade-long transition to this

---

63. J. Pisani-Ferry, Ph. Aghion, M. Belka, J. von Hagen and A. Sapir, 'Coming of age: reform in the euro area', *Bruegel Blueprint Series*, 2008, Volume IV, p. 10.

64. European Council, European Council 28/29 June 2012 Conclusions', EUCO 76/12, Brussels, 29 June 2012 (accessed 5 August 2012). Online. Available: http://www.consilium.europa.eu/uedocs/cms_data/docs/pressdata/en/ec/131388.pdf; European Council, European Council 18/19 October 2012 Conclusions', EUCO 156/12, Brussels, 19 October 2012 (accessed 25 October 2012) . Online. Available: http://www.consilium.europa.eu/uedocs/cms_data/docs/pressdata/en/ec/133004.pdf; European Council, 'Towards a genuine economic and monetary union: report by President of the European Council Herman Van Rompuy', EUCO 120/12, Brussels, 26 June 2012. Online. Available: http://ec.europa.eu/economy_finance/focuson/crisis/documents/131201_en.pdf.

union, it is fair to say that, over the last two and a half years, the kind of institutional engineering that has been taking place, beginning with the Greek special financial vehicle in 2010 – falls short of being either 'genuine' or of promoting 'union'. With the fear of institutionalising moral hazard hanging over their heads, Eurozone authorities have continuously opted for institutions and instruments that promote conditionality at the expense of solidarity: the Treaty on Stability, Coordination and Governance (TSCG), the reformed SGP, the 'European Semester', the 'Euro-Plus-Pact', even the ECB's Outright Monetary Transactions. Granting that it is fair to safeguard the interests of the (taxpayers and the elected politicians of the) 'core', the inability to frame the PIIGS situation (with all the differences in their adjustment needs) as a *common* problem for the Union speaks volumes about the possibility of this 'genuine monetary union' succeeding. It also seems to send the wrong signals to the very markets whose 'favours' Eurozone authorities have tried really hard to regain; one only needs to compare the crippling risk premiums still paid by the periphery with the rates paid by the most creditworthy countries, Germany in particular. The more the Eurozone is divided in two 'zones', the core and the periphery, the more the report's 'vision for the future' of EMU and how it can contribute to 'growth, jobs and stability' will be considered limited and irrelevant.

In reality, the centralisation of control comes without any compensating features. Even though fiscal discipline by rules failed, the *new* EMU governance has created new rules and strengthened existing ones, pushing on down the same path. How has it been possible for Eurozone authorities to administer bigger doses of the same failed 'medicine'? This is the first question. One answer could be that they haven't grasped the causes of the euro crisis *or* that they continue to frame the operation of EMU along the pre-crisis lines of 'sound public finances'. With the exception of Greece and its fiscal derailment, however, the real problem tearing up the Eurozone has been the loss of competitiveness and increasingly large current account imbalances (Greece has, of course, suffered from failing competitiveness too), together with an inter-connected banking system. In reality, this asymmetry built in the proposed 'solutions' to the euro crisis is indicative of the prevailing attitude: creditors refuse to share responsibility for the imbalances present in the Eurozone, shifting the whole burden of adjustment to debtors.

There is a second question. How have Eurozone authorities been able to proceed with making so many rules that encroach on national economic governance – inadvertently touching upon issues of national sovereignty – without offering, at minimum, some kind of fiscal backstop or transfer? This is particularly pertinent given the seeming futility of the rule-based approach:[65] ongoing excessive-deficit procedures show that, out of the 17 countries that have adopted the euro, 13 are under such a procedure, with correction deadlines ranging from 2014 for

---

65. E. Panagiotarea, 'National economic policy and the sovereign debt crisis: will a crisis of democracy follow?', in E. Panagiotarea (ed.) *Greek Review of Political Science*, 2012, no. 39, special issue : 'The Politics of the Eurozone Crisis: Balancing between National Independence and Supranational Interdependence' [in Greek].

the Netherlands to 2015 for France, Portugal, and Ireland to 2016 for Spain and Greece. Quite how fiscal discipline can be administered in the light of such euro-wide delinquent behaviour remains to be seen.

The second debate relates to the IMF/EU experiment in problem-solving. The bailouts-cum-austerity strategy has so far appeared to have failed; nowhere is this more evident than in Greece. Progress made in closing its budget gap has come at the cost of a collapsing economy and a ballooning debt – with the gains of the recent debt-restructuring having been significantly reduced. The other programme countries are also facing bigger overall debt loads: Portugal's debt has risen to 108.1 per cent and Ireland's to 106.4 per cent.[66] If anything, serious questions can be raised regarding whether these countries will be able to pay back their creditors as along as growth remains stagnant and the interest demanded on their bailout loans is relatively punitive. 'Growing out of debt' – the new mantra – is as believable as the prevailing German-led and Commission-approved 'frame', namely that austerity holds the key to market confidence. Even in Italy, where tax increases and spending cuts have been staunchly administered and accompanied by moves to reform the pension system and the rigid labour market, debt has reached 120.7 per cent of GDP.

In spite of this apparent failure, however, the options for taking a different path are virtually nonexistent. Greece is expected to implement a 'new' €13.5 billion austerity package, when almost every item in it has been 'implemented' before and failed. Even if it all boils down to Greek delinquency, the fact that the economy has shrunk by 25 per cent since 2008 – another 6 per cent is expected for 2013 – suggests that the higher tax revenues required to pay off debt will not be raised. Of the other programme countries, Portugal has been given a 2015 deadline to meet previously agreed deficit-reduction targets under its €78bn bailout programme. Justified in terms of the country's 'enhanced credibility',[67] it was still an extension. Ireland is, once more, the 'model' student but the price paid for programme adherence is heavy: real GDP growth has slowed to a projected rate of 0.5 per cent in 2012, while unemployment remains unacceptably high, especially among the youth.[68]

In a 2012 report, the IMF appears to pick up on this absurdity, acknowledging that it has underestimated the impact of austerity on economic growth, but failing, however, to move beyond it: 'If history is a lesson, the path to restoring fiscal sustainability will be long and arduous for most advanced economies'.[69] The

---

66. Eurostat, 'Provision of deficit and debt data for 2011 – second notification', 149/2012, 22 October 2012 (accessed 12 February 2012). Online. Available: http://epp.eurostat.ec.europa.eu/cache/ITY_PUBLIC/2-22102012-AP/EN/2-22102012-AP-EN.PDF

67. 'Statement by Vice President Rehn following the conclusion of the fifth review mission to Portugal', MEMO/12/657 (accessed 1 November 2012). Online. Available: http://europa.eu/rapid/press-release_MEMO-12-657_en.htm

68. 'Statement by the EC, ECB, and IMF on the Review Mission to Ireland', MEMO/12/808, 25 October 2012, 1 November 2012. Online. Available: http://europa.eu/rapid/press-release_MEMO-12-808_en.htm

69. International Monetary Fund, 'Taking stock: a progress report on fiscal adjustment', *Fiscal Monitor*, October 2012, p. 24.

Commission, on the other hand, has adopted a far less conciliatory tone; the prevailing sentiment appears to be that 'the growth effect of a given consolidation effort depends on a number of factors (such as the composition of the fiscal effort, the credibility of the adjustment and financing conditions of the private sector)'; even if it is worse for the countries hit hard by the crisis, 'the design of fiscal measures as well as their credible medium-term orientation are crucial to mitigate this impact'.[70] This is a convenient conclusion that goes against the evidence cited above. In fact, as growth is forecast to contract by 0.4 per cent in the euro area in 2013, budget consolidation seems to be breeding more consolidation. Spain is a particular case in point, expected to engage in more budget-cutting activity, to get its deficits back in line with the already upwardly revised targets. If anything, this 'exercise' is beginning to seem like shooting at a moving target, with France and Belgium, whose efforts are considered slightly off track, possibly having to follow suit.

The third debate touches upon the growing democratic deficit: measures for centralising governance mechanisms and co-ordinating fiscal and economic policy certainly impinge on who owns national economic policy; popular unrest may have toppled governments in Portugal, Spain, Greece, Italy[71] and Ireland but, if there is one economic policy to be followed and one standard approach to attaining it, how exactly does the electoral process affect a new government's economic programme?[72] Over time, the debt crisis has become a crisis of trust; it began with a lack of trust in the EMU edifice – which generated crippling macro-economic imbalances rather than the promised real convergence – and it is now threatening to engulf every new institutional initiative that promises to remove economic policy further from democratically accountable governments. Allowing for the 'carrot' provided by the European Stability Mechanism, citizens are no longer comfortable with the 'the use of the discretionary power which both political and non-political actors hold in the EU set-up';[73] the *carte blanche* previously given by citizens on the future of European integration, had, in any case, already been taken back during the last attempt at treaty revision.[74]

The language of budget containment may have pushed to the side serious questions relating to the problem of trade deficits, fiscal transfers, collective debt issuance and the role of the ECB. These questions will not go away, however, particularly as unemployment rates have now significantly diverged along core–periphery lines; according to the April 2013 Eurostat data, the lowest unemployment rates were recorded in Austria (4.9 per cent), Germany (5.4 per

---

70. European Commission, 'European economic forecast Autumn 2012', p. 4.

71. In November 2011, the technocratic governments of Lucas Papademos in Greece and Mario Monti in Italy were formed without the calling of elections.

72. E. Panagiotarea, 'National economic policy and the sovereign debt crisis'.

73. O. Cramme, 'The changing space for EU politics: democracy and ideology in times of crisis', *Policy Network Paper*, October 2011, p. 10.

74. L. Tsoukalis, 'The JCMS Annual Review Lecture: the shattering of illusions – and what next?', *Journal of Common Market Studies*, 2011, vol. 49, Annual Review, p. 21.

cent) and Luxembourg (5.6 per cent), and the highest rates in Greece (27.0 per cent in February), Spain (26.8 per cent) and Portugal (17.8 per cent).[75] The prescribed medicine is becoming increasingly hard to swallow, as austerity programmes appear to be causing debt spirals, tearing apart, in the process, the very societies they are supposed to help. In the face of evidence of increased economic inequality, social alienation, the rise of left and right extremism, it is quite perplexing that Eurozone authorities fail to ask yet another question: how can countries with these levels of unemployment be required to raise taxes and cut social transfers?[76] If new institutions, including the recently heralded 'Compact for Growth and Jobs', encompassing action to be taken by the Member States and the European Union with the aim of relaunching growth, investment and employment as well as making Europe more competitive'[77] has a chance of sticking, they must offer a new contract between members participating in the Eurozone; they will also probably require a new contract between citizens and their respective governments, particularly if more powers are to be parcelled off to Brussels.

The story of Greece's delinquency is far more appealing and believable than the story of EMU's systemic failure. In reality, however, the two stories intersect; the Greek sovereign debt crisis shows that EMU was always going to be about *owning and sharing responsibility in a less-than-optimal monetary union in a more-than-troubled world.* The proposed move towards a 'Genuine Economic and Monetary Union' will theoretically balance the need for more responsibility, with the need for more solidarity. The logic behind it offers a cosy narrative of 'four essential building blocks'[78], an integrated financial framework, an integrated budgetary framework, an integrated economic policy framework and strengthened democratic legitimacy and accountability. Without the last block, the other three will not stand the scrutiny of national electorates, be they in creditor or in debtor countries. Without creating a state of symmetry and 'fair play' between the core and the periphery, the first three blocks will fall prey to rule-dodging, noncompliance, credit booms and self-fulfilling marketing sentiments; alternatively, they might create a union of institutionalised inequalities and permanent economic divergences. If anything, the lessons provided by 'Greece in the euro' will not go away anytime soon: unless all members begin to act as if belonging to the Union matters, then its break-up will always be a possibility- regardless of its genuineness, actual cost or, more importantly, the cost to the European integration project.

---

75. Eurostat, 'Unemployment Statistics' (accessed 15 May 2013).Online. Available: http://epp.euro-stat.ec.europa.eu/statistics_explained/index.php/Unemployment_statistics

76. *See* M. Feldstein, 'Europe's empty fiscal compact' (accessed 18 August 2012). Online. Available: http://www.project-syndicate.org/commentary/europe-s-empty-fiscal-compact

77. European Council, European Council 28/29 June 2012 Conclusions', pp. 7–15.

78. European Council, 'Towards a Genuine Economic and Monetary Union', p. 3.

appendix a | biographical data

Konstantinos G. Karamanlis (8 March 1907–23 April 1998) towered over Greek politics, serving as Prime Minister for fourteen years (1955–1963 and 1974–1980) and as President of the Third Hellenic Republic for ten (1980–1985 and 1990–95).

Karamanlis founded the New Democracy Party, which became the main centre-right party in Greek politics and one of the two major parties (the other was the socialist PASOK) that typically formed majority governments during the *metapolitefsi*, the term initially used to signify the regime change of the mid-seventies, which, however, has come to define Greece's political life over the past 39 years. Following the fall of the military dictatorship (1967–1974), Karamanlis, who engineered the smooth transition to democracy, created an entirely new political landscape, with the legalisation of the Communist Party and the 1974 December referendum abolishing the monarchy.

With the Constitution of 1975, Karamanlis introduced a presidential/parliamentary democracy, wherein the head of state (President) maintained the right to interfere in politics. Its first revision in 1986 saw the significant curtailment of presidential powers, introducing a clear parliamentary system of governance, while its second revision in 2001 introduced new individual rights and new rules of transparency in politics. The latest revision in 2008 amended provisions that pertained to MPs' professional incompatibility and endowed Parliament with the power to proceed with proposals to amend the budget under certain preconditions, together with an *ad hoc* procedure for the parliamentary oversight of the budget's implementation.

Soon after the establishment of the 1975 Constitution and the founding of the Third Hellenic Republic, Karamanlis tabled a formal application for the swift accession of Greece to the European Community, re-activating the 'frozen' Association Agreement of 1961. 'Greece belongs to the West' was his motto, as he set out his strategy of securing Greek membership, which would entrench national security and promote economic and cultural development. The Treaty of Accession was signed in 1979 and subsequently validated by parliamentary majority: the two major opposition parties, Panhellenic Socialist Movement, PASOK, and the Communist Party of Greece, KKE, abstained. Greece became the tenth member of the EC on January 1, 1981. Having attained the central goal of his premiership, Karamanlis left office in 1980, a year before the end of his tenure. He was elected to the presidency in 1980 and subsequently re-elected for a second term (1990–1995), solidifying his achievements as a conservative patriarch and as one of Europe's most respected politicians.

Andreas G. Papandreou (5 February 1919–23 June 1996) was a Greek economist, who ruled the country as its first socialist Prime Minister from 1981–1985, 1985–1989 and 1993–1996. In the process, he defined an entire political era.

The son of Prime Minister Georgios Papandreou (1944–1945, 1963, 1964–1965) and a member of his cabinet (Minister to the Prime Minister and subsequently Alternate Minister of Co-ordination), Papandreou founded the Panhellenic Socialist Movement (PASOK) in 1974, turning it into a national, mass, grass-roots organisation. Contradicting Karamanlis's 'Greece belongs to the West' with 'Greece belongs to the Greeks', Papandreou campaigned for 'change' in the 1981 elections. With its landslide victory, PASOK became the first socialist party to form a government in Greek constitutional history.

As Prime Minister, Papandreou introduced expansionary economic policies – bloating the public sector and effectively carrying out a strategy of income redistribution – together with significant liberalising laws as part of his 'Contract with the People'. One of his main election promises – to engineer Greece's withdrawal from NATO and the EC – was effectively dropped, the U-turn justified on account of the government's promise to renegotiate the respective agreements. Papandreou was re-elected in 1985, but his second term (1985–1989) was marred by a deteriorating economy – huge budget deficits led to rising levels of inflation and a growing foreign debt – and weakened by a grave financial scandal, in which he was implicated but later acquitted. In the June 18 1989 elections, PASOK lost its majority in parliament and Papandreou resigned from office. He returned triumphantly to power in October 1993, when PASOK won in the national elections, the landslide victory widely credited as testament to his charismatic personality. He served until ill health forced him to retire in January 1996. He died a few months later.

For all his modernising rhetoric and his undisputed charisma, Papandreou was a traditional Greek politician, the son of a Prime Minister, who eagerly appointed his own son to top ministerial posts. His party was held together by the force of his personality, with the party machine dispensing patronage and favours on an unprecedented, massive scale, effectively capturing the state apparatus. With a complex legacy, he remains today one of Greece's most revered politicians and a dominant figure in Greek political history.

Konstantinos K. Mitsotakis (18 October 1918–), came from one of the older political families of Crete, with family connections going back to Elefherios Venizelos, known as the 'ethnarch', leader of the nation in the early twentieth century.

A traditional Greek liberal and a member of George Papandreou's Centre Union Party, Mitsotakis left the party with a group of dissidents in 1965, causing the government to fall and triggering bitter animosity with the Papandreou family and political supporters that was to last for decades. Arrested by the military junta in 1967, he lived in exile until its fall in 1974. Mitsotakis, who was elected in parliament in 1977 with his Party of New Liberals, joined New Democracy in 1978 and became party leader in 1984. Having fought two inconclusive elections in 1989, he finally became prime minister in April 1990. Mitsotakis prioritised the stabilisation of the economy, including the reduction of budget deficits and inflation, and the privatisation of state-owned enterprises. Determined to break with what he perceived as the legacy of PASOK's international isolation, he was a staunch supporter of European integration at Maastricht and rekindled Greek-US relations. Mitsotakis was not able to prevent the major internal crisis which erupted over the name of the newly independent former Yugoslav Republic of Macedonia, as several ND parliament members, led by former Minister of Foreign Affairs Antonis Samaras, withdrew their support from the government. Mitsotakis lost the premature 1993 elections and resigned as ND's leader. He became the party's honorary president a year later, a position he still holds today. In the 2004 elections, he decided not to stand, bringing to a close 58 years of active political participation.

Costas G. Simitis (23 June 1936–) was a founding member of PASOK, who became its leader between 1996 and 2004.

A law professor, Simitis participated in the first PASOK government in 1981 as Minister of Agriculture, a position he held until 1985, when he became Minister of National Economy. His efforts to implement Greece's first serious stabilisation programme met with serious resistance both within the government and the party, causing him to resign in 1987, when Prime Minister Papandreou publicly abandoned fiscal prudence. He subsequently joined the 1993 PASOK government, as Minister for Industry, Energy and Technology and Minister for Commerce. Simitis was elected to PASOK's leadership in 1996, winning the 1996 elections. Under his leadership, PASOK also won the 2000 national elections. Simitis was credited with having successfully engineered Greece's entry to the Economic and Monetary Union.

His major political project was to bring about the 'modernisation' of Greek society, particularly through the stabilisation and development of the Greek economy and an enhanced role for Greece in Europe and the international environment. In January 2004, he announced his resignation from PASOK's presidency and he was succeeded by the only candidate, then Minister of Foreign Affairs George Papandreou, remaining Prime Minister until the March 2004 national elections. PASOK lost these to Kostas Karamanlis's ND party. He remains today a member of the Greek parliament. He has also authored a number of books covering his political career and his political and economic interests.

Kostas A. Karamanlis (14 September 1956–) was born into the Karamanlis political dynasty, the nephew of Konstantinos G. Karamanlis, founder of New Democracy, prime minister and president of the Hellenic Republic.

A lawyer with a PhD in international relations, he was first elected ND deputy for Thessaloniki in 1989, becoming leader of the party in 1997. Karamanlis served as leader of the opposition between 1997 and 2004 and as Vice-President of the European People's Party (EPP) between 1999 and 2006. He was elected Prime Minister in the 2004 national elections, on an agenda to 're-establish the Greek state'. He was subsequently re-elected in the 2007 on promises to fight corruption and make Greece's bloated government more efficient, with large-scale privatisation of state enterprises and the rationalisation of public sector employment and social security systems. In 2009, he called snap elections, seeking a clear majority to pass the serious austerity measures that the onset of the financial crisis required. For all his hard rhetoric, Greece's budget deficit widened significantly during his watch and public debt continued to mount. He lost the 2009 elections to George Papandreou's PASOK, also resigning as president of New Democracy party. He is today a member of parliament.

George A. Papandreou (16 June 1952–), a sociologist, was born into the political dynasty founded by his grandfather Prime Minister G. Papandreou.

First elected to parliament in 1981, the year his father Andreas became Prime Minister, he soon had a burgeoning political career. He was Under-Secretary for Cultural Affairs in 1985 and Minister of Education and Religious Affairs between 1988 and 1989. He became Deputy Minister of Foreign Affairs in 1993, Minister for Education and Religious Affairs in 1994, Alternate Minister of Foreign Affairs in 1996 and Minister of Foreign Affairs between February 1999 and 2004, earning international praise for his Greek–Turkish rapprochement. He was elected to PASOK's leadership in February 2004 – he was the only candidate – a position he retained in a 2007 leadership contest, following the party's defeat in national elections.

Papandreou became Prime Minister in October 2009, his election campaign centring on the slogan 'money exists'. Following a revision of the Greek public deficit figure, Papandreou's new government soon became embroiled in a bitter battle with Eurozone authorities over Greece's statistical data, negatively affecting the country's access to the markets. A series of tough austerity measures, adopted between January 2010 and April 2010, failed to reverse Greece's credibility deficit or narrow the unsustainable bond yields, prompting Papandreou to request the activation of the €110 billion Greek Loan Facility, agreed in May with the euro area member states and the International Monetary Fund. Due to implementation failures, and a deeper than expected recession, a second €130 billion bailout loan was offered to Greece in October 2011, conditional on the implementation of another austerity package and high private-sector involvement (PSI) in a debt-exchange offer. Papandreou announced his decision to put the new bail-out plan to a referendum but was forced to back down, following upheaval in the government and the intense disapproval of his European partners. With immense damage incurred to his standing internally and abroad, he resigned as Prime Minister on 10 November 2011. After days of political wrangling, the two major parties, PASOK and ND, together with the Popular Orthodox Rally, agreed to give Lucas Papademos, former Vice President of the European Central Bank, the mandate to form an interim coalition government that would implement the tough terms envisaged in the €130 billion bail-out programme.

Papandreou is today a member of parliament for PASOK, having resigned from the party's leadership in March 2012. He is President of Socialist International, having first been elected to the post in 2006.

Lucas D. Papademos (11 October 1947–) is an economist who served as Prime Minister between November 2011 and May 2012. Previously, he was the Vice-President of the European Central Bank from 2002 to 2010 and the Governor of the Bank of Greece from 1994 to 2002.

With the political backing of PASOK, ND, and the Popular Orthodox Rally parties, Papademos, an authority in macroeconomics, headed an interim coalition government, whose main priority was to implement the tough terms envisaged in the €130 billion bail-out programme agreed at the October 2011 EU Summit. Papademos oversaw the high private-sector involvement (PSI) in Greece's debt-exchange offer, making a significant contribution to improving Greece's debt sustainability.

He called a general election in May 2012, which resulted in a hung parliament. President of the Council of State Panagiotis Pikrammenos replaced Papademos as caretaker Prime Minister, until a second general election was held in June 2012. On 20 June, a national unity government was formed, comprising ND, PASOK and DIMAR (Democratic Left), with Antonis Samaras, Leader of New Democracy, the party which won 30 per cent of votes, serving as Prime Minister.

Papademos is professor of economics at the University of Athens, currently Visiting Professor of Public Policy at Harvard Kennedy School and Senior Fellow at the Centre for Financial Studies, Goethe University, Frankfurt.

appendix b | list of interviewees

Personal interviews (one or more) were conducted with those listed below. They are presented in alphabetical order and the professional capacity on the basis of which they were interviewed[1].

Prof. George Alogoskoufis, Member of Parliament for ND; President of the Council of Economic Experts (1992–93); Minister of Economy and Finance (2004–9)

Nikos Analytis, Vice President of the Federation of Greek Industries – social and labour affairs (1988–2004) [Deceased]

Gerassimos Arsenis, Minister of National Economy (1982–5); Governor of the Bank of Greece (1981–3)

Stefanos Augouleas, Adviser to the Minister of National Economy (1997)

G. Bakatsianos, Economic Adviser, C2 Directorate of European Integration and Economic and Monetary Policy, Ministry of Foreign Affairs

Dimitris Chalikias, Governor of the Bank of Greece,(1984–92)

Prof. Nicolaos Christodoulakis, Deputy Minister of Finance (1996–9); Minister of National Economy (2001–4)

Timos Christodoulou, Minister of National Economy (1991–2)

Petros Doukas, Deputy Minister of Finance (1992–3)

Apostolos Fotiadis, Deputy Minister of Finance (2000–4)

Nicolaos Garganas, Deputy Governor of the Bank of Greece (1996–2002)

Georgos Glynos, Adviser to Prime Minister on European Affairs (2011) [deceased]

Prof. Panayiotis Ioakimidis, Policy Expert, C2 Directorate of European Integration and Economic and Monetary Policy, Ministry of Foreign Affairs (1997–2000)

Theodoros Karatzas, Deputy Minister of National Economy, (1987–8) [Deceased]

George Katiforis, Economic Adviser to the Prime Minister (1987–9 and 1993–4)

Stefanos Manos, Minister of National Economy (1992–3)

Constantinos Mitsotakis, Prime Minister (1990–3)

Prof. Lucas Papademos, Governor of the Bank of Greece (1996–2002)

Giorgos Papakonstantinou, Minister of Finance (2009–11)

Theodore Papalexopoulos, President of the Federation of Greek Industries (1982–8)

Yannos Papantoniou, Minister of National Economy (1994–6), Minister of National Economy and Finance (1996–2002)

Yannis Papathanasiou, Minister of Economy and Finance (2009)

---

1. Professor G. Alogoskoufis and Governor of the Bank of Greece G. Provopoulos are recorded twice in the text, as separate interviewees, because of the time lapse between the interviews and the different positions that they held.

Manolis Patestos, President of OSPA (Federation of Unions of Civil Aviation) (1999–2008)

Prof. Stelios Perrakis, Secretary-General for European Affairs, Ministry of Foreign Affairs (1997–2000)

Associate Prof. Ilias Plaskovitis, Secretary-General for Investment and Development, Ministry of National Economy (1993–8)

Prof. George Provopoulos, Deputy Governor of the Bank of Greece, (1990–3); Governor of the Bank of Greece (2008–)

Christos Poluzogopoulos, President of GSEE (1996–2006)

Eleni Psarrou, Directorate of Relations with the European Communities, Ministry of National Economy

Prof. Vassilis Rapanos, Chairman of the Hellenic Telecommunications Organisation (1998–9)

Yannis Sidiropoulos, Director of Economic Policy, Ministry of National Economy (1999–2007)

Eleni Skolarikou, Diplomat, Diplomatic Office of the General Secretary of European Affairs

Yannis Spraos, Committee for the Long-Term Examination of Macroeconomic Policy (1996–9)

Prof. Yannis Stournaras, President of the Council of Economic Experts (1996–2000)

Dimitris Tsovolas, Minister of Finance (1985–89)

Yannis Varvitsiotis, Vice-President of New Democracy (1994–7)

Christos Verelis, Minister of Transport (2000–4)

Prof. Tasos Yannitsis, Economic Adviser to the Prime Minister (1994–2000)

Prof. George Zanias, President of the Council of Economic Advisors, Ministry of Finance (2009–12)

index

Almunia, J. 110
Alogoskoufis, G. 103 n.30, 110
Arsenis, G. 36 n.21, 67 n.54, 117 n.88
Athens Stock Exchange 155
Austria 90

Bank of Greece (BoG) 11, 33, 75–6,
  179
  EMU and monetary control 75–6,
    77, 80, 92, 94, 115
  central bank independence and
    69, 80–2, 90
  deficit warnings and 129
  interest rate intervention and 78,
    82, 84
Barroso, J. M. D. 138
Belgium 4, 173
Bundesbank 67, 77

capitalist economies
  centre/periphery development and
    36
  dependency theory and 36
  Mediterranean type and 26, 93, 158,
    168
Christodoulou, P. 141 n.81
Christodoulou, T. 50 n. 80, 57, 58, 64
  n.37
Christopherson, H. 46
Chrysohoidis, M. 145
clientelism 19, 38, 157, 167
  bureaucratic 156
corruption
  Corruption Perception Index (CPI)
    and 159
  Greece and 123, 155, 158–9
    economic crisis, contribution to

      158–9, 164, 167, 168
    Eurobarometer poll and 159
    government bribery and 158
    pension fraud and 162
    shadow economy and 168
    2011 survey and 158–9
  tax evasion and 160–1
Council of Ministers 43
  Integrated Mediterranean Pro-
    grammes (IMPs) 43
Credit Default Swaps (CDS) 1, 6
Cyprus 1, 3

Dallara, C. 6 n.16
Damanaki, M. 61 n.26, 68
Delors, J. 43 n.49, 46
Delors Report (1989) 46
DIMAR 7

Economic and Financial Affairs
  Council (Ecofin) 59, 63 n.30, 90,
    91, 121, 122, 140, 146, 170
economic performance, analysis of
    10, 15–16
  complementarity, absence of and
    26, 148, 149
  imposed change, resistance to 17, 24
  institutional effect on 15
  market performance and 16
  policy formation 9, 17–18, 25
  see also institutions; new institu-
    tionalism
EEC, Greek entry (1981) 27, 29, 32,
    33, 34–5, 39–40, 50, 51, 66, 167,
    175
  Association Agreement (1961) 32,
    33, 175

Community policy compliance and
30, 47, 50, 51
economic-policy change, effect on
51, 167
export competition and 40, 167
institutional change and 29–30,
42–3, 167
membership application (1975) 32, 33
Memorandum (1982) and 11, 40
net entry receipts/loans and 29
transition period and 40
Treaty of Accession (1979) 34,
39–40, 175
EMU (Economic and Monetary
Union)
Broad Economic Policy Guidelines
(BEPGs) 8, 25, 86, 87, 121
Cohesion Fund and 61, 70
Council of Economic Advisers 11
democratic deficit and 27, 170, 173,
174
establishment of (Delors Report)
46–7, 62
introductory stages of 62–4
Treaty on European Union
(1991) and 46, 62
fiscal discipline and 116–17, 121–5,
150, 171
delegation/contract approaches
and 116–17, 169
Stability and Growth Pact 117,
121, 127, 150
success of 108–9, 117, 121–2,
150–1, 171–2
future of 170–4
core/periphery divisions and 171,
173, 174
debt management and 171–3
economic growth, contraction
of 173
symmetry, creation of and 174
Van Rompuy Report (2012) and
170–1
institutionalisation process and 10,
16, 171

change agents and 123
logic of change and 23
national interaction with 16, 27,
53
national/supranational balance in
27, 163, 170
north/south imbalance and 119
policy framework/rules 2, 22, 62–4,
71–2, 97, 124, 171
asymmetric shocks, provision
for 97
excessive deficit procedures and
63–4, 109, 171–2
'no-bail-out' rule and 70, 97
political union (EPU) and 56, 58–9,
66, 70
single currency (euro) and 10, 46,
62, 63, 85, 88, 89 n.63, 98, 119,
123, 125
ostrichism and 121, 122, 123,
124, 164
trust crisis and 173
see also EMU, application Greece;
EMU governance; EMU entry
Greece; Eurozone crisis
EMU application, Greece 1, 8, 11,
12–13, 55–95
application submission (2000) and
88
commitment to 58–9, 71–2
ERM entry and 84–5
foreign and security interests and
65–6
as opportunity for domestic
reform 64–5, 71–2, 73, 84,
94
PM Mitsotakis and 65–7
convergence programme and 59, 68,
72, 73–88, 89, 100, 145
criteria of 60, 62, *63,* 67, 68, 73,
78, 84, 88, 94
ECB/ESCB 1999 reports and 88
ERM entry and *see* under
Exchange Rate Mechanism
(ERM)

as nominal 64, 65, 73, 90, 97,
118, 121, 163, 168
public debt strategy and 86
see also under Bank of Greece
entry negotiations and 8, 29, 55,
56–61, 68–70, 71, 72
autonomy/size and status effects
60, 68–9, 72
aspirations/outcomes table *63*
extended transition period and
59, 61, 67, 70, 90
financial support issue and 59,
61, 67–8, 70
fiscal discipline, imposition of
60, 65, 72, 91, 92
opposition parties, views of 67–8
prime ministerial control and
57–8, 66–7
as two-level game 68–9
as external-constraint strategy 55,
64, 69, 71, 72, 73, 90, 93, 118,
126, 163–4, 167
convergence, use of for 83–4, 163
EMU institutionalisation and 70,
90, 92, 93
policy competence delegation
and 73
power asymmetry and 69–70,
122
formal rules of 56, 64, 167
global level changes, effect on 72
Memorandum (1991) 11, 47, 56, 60
national politics and 8, 56, 64–5,
168
disinflation, consideration of
64–5
economy, expected effect on
64–5, 67
EU politics, attitude/knowledge
and 56, 57, 69
inter-ministerial co-ordination
and 56–7, 58, 65
personalisation of leadership and
70, 167
as policy path 65

Treaty ratification and 66–8
government goals and 66–7
opposition parties and 66, 67–8
see also under Exchange Rate
Mechanism (ERM)
EMU governance 10, 13, 22, 164
Excessive Imbalance Procedure
(EIP) 4
The Euro-Plus-Pact and 4, 171
European Semester 4, 171
macroeconomic imbalances and 4,
12, 22, 72, 98, 164, 169, 171,
173
six-pack 3
Treaty on Stability, Coordination
and Governance (TSCG) 3, 22,
171
two-pack 4
EMU entry, Greece (2001) 89–95,
97–124, 177
debt-to-GDP ratio and 101–2,
110–11
entry criteria and 90, 94
EU support for 89–90
fiscal deficit and 91, 93–4, 102–113,
114, 119, 121, 123–4, 165
elections and deficit graph
1991–2010 *112*
EMU members' disregard of
23–4
Eurostat audits 103–4, 105,
110–11
2004 Excessive Deficit
Procedure (EDP) and 102–3,
106, 108, 110, 111, 112, 114,
121, 122, 123, 124, 126, 127,
130, 135, 141, 149, 150
2005 National Reform
Programme 107–8
Stability and Growth Pact
discipline and 108–9, 121,
122
see also under Greek sovereign-
debt crisis (2009-)
national optimism and 89, 90

New Democracy government
(2004–09) 102–13
budget deficit graph *112*
fiscal audit and reform 2004
102–11
procrastination v. adjustment by
113
2006 Draft Budget Bill and 107
privatisation programme and 100–1,
105, 164, 165
Hellenic Republic Asset
Development Fund
(HRADF) and 164
social security/welfare reform and
100, 101, 104, 105, 107, 111–113
National Fund for Social
Cohesion and 113
pension expenditure and 2,
112–13, 155, 157, 161, 162,
164
taxation policy and reform 101, 104,
105, 106, 107, 112, 114
see also Greek sovereign-debt crisis
(2009–)
European Agricultural and Guarantee
Fund 29
European Central Bank (ECB) 4, 11,
22, 63, 91, 138, 150, 173, 178, 179
Convergence Report (2000) and 123
fiscal deficit discipline and 70, 109,
127, 128, 133
Greece monetary policy and 11–12,
63, 64, 71, 88, 94, 98, 119, 136,
138, 140, 143
1999 Report, EMU entry criteria
88
IMF negotiations and 144, 146
Maastricht Treaty and 71
OMT Programme and 4, 171
European Court of Justice 108 n.49
European Investment Bank 122
European Monetary Institute (EMI) 62
European Monetary System (EMS) 22,
39, 64, 83, 85
1992–3 crisis and 74

use as national constraint 83–5
European System of Central Banks
(ESCB) 63, 88
Eurostat 12, 100, 103–4, 110–11, 114,
122, 124, 126, 130, 140, 149, *152*
deficit and debt data (2009) 5 n.8
enforcement power of 122, 130
methodological visits 103, 124
revisions 100, 103, 110, 127, 141, 149
unemployment data (2013) 173–4
Eurozone crisis (2008-)
competitiveness, loss of 171
as core/periphery chasm and 27,
125–6, 151, 170, 171
inflation differences and 125
country debt analysis 4–5
as crisis of trust 173
crisis-management strategy and 125,
126, 147
credibility deficit and 150
European Stability Mechanism
(ESM) and 4, 22, 173
European Financial Stability
Facility (EFSF) and 3, 6, 7,
147
European Financial Stability
Mechanism (EFSM) and 3,
147
reactive approach of 126
deficit 1999–2007 *109*
Excessive Deficit Procedure (EDP)
26, 150, 171–2
see also under EMU entry, Greece

fiscal stimulation package and 114
as 'Greek crisis' 126
IMF involvement in 137–8, 139,
140–7, 172
institutional interaction and 16–17,
25, 166
civil service accountability and
156
credibility deficit and 150
national sovereignty and 17, 25,
171

personalisation of politics and
156
institutionalist analysis and 17,
22–4, 25, 170–4
crisis as critical juncture 22
delegation and contract approaches and 26–7, 169
ECB-centric setup of 22
national deficit as % of GDP *152–3*
north/south imbalance and 2, 25,
119
adjustment mechanisms and 2–4,
16–17, 25, 119, 171
rule-breaking 110, 121, 122, 124
social effects of 173–4
Stability and Growth Pact (SGP)
and 3, 8, 15, 25, 26, 171
failure of 150, *152–3*
as systemic failure 3, 11, 13, 27,
146, 149, 151, 155–6, 166, 170,
174
Exchange Rate Mechanism (ERM) 67,
69, 84
Greek Drachma entry to 78, 80,
81–7, 90
'code of conduct', adherence to
90
devaluation and 82, 83, 85, 86,
88, 94, 98, 115 n.76
ERM II and 85, 88
rate at entry 83
Greek euro and 83

Finland 140, 141
Fitch 126, 130, 132, 139
France 26, 90, 121, 131, 160–1, 173
Mitterrand government 3
Stability and Growth Pact reform
and 108
deficit 1999–2007 *109*

Garganas, N. 83 n.36
General Confederation of Greek
Workers 11
Germany 136, 137, 139, 174

EMU and 119, 121
excessive deficit and 108, 109
Greek crisis and 137, 139–40, 144
Stability and Growth Pact reform
and 108, 109
Greece
as clientelistic state 150
Coalition Party 68
Cyprus dispute 33 n.15
democracy, restoration of (1974) 29,
30–1, 32, 50, 167, 175
Constitution (1975) 175
governance changes and 30–1
DIMAR (Democratic Left) 179
Ecology Party 66, 68
economy *see* Greek economy
KKE (Communist Party) 34, 45
n.60, 66, 68, 175
Left Coalition 45
Mediterranean capitalism in 26
military dictatorship (1967) 32, 175
Olympic Games and 101, 107–8
Popular Orthodox Rally 178, 179
see also New Democracy Party
(ND); PASOK
Greek economy
agricultural sector dominance and 34
EEC accession, effect on 40
Eurozone participation and 98
budget deficit growth 12, 29, 31, 34,
35, 38, 41, 42, 45–6, 49, 50–1
election years, graph of 38, *39*
EMU convergence programme
78–9, 86, 87, 91
Eurozone accession and 93–4,
98, *109*
1971–83 government graph 50,
52
see also under EMU entry,
Greece; Greek sovereign-
debt crisis
EEC entry *see* EEC, Greek entry
electoral-fiscal cycles and 12, 38,
39, 41, 45, 50, 51, 111, 163
budget deficit graph and *112*

revenue loss per election and 163
EMU and *see* EMU application,
   Greece; EMU entry, Greece
euro, introduction of (1999) 83, 86,
   87, 88, 98, 163
   budget deficit and *109*, 115
exchange-rate policy 73–4, 76–8, *89*
   Convergence Program 1993–8
      74, 85
   ERM entry and 78, 80, 81–7,
      88, *89*
   'hard-Drachma policy' 1986–7
      74, 76–7
   see also under Exchange Rate
      Mechanism (ERM)
GDP growth
   1960–79 30, 33
   1981–1992 29, 37, 41, 44, 48,
      76 n.8
   2000–2008 1, 94, 98–9, 108,
      115–16
industrial structure and 33, 34, 50
   Industrial Restructuring
      Organisation (IRO) 37
   nationalisation and 36–7
inflation rate 32, 34, 37, 41, 42, 45,
   47, 48, 51, 73
   EMU membership and 73, 74,
      75, 77–8, 80, 81, 86, 87, 88
   ERM entry and 83, 86, 98
   1986–7 stabilisation and 44, 74
   1996–2000 graph *79*
   2004–9 reform and 108, 115
national economic governance and
   30, 171
   General Directorate of Fiscal
      Audits and 107
   Hellenic Statistical Authority
      138, 165 n.49, 166 n.50
   macroeconomic imbalances and
      31, 36, 38, 42, 47, 50, 65, 72
   National Statistical Service 106,
      107, 110, 138, 149
   Public Debt Management Office
      and 102

1974–81 and statism 29, 30–5
   redistribution/social security and
      31–2, 36 n.24, 50
1981–90 debt growth 29, 35–53
   Drachma devaluation and 42
   EC loan (1985) and integration
      42–3, 44, 46, 51
   nationalisation and 36–7, 50
   privatisation programme and 48,
      49–50
   wage adjustment/indexation,
      effect of 36, 37, 42, 47, 50
   1991 adjustment programme 47–8
   1991 EC loan 48, 50
   non-reform and 123, 164
   oil shock (1973) effect on 30, 32
   patronage politics and 13, 51, 164
   politicisation of economy and 29,
      34–5, 44, 50, 51, 163, 166
   see also unemployment; Greek
      sovereign-debt crisis
Greek sovereign-debt crisis (2009-)
   1–2, 5–8, 113–124, 125–74
   Budget Laws and 116
   civil discontent and 1, 5, 155, 173
      union protest and strikes 1, 133,
         136, 146, 155
   competitiveness, loss of 115, 121,
      145, 158, 169, 171
   credit ratings and 126, 130, 132,
      139, 140–1, 143
   crony capitalism and 158
      see also corruption
   default possibility of 137, 143, 144
   deficit (2007–10) in 4–5, 13, 15,
      112, 115–16, 123, 125, 127, 140,
      147, 155, 165
      Council Conclusion (2009) 127,
         131
      future reduction of 172
      German involvement and 137
      trust in reporting of 130, 132, 149
      warnings and reducing measures
         126, 128–31, 135
Euribor 139

euro membership exit and 5, 6, 89
Europeanisation, effect on 155
fiscal discipline and 116–17, 121,
    123, 124, 150, 170
    EC procedures and 127, 131, 133
    Finance Minister, efforts of 118
    Prime Ministerial power and 117
    Stability and Growth Pact,
        attitude to 121, 122, 168
general elections (2010) and 129
Greek Loan Facility (GLF) and 2
    n.3, 3, 7, 142, 146, 147, 149, 178
IMF emergency involvement in
    (2010) 136–8, 139–40, 143–7
    deficit adjustment targets and
        144, 147
    as divergent adjustment 26
    effectiveness of 172
    EU countries opposition to
        139–40, 143
    EU/IMF adjustment programmes
        1–2, 5, 6, 17, 27, 126, 138–
        40, 142, 147, 160, 165, 178
    PASOK government, effect on
        145
    public opposition to 146
    troika negotiations and 144–5
income inequality/material depriva-
    tion and 165–6
institutionalist analysis of 17–19,
    51–2, 124, 166–70
    'adjustment' process and 17, 18,
        148, 166, 167, 170
    change, resistance to 18–19, 124,
        167, 169
    economy, politicisation of and
        166–7
    growth, framework choice and
        166
    institutional divergence and 168
    preference-formation and 168
    rule-breaking practices and 169
macroeconomic imbalances and
    108, 114, 115, 121, 125, 126
national savings rate decline 116

PASOK government measures and
    129–30, 131–3, 136, 142
policy making, effectiveness of 10,
    24, 116–18, 123–4, 126, 128,
    136–9, 134, 142, 148–51, 168–9
    accountability/transparency and
        118, 135, 156, 158, 161, 169
    auditing/evaluation and 118, 124,
        161–2
    credibility, loss of 124, 130, 132,
        133, 135, 136, 149–50
    informal norms 52, 121, 161, 167
    legal formalism and 157
    ostrichism and 119, 121, 123,
        128, 148, 164, 169
    policy monopolism and 149
    2011 OECD report and 157–8
political institutions, role in 5, 15,
    118, 148, 156, 164, 169
    civil service and culture of 157,
        165
    bureaucratic clientelism and
        156–7
    delegation and control within 169
    institutional complementarity
        and 148–9, 160–70
    ministerial co-operation/co-
        ordination and 157–8, 169
    political personalisation and 156
    public sector enterprises and
        162–3, 167
private sector involvement (PSI)
    and 5–6, 178
SMEs, loss of 155
social security/pensions and 114,
    121, 132, 150, 155, 157, 161,
    162, 164, 167, 168–9
sovereign bonds spreads *140*,
    141–2, 146
Stability and Growth Pact compli-
    ance 10, 11, 12, 15, 17, 26, 116,
    122, 128
    Updated Stability and Growth
        Programme (2010) 132, 135,
        140, 149–50

tax evasion/property tax and 114, 124, 129, 136, 143, 159–61
unemployment and debt (1999–2008) *120*
vested interests and 3, 25, 131, 155, 158, 160, 164
Grivas, I. 45

institutions 15
definition of 17–18
economic performance, role in 15–16, 24–5, 166
historical context, effect on 16, 18
informal 10, 18, 19 n.11
representative democracy and 15
stability of 17, 18, 19, 24
'varieties of capitalism' approach to 26, 148, 149
comparative advantage 10, 26, 93 n.83, 168 n.55
complementarity, concept of 10, 26, 93, 148, 168, 169
see also new institutionalism
Integrated Mediterranean Programmes 29, 67
International Monetary Fund (IMF) 1, 18
Greek crisis and 3, 6, 8, 103, 133–40
2012 progress report and 172–3
see also under Greek sovereign-debt crisis
Ireland 159
EDP and 172
EMU and 61, 72, 119
financial crisis in 1, 3, 4, 83, 125, 128, 140, 143, 150, 169, 172, 173
GDP (2000) and 94
Italy 26, 159
EMU and 83
financial crisis in 4, 5, 127, 172, 173
deficit 1999–2007 *109*

Juncker, J.-C. 6 n.17, 123

Karamanlis, K. A. 102, 113, 129, 177–8
Karamanlis, K. G. 31, 32 n.11, 34 n.16, 38 n.30, 175, 176, 177
Katseli, A. 145
Kohl, H. 71 n.72
Kostopoulos, D. 68 n.56

Lagarde, C. 160
Lehman Brothers 139, 147
Lisbon Treaty (2007) 107

Maastricht Treaty 55, 57, 61, 71
Merkel, A. 134, 137–8, 142
Mitsotakis, K. 47, 48 n.73, 57–8, 65–7, 176–7
EMU commitment and 65–7
Moody's 132, 140–1

Netherlands, the 139, 140, 172
New Democracy Party (ND) 7, 32, 33, 36, 38, *52*, 58, 66, 74, 175, 176–7, 179
EMU, position on 66, 67–8
1989 coalition 45
1990–3 government 46, 47
neo-liberalism/pro Europe stance and 48
2004–9 government 102
new institutionalism 17–21, 25
actor centrality and 19–21
historical institutionalism and 18, 19, 20, 92, 166
institutional framework, choice of and 23, 25, 35, 51, 166
overarching context, notion of 35
institutional change and 20, 21, 23–4, 29–30, 123
adjustment pressures and 19, 52
change agents, typology of 123
critical junctures and 22, 51
four modal types of 24
path dependence, notion of and 17, 21–3, 52
resistance to 17–19, 21
reform processes and 12, 17, 23

change and stability of 23–4, 25
unanticipated consequences of 70–1
see also rational-choice institutionalism; sociological institutionalism

Obama, B. 147
OECD 26, 157–8, 159–60, 162, 165

Paleokrassas, Y. 57
Papademos, L. 81, 173 n.71, 178, 179,
Papandreou, A. G. 33 n.11, 61 n.26,
176, 177, 178
EMU position and 66, 67 n.54
government (1981–89) 3, 35–6, 37,
41, 43, 45, 117
'redistributive Keynesianism' of
3, 35–6, 40–1
Papandreou, G. A. 129, 133, 134–6,
142–3, 159 n.23, 176, 178
Papakonstantinou, G. 129–30, 131–2,
134 n.45, 143, 149 n.123, 161
Papantoniou, Y. 36 n.21, 117 n.87, n.89
PASOK (Panhellenic Socialist
Movement) 7, 33 n.11, 34, 35–7,
38, *52*, 107, 112, 175, 176, 177, 178
EMU position and 59, 66, 67–8
Eurozone accession and 99
1981–9 government 35–8, 176, 177
Keynesian approach of 3, 36, 41
Single European Act (1986)
effect on 43–4
stabilisation programmes 42–4,
50 n.79, 51, 56, 74 n.2, 163,
177
structural reform and 36–7, 38
1993–2004 government 50, 74, 79,
176, 177
budget deficit under *112*
fiscal discipline and 117
2009 government 129–30, 131–4,
178
reform measures and 129–30,
131–3, 136, 142
IMF involvement effect on 145

Pikrammenos, P. 179
policy change 21–3, 24
institutional change and 24
path dependence and 17, 21–3
Portugal 2, 26, 159
EEC accession and 43
EMU and 61, 72, 102 n.25, 119
financial crisis in 1, 3, 4, 5, 116,
136, 143, 144, 146, 173, 174
deficit 1999–2007 *109*
EDP and 172
GDP (2000) and 94
Prodi, R. 88
Provopoulos, G. 129, 140

Rallis, G. 38
rational-choice institutionalism 18, 19,
35, 92
actor interaction and 19–20, 21
decision-making and 52, 121, 167
new institutionalism and 20, 21, 92,
168
preference formation and 92, 168
Rehn, O. 7 n.22, 143, 146
Russia 84

Samaras, A. 7, 57, 58, 177, 179
Schäuble, W. 139
Securities Market Programme (SMP)
4, 7
Simitis, C. 43 n.49, 79, 88, 89, 102, 177
Single European Act (1986) 43
sociological institutionalism 20
Solbes, P. 88
Spain 159
EEC accession and 43
EMU and 61, 72, 90, 119
financial crisis in 1, 2, 3, 4, 5, 125,
143, 146, 150, 169, 173, 174
EDP and 172
GDP (2000) and 94
Standard & Poor's 126, 132, 143
Stournaras, Y. 83 n.36
Strauss-Kahn, D. 137 n.65, 139 n.74,
143, 146

trade unions 50, 74
    austerity, protest and strikes 1, 133,
       136, 146, 155
    EMU membership effect on 91, 92
    exemptions and benefits 92
Transparency International Greece
    158–9
Treaty on European Union (TEU)
    (1991) 46, 55, 62, 66, 78
Treaty on the Functioning of the
    European Union (TFEU) 135, 138
Trichet, J.-C. 109 n.53, 122 n.101,
    127, 128, 143, 146–7
Turkey 26
Tzanetakis, T. 45

unemployment 172, 173–4
    Eurostat 2013 report 173–4
    Greece and 2, 25, 38, 155, 165, 174
       EMU entry and 52, 67, 71, 73,
          120
       inflation as trade-off 37 n.28
       youth level and 165

United States 113

Van Rompuy, H. 170
Venizelos, E. 161
Vlachos, G. 58

Waigel, T. 71 n.72
World Economic Forum 133

Zolotas, X. 33, 45, 46

www.ingramcontent.com/pod-product-compliance
Lightning Source LLC
Chambersburg PA
CBHW072129020426
42334CB00018B/1731